CHILDREN WRITING STORIES

"Here's a book, a wonderful book that enables the enabler to enable. The first book I ever compiled 35 years ago was a collection of children's writing. I was a teacher at the time, and I was fired by the freshness, the eagerness, the honesty of the writing my students were producing. Here is a worthy successor to Ted Hughes' *Poetry in the Making*, the book that enabled me to gain the confidence to begin to find my own voice as a story teller.

Children Writing Stories confirms that we all have a story to tell if we are enabled to develop enough self-belief. So much of our natural creativity is smothered during our school years. Teachers and children feel hemmed in by the strictures of a curriculum which simply does not allow room for creativity to breathe. Unlock the chains, let the light in, and this is the kind of writing that will flow, this is the kind of intellectual and emotional growing that can transform young lives."

Michael Morpurgo, Children's Laureate 2003–2005

Pay Attention!
"What a splendid book! Michael Armstrong pays attention – thirty years of it – to the stories that children write. We get two for one: the children's own delightful and intriguing work – I want to rush off and write some Wally (age 5) stories of my own – and Michael Armstrong's intense interpretations. There's added depth here too; he was their teacher. His knowledge of the child behind the story enriches his close observations, rounds them out. My favourite tale is, probably, 'Girl Today, Hare Tomorrow' by Rebecca (age 11). You'll assuredly find yours. Read on!"

Allan Ahlberg

"A genius observer of young children, Michael Armstrong inspires all teachers to look, listen, and enter into conversations with children, their art, and their writings. His patience, unique insights, and close readings of children's stories bear witness to the power of teacher intuition open to the wisdom that comes from years of learning with and from children."

Shirley Brice Heath

"The book is both timely and timeless, towering above the banality of official endorsements of children's creativity and the current structures of classroom literacy. Armstrong most beautifully demonstrates, once and for all, that children are not the little ghosts of adults, but powerful thinkers, dreamers, social critics, satirists and visionaries in their own right, and in ways of their own invention. This is not a textbook, but one of those rare books that will excite and inspire; it will be read for personal as well as professional benefit, not in order to pass exams, or meet standards of competence."

Mary Jane Drummond

"Michael Armstrong's brilliant interpretations of narratives by children teaches us that children's stories can be analysed with the same rigor as those written by adults. Along the way, he also makes an important, even radical, point: Young children think like artists, and the best teachers take advantage of this natural passion by putting creativity at the center, rather than the periphery, of education."

Sam Swope

"One of Michael Armstrong's strong themes – 'teaching as interpretation' – may seem at first a surprising idea. I know from personal experience how Michael's intense respect for each individual story-maker has profoundly influenced 20 summers of teachers in his classes at the Bread Loaf School of English. Now, with this book, many more can learn from this gifted teacher."

Courtney Cazden, Harvard Graduate School of Education

"What a joy! Homage to Tolstoy apart, a whole book dedicated to insightful analysis of children's written stories by a gifted teacher. Armstrong taught us in *Closely Observed Children* how to look and listen to children and take their artistic endeavours seriously. This book lives up to its excellent predecessor. Forget the tangled webs of the National Literacy Strategy wasting millions of trees and pounds with its prescriptive, mechanistic message. This is real learning at its best, teaching by example, through painstaking scrutiny of the art of young writers. Absorbing, moving, enlightening, inspiring."

Morag Styles

CHILDREN WRITING STORIES

MICHAEL ARMSTRONG

Open University Press

Open University Press
McGraw-Hill Education
McGraw-Hill House
Shoppenhangers Road
Maidenhead
Berkshire
England
SL6 2QL

email: enquiries@openup.co.uk
world wide web: www.openup.co.uk

and Two Penn Plaza, New York, NY 10121-2289, USA

First published 2006

A catalogue record of this book is available from the British Library

ISBN-10: 0 335 021976 4 (pb) 0 335 21977 2 (hb)
ISBN-13: 978 0335 21976 6 (pb) 978 0336 21977 3 (hb)

Library of Congress Cataloguing-in-Publication Data
CIP data applied for

Typeset by YHT Ltd
Printed in Poland by OZGraf S.A. www.polskabook.pl

CONTENTS

for Jenny Giles
and
in memory of
Brian Simon

PREFACE:
THINKING ABOUT
CHILDREN'S STORIES

This is a book about the stories that children write: about their literary form, about their aesthetic and ethical content, about their significance for an understanding of intellectual growth, learning and teaching, education as a cultural enterprise. The book is the sequel to an earlier work, *Closely Observed Children*, first published in 1980. In *Closely Observed Children*, I set out to describe the intellectual life of a class of eight- to nine-year-old children in a primary school in rural Leicestershire. In particular I wanted to document the seriousness of purpose which I witnessed in children's thought and action, their 'high intent', as I called it (Armstrong 1980: 206). That seriousness, at once earnest and playful, was evident in every aspect of these children's work: in their writing, their art, their mathematics, their model making, their nature study. I was led to conclude that

> from their earliest acquaintance with the various traditions of human thought, with literature, art, mathematics, science, and the like, [children] struggle to make use of these several traditions, of the constraints which they impose as well as the opportunities which they present, to examine, extend and express in a fitting form their own experience and understanding.

> (1980: 129)

The life of reason, I argued, was coterminous with the beginnings of learning.

The present book takes children's high intent for granted. My purpose is to explore the ways in which that intent is manifested in one particular domain, that of written narrative. What follows is a sequence of studies in literary imagination, an investigation into the natural history of narrative during the years of childhood. In the preface to his three-volume masterpiece, *Time and Narrative* (1984), Paul Ricoeur defines narrative, or, more precisely the plot, as 'the privileged means by which we reconfigure our confused, unformed and at the limit mute temporal experience' (1984: xi). Ricoeur draws his examples from the masterpieces of modernism, *Mrs Dalloway*, *The Magic Mountain*, *Remembrance of Things Past*. My ambition is to demonstrate that the stories written by children, for all their acknowledged immaturity, serve the same purpose and follow the same procedure.

The method of my inquiry is descriptive and interpretive, based on the close reading of a limited number of stories, informed by a knowledge of the context in which they were composed. It is only through the sympathetic scrutiny of individual works that it seems to me possible to discover the creative and critical force of children's narrative imagination. My procedural principle might best be summarized in words used by Walter Benjamin in connection with the principle of montage as he chose to practise it in his *Arcades Project*: 'to discover in the analysis of the small individual moment the crystal of the total event' (1999b: 461). The stories that I have chosen to discuss are drawn from a variety of sources, but chiefly from my own experience as headteacher and classroom teacher at Harwell Primary School in Oxfordshire where I worked from 1981 until 1999 and where I became ever more absorbed in the excitement of understanding children's understanding. Each chapter is preceded by the particular story or stories which the chapter goes on to examine. My intention is that readers should have the opportunity to respond to the stories for themselves before reading my own interpretations. Interpretation is necessarily a collective pursuit and my own readings are both a product of discussions with friends and colleagues, and many of the writers themselves, and an incitement to further discussion. The book may thus be seen as both a select anthology of children's stories and a critical, though always provisional, account of children's narrative practice.

My interest in children's stories was first aroused, many years ago, by a reading of Tolstoy's essays on education, written in his early thirties when for a few years he ran a tiny village school for peasant children on his country estate at Yasnaya Polyana, 130 miles south of Moscow. Among these extraordinary essays one in particular caught my imagination, the impassioned account of how Tolstoy, himself already by then a leading figure in Russian literature, came to discover, almost by chance, the literary power and precision of which his young pupils were capable as they entered 'the world of art' (Tolstoy 1982: 222–47). Tolstoy was overwhelmed, not so much by the charm of his pupils' stories, two of which he describes and interprets with incomparable vivacity, as by what he calls their 'conscious creativity'. Their stories, he argues with a characteristic mixture of amazement and assurance, are the product not of a spontaneous gift or happy accident but of a deliberate design, a design which callenges his own literary understanding. Tolstoy's experience leads him to call into question both the nature of literary learning and the practice of literature as a whole. It is altogether without irony that he entitles his essay 'Who Should Learn to Write from Whom? Should the Peasant Children Learn to Write from Us or Should We Learn to Write from Them?'. Tolstoy's conclusions are so radical that they have been almost entirely overlooked in the century and a half since his essay was published. Yet they raise, in dramatic form, fundamental questions that lie at the heart of any authentic discussion of literary consciousness and its growth. I see my book as an extended gloss on Tolstoy's essay, an attempt to revive and extend its seminal argument.

The book opens with a reflection on Tolstoy's great essay and a reinterpretation of the second of the two stories on which that essay is based. Chapters 2 to 6 explore a series of stories written by children between the ages of 5 and 16 and trace the growth of literary consciousness from the dawn of written narrative in the kindergarten through the early years of schooling and on into adolescence. Chapter 2 is devoted to the work of Vivian Paley, whose book *Wally's Stories* (1981) offers an unrivalled glimpse into the narrative world of a child on the edge of literacy. The following four chapters are derived from my own experience and that of my colleagues at Harwell Primary School. A final chapter draws from the stories presented, interpreted and discussed in earlier chapters a set of conclusions as to the nature of children's narrative thinking and what this means for a pedagogy of the imagination. This concluding discussion leads the argument back to Tolstoy's essay and the book closes with Tolstoy's own tale of childhood, imagination and the mutuality of learning.

My work is indebted to two very special institutions. The first of these is Harwell Primary School. The children, teachers, support staff, parents and governors of Harwell School have been my inspiration and guide for the past 25 years. Only a minute fraction of the children's stories have found a place in this book but its argument depends upon the storytelling of the several hundred children who passed through the school between 1981 and 1999. The stories of any one of them might have featured here, just as they featured week by week in the newsletter distributed to the children's families. I believe there is no child who does not have a good story to tell. The second institution is the Bread Loaf School of English at Middlebury College, Vermont, USA. Every year except one since 1986 I have taught courses on narrative and the teaching of narrative to students, most of them classroom teachers, who have spent their summer vacations studying at Bread Loaf for an MA in Literature. Every story recounted in this book has been pored over again and again in my Bread Loaf classes. My debt to the students, faculty and staff of the Bread Loaf School of English, like the debt to Harwell School, is incalculable.

Beyond these primary debts I would like acknowledge a few of the many friends and colleagues whose experience and conversation have guided my work over the years: Brian Simon, Raymond King, Roy Waters, Alan Pinch, Michael Young, Tim McMullen, John and Pat Darcy, Tony Kallett, Allan Ahlberg, Byron Thomas, David Hawkins, Brenda and Monroe Engel, Maggie Gracie, Lesley King, Peter Hollis, Mary Brown, Stephen Rowland, Myra Barrs, Jenny Giles, Jim Maddox, Dixie Goswami, Courtney Cazden, Michele Stepto, Eleanor Duckworth, Steve Seidel and Marty Rutherford.

My final debt is to Isobel Armstrong. There is hardly a sentence or a thought in the book that has escaped her scrutiny.

CONSCIOUS CREATIVITY: REFLECTIONS ON AN ESSAY BY LEO TOLSTOY

THE LIFE OF A SOLDIER'S WIFE

Fyedka, age 11

The farthest back I can remember, I was about six; we were poor and lived on the edge of the village. There were my father, my mother, my grandmother and my sister. I remember, as if in a dream, how my grandmother loved me more than my mother did. She used to go around in an old white robe and a shabby check skirt, and she had an old linen rag round her head. Whenever I started running off anywhere she would say, "Mind you don't hurt yourself, Fyedka!" My mother was a weak woman. Father used often to wallop her when he came in drunk. She used to weep a few tears and say nothing. She wore a calico kerchief, went barefoot in summer and wore bark sandals in winter.

My father was about thirty; he was of middle height, thickset, with a broad chest. His beard was small; he wore a short blue jacket. On his head he wore a post-driver's cap. I was afraid of him; when I got up to mischief he gave me a good hiding and swore at me. When he began to hit me I would go running straight up to my grandmother; she would protect me.

My sister was always excitable. When something really excited me I always went to my big sister to let off steam.

For as far back as I can remember our cottage had been in a tumbledown way; we held it up with props. The cottage had been cramped anyway, and when it was propped up it became still worse. Then I remember me and my mate Tarasok climbing up on to a support. Grandmother said to me, "Don't you climb on the support, you young devils, or you'll knock the cottage down." Tarasok and I went into the yard birdnesting. I was daring enough for anything; I caught hold of the fence and jumped right over it. Then I caught hold of a stick with both hands and wanted to climb up some more – the stick broke and I went flying head over heels. It just happened there was a shaft lying there. When I fell off I hit my cheek right against the shaft and yelled blue murder. And that mark is still on my cheek.

The yard was crowded and open at one end and had heaps of rotten straw in it here and there. In the yard there was only one miserable old lop-sided horse. We had no cow; there were two wretched little sheep and one lamb. I always slept with that lamb; he used to make me all greasy. We ate dry bread and drank water; we had no-one to do the work; my mother was pregnant and kept complaining about her stomach. Grandmother was always near the stove, and always had a headache. The only one who worked was my sister, and that was not for the family, but on her own account – she was buying herself fine clothes and preparing to get married. As for my father, it went without saying – whatever he earned he drank.

I remember old Nefed coming to us – he was the village elder – and starting to curse my father for something. I just heard Nefed say, "Everyone's paid the tax money; you're the only one who hasn't. Look out for yourself, Gordyushka, my lad, the meeting will be called and they'll send you for a soldier." I heard him mention a pillow. I was sorry they were going to have my father shot. I snatched up my own pillow, put it on the elder's knees and said, "Here you are, here's a pillow, only don't send my father for a soldier." Everyone burst out laughing. The elder said, "You see, Gordei, whatever you earn you drink, but your son looks after you so, he'll even give up his last pillow for you." My father threw up his hand and went out into the yard. And grandmother said to the elder, "That's just what he wants; to leave his family and his house and not think about anything."

My father was not at all afraid and I remember that he went on going to the tavern. A month later the elder called a village meeting. A lot of people came to our yard, and people began to shout something. "He ought to be sent for a soldier." My mother was standing beside the people, crying. I went up to her and said, "Ma, what are you crying about?"

My mother caught me in her arms and started to cry harder, and said, "You're not sorry for him, and they want to send him for a soldier."

Then they sent old Yefim to fetch my father. Old Yefim brought him along drunk. I said, "Ma, what will he do there?"

Mother said to me, "The soldiers will bayonet him."

I felt sorry. I took fright and started to cry. Old Nefed looked at my father and said, "Well, what's your judgement?"

The people shouted, "Make him a soldier."

My father threw up his hand again and said, "That's just what I need, only don't forget my son."

Then a cart came up to us; they put my father in the cart and drove off. My mother clung round my father's neck and started to cry. The cart set off gently; my mother and my mother's sister Agafya and old Tatyana walked after the cart, and they were all crying. And I was sitting on my father's knees. So we got as far as the church; my father and the relations prayed, and he made me get out of the cart. We said goodbye; my mother and relations just burst out sobbing and cried all the way.

So we arrived home; grandmother was sitting by the window crying, and my mother flopped down on a bench and went on sobbing right up to dinner-time. Grandmother began to soothe my mother and said, "That's enough now Matryona. What can you do about it?" – but she was sighing herself – "it seems it is God's will. After all, you are still young; God may yet bring him back to see you again. But at my time of life I am always ailing, in no time at all I shall be dead."

My mother said, "Oh mother! I do feel bad! I do feel bad!" and she burst out sobbing.

And grandmother said, "Well, what are we to do now? There's no getting him back you know!"

My sister was sitting crying by the step too; her eyes were red with tears.

So we started a poor sort of life, three times worse than when my father was there – nothing to eat, the sheep were sold to buy bread, and they sold my pretty little lamb; all we had left was the lop-sided mare, and she had broken a leg.

* * *

After my father had been sent for a soldier, a month later my mother had a baby. Grandmother went out to fetch a woman. Then she borrowed some groats from her father-in-law and sent her son to get a priest. Then she stoked up the stove and began to cook porridge. My sister went to collect people for the christening. She fetched the people and a cottage-loaf apiece, and they sat down on the benches. Our relations began to set out the tables and cover them with cloths. Everything was ready and the benches had been fetched. We all sat down in our places; the priest arrived and read from a book. The boy was passed over to him and a tub of water was set down. All of a sudden he plunged the boy into the water.

I thought he wanted to drown him and shouted out, "Give the boy here!"

But grandmother made as if to hit me and said, "Don't shout or he'll hit you!"

I fell silent. And he plunged him in three times, and then gave him to Auntie Akelina.

My aunt wrapped him up in muslin and gave him to mother.

Then we all sat down to table; grandmother placed the two bowls of porridge on the table and served people with it. When everyone had eaten their fill they got up from the table, thanked grandmother and all left.

I went up to mother and said, "Ma, what's his name?"

Mother said, "Same as yours."

The boy was thin; he had puny little legs and kept on screaming.

Mother said, "Lord, when will that brat be dead?"

A week passed. Grandmother said, "Well, thank God that's the christening over." But the boy was doing worse and worse all the time.

At midnight mother started crying for some reason. Grandmother got up and said, "What's the matter? Christ be with you!"

Mother said, "My son is dead."

Grandmother lit a lamp, washed the boy, dressed him in a shirt, girded him up and placed him beneath the ikons. When dawn came my grandmother went to old Nefed's and told him. Old Nefed arrived with some planks and began to make a coffin. He made the little coffin and laid the boy in it. Then my mother sat down and began to keen and wail in a thin voice, and went on wailing for a long time. Then old Nefed took the boy and carried him off to be buried.

* * *

The only rejoicing we had was when we gave my sister to be married. A husband called Kondrashka was found for her. So they came courting and brought a loaf of white bread and a lot of vodka, and all sat down at a table, and mother sat down too. Then old Ivan poured some vodka into a glass and brought it to my mother; mother drank it. Then he sliced some bread and gave it to mother.

I was standing by the table, and I did so want a bit of bread. I bent mother down and spoke into her ear. Mother burst out laughing and old Ivan said, "What does he want, a bit of bread?" and went and cut me off a big piece. I took the bread and went off into the store room.

Then old Ivan poured some more out into a glass and took it to my mother. Mother said, "No, no more for me."

But old Ivan insisted; mother took it and drank it down. When everyone had gone out, old Ivan said, "Well, tomorrow we'll begin."

Mother said, "All right," and he went home.

I got up early next morning; I saw my sister dressed up in her new shoes and a nice kerchief and a new fur coat. Then I saw that mother was also dressed up nice and was stoking up the stove, and Kiryushka's mother was washing beef. When the cottage was warmed up a lot of people came to see us, a whole houseful. Then I saw three troikas coming, and the bridegroom Kondrashka in a new kaftan and a tall cap, and he drove right into our yard. Straight away the bridegroom got out of the cart and then came into the cottage. Then they brought my sister out, and the groom took her by the hand. They were made to sit at the table, and the women began to recite the greetings, and went on for a long time reciting them. Then they left the table, said a prayer, went into the yard, and went up to the troika. Kondrashka took my sister and made her sit in the cart, and got into the other one himself. When they had all taken their places they crossed themselves and set off.

I went out into the street and watched; they galloped away to the church and disappeared from sight. Then I went into the cottage and mother gave me a piece of bread. Then I sat down by the window and waited for them to come, and said, "Mum, when is my sister coming?"

Then I heard someone shout, "The wedding party's coming!"

I was delighted and went out to have a look; I saw a lot of people standing by the porch playing a song which went, "Why were you so long a-coming?" Then they drove into the yard again. The bridegroom got out and helped my sister out, and they went into the cottage. They were going to sit down at the table, but people were at the table, and I was sitting there with a rolling pin. Then Uncle Gerasim said, "Get up from the table."

I felt afraid and wanted to be off. Grandmother said, "You show him the rolling pin and say, 'What's this then?' and he'll give you some money."

Gerasim said, "I'll hit you with my whip!"

"And I'll hit you with the rolling pin," I said.

Then Gerasim poured out a glass of vodka and put some money in it and handed it to me. I drank it down and took out the money, and served vodka to everyone; the other people stood up and they sat down.

Then people began to play songs and dance. Mother gave me some beef. Then they served Uncle Gerasim with some vodka. He drank a little and said, "It's bitter!"

My sister took Kondrashka by the ears and they began to kiss. And they went on playing for a long time. When they had done playing and everyone had gone the bridegroom took my sister home. And mother said, "Now we are ruined and done for!"

A year passed; we did not have anything to eat at all. So my mother went and begged some flour from the village elder, and each month they used to give us two poods of flour. Half a year later my grandmother began to be very ill, and lay on her bed saying, "Now I shall never see Gordei," and kept on crying. Then she would say, "God be with him," and said to my mother, "If he comes – and God grant – don't quarrel with him."

A month later my grandmother died; only my mother was left. They laid grandmother out beneath the ikons; my mother sat down beside her and started to cry. I remember my mother crying beside her and saying, "O my dear mother, who will care for your wretched child now? What am I to do now? How can I take counsel? How shall I live out my life?" And my mother went on crying like this for a long time.

They brought a coffin and started to lay grandmother in it. The priest was sent for. The priest came, recited the dead mass and she was carried off to be buried. My mother went too and cried all the way. When grandmother had been buried my mother came back, and I saw that she was so pale. Just the two of us remained, mother and I, and for a long time we lived in poverty.

* * *

And now six years had passed since the time when my father had been sent for a soldier; I was twelve years old.

One day Mother sent me out to feed the lop-sided mare. I watched over it for a long time. Soldiers were going past. Then I saw a soldier coming who was like my father; he came up to me and said:

"Where are you from?"

I said, "From Yasnaya."

"Well now, do you know Matryona Shintyakova?"

I said, "Yes."

"Hasn't she got married?"

"No."

Then I asked, "And would you have seen my father in the army? His name is Gordei Shintyakov."

"Yes, I have. We were in the same regiment, and the colonel didn't half beat him." As soon as I heard this I felt sorry and began to cry. Then I noticed tears running down the soldier's cheeks; he started crying too. So I took him to our house. He prayed and said, "How d'ye do." Then he took his coat off and sat down on the chest and started to look hard at everything. Then he said, "Well now, is this all the family you've got?"

My mother said, "That's all."

At that the soldier began to weep and said, "Where's my mother then?"

Mother ran up to my father and said, "Your mother died a long time ago."

I ran up and started to kiss my father. My father was weeping, but in spite of that I started looking at everything that was in his packs and his pockets. In the pack I found two nice medals and slipped them inside my shirt. Then people arrived and kissed my father. Father stopped crying and looked at the people and just could not recognize them. Then my sister came along and kissed my father. Father said, "Which is this young woman?"

Mother burst out laughing and said, "He's a fine one; he doesn't know his own daughter."

Father called her over to him again and kissed her again and asked mother how long she had been married.

Mother said, "A long time now."

Then all the folk went home, only my sister stayed. Mother started to stoke up the stove and cook an omelette, and sent my sister out for a pint of vodka. The liquor was brought in and put on the table.

Father said, "What's this?"

My sister said, "It's vodka for you."

Father said, "No, I've stopped drinking now."

Mother said, "Now thank Heaven you've stopped."

Then the omelette was served up. Father said a prayer and sat down to table. I sat down next to him; my sister sat on the chest, and Mother stood by the table and looked at Father and said, "Just fancy, you've got younger! You've no beard."

Everyone began to laugh. When we had had supper my sister kissed Father again and went off home. Then Father began to rummage in his pack, and Mother and I watched. Then Mother caught sight of a book in it and said, "Learnt to read, have you?"

Father said, "That I have."

Then Father took out a big bundle and gave it to Mother.

"What's this?" says Mother.

"Money," says Father.

My mother was glad, and hastened, she put it away safe. Then my mother came back and said, "Where did you get it from?"

Father said, "I was an officer and had the army money. I gave it out to the soldiers and there was some left so I took it."

My mother was so glad she was running about like mad. The day was over by now; evening was coming on. A lamp was lit. My father took up the book and began to read. I sat beside him and listened, and Mother shone the lamp on to it. And my father read the book for a long time. Then we went to bed. I lay down on the back bench with my father, and my mother lay at our feet, and they were talking for a long time, almost till midnight. Then we went to sleep.

In the morning my mother got up, went up to my father and said, "Up you get, Gordei, we need firewood for the stove." Dad got up, put on his boots and cap and said, "Got an axe?"

Mother said, "Yes, but it's jagged, maybe it won't chop."

My father took the axe firmly in both hands, went up to the block, set it upright and hit it with all his might and split the block in two; he chopped up the wood and brought it into the cottage. Mother set about stoking up the stove; she filled it right up and it gave out a good glow. When it was glowing nicely my father says:

"Matryona!"

My mother came up and said, "Well, what is it?"

Father said, "I'm thinking of buying a cow, five lambs, two horses and a cottage – this one's falling down you know – so it'll come to about a hundred and fifty roubles in all."

My mother seemed to ponder; then she said, "Then we shall run through the money."

Father said, "We shall work."

My mother said, "Well, all right, we'll buy it, but I'll tell you what – where do we get the framework?"

Father said, "Hasn't Kiryukha got one then?"

My mother said, "That's just it, he hasn't. The Fokanichevs have grabbed it."

Father thought for a bit and said, "Well, we'll get one from Bryantsev."

My mother said. "I'd be surprised if he's got one either."

Father said, "'Course he will, he's from the state forest."

Mother said, "I'm afraid he'll charge a lot. Look out, he's a proper rogue."

Father said. "I'll go and take him some vodka and talk it over with him. And you bake us an egg in the ashes for dinner."

Then Mum got up a nice bit of dinner; she borrowed it from her folks. Then Father took some vodka and went off to see Bryantsev, and we stayed behind and sat waiting for a long time. I got bored without my father. I began to ask my mother to let me go where Father had gone. Mum said, "You'll get lost."

I started to cry and made to leave, but my mother hit me, and I sat down on the stove and cried still more. Then I saw my father come into the cottage and say, "What are you crying about?"

Mother said, "Fedyushka was going to run off after you, and I hit him."

Father came up to me and said, "What are you crying about?"

I began to complain about my mother. My father went up to my mother and started to beat her, made out he was anyway, and he keeps on saying, "Don't you hit Fyedka! Don't you hit Fyedka!" Mum made out she was crying. And I sat on Dad's knee and was glad.

Then Dad sat down to table and put me next to him and shouted, "Now Mother, give me and Fyedka our dinners; we're hungry."

So Mother gave us beef, and we began to eat. We finished dinner, and Mother said, "Well, what about the frame?"

Father said, "Fifty silver roubles."

Mother said, "That's nothing."

Father said, "Yes, there's no doubt about it, it's a first rate frame."

The End

Translation by Alan Pinch
(Tolstoy 1982: 262–70)

I felt that from that day onwards a new world of delights and sufferings had opened for him – the world of art.

(Tolstoy 1982: 227)

'Who should learn to write from whom? Should the peasant children learn to write from us, or should we learn to write from them?' This is the paradoxical title of an essay written by Tolstoy in 1862 (1982: 222–47). The essay marks the culmination of Tolstoy's fleeting but passionate interest in education between the years 1859 and 1862. These were critical years for Tolstoy. He had grown dissatisfied with his own writing, if not with literature in general, and he was uncertain of the extent of his political commitment in the face of the imminent emancipation of the serfs. His response was to withdraw to his family estate at Yasnaya Polyana, busy himself in estate management and open a free school for the peasant children from Yasnaya Polyana and the neighbouring villages. The school opened in Tolstoy's house in the autumn of 1859. By March 1860 there were around 50 pupils and the school was fast becoming 'the one interest that attaches me to life' (Maude 1929: vol 1, 250). Tolstoy's teaching was interrupted in the summer of 1860 when he left Yasnaya Polyana to tour Europe, partly in order to visit his dying brother and partly in search of educational ideas and the latest teaching practices. On his return home in the spring of 1861 he took up teaching again with renewed enthusiasm.

A letter to his distant relative and confidante, Countess A. A. Tolstaya, gives a lyrical picture of the school at this time:

I also have a charming and poetic occupation which I can't tear myself away from, and that's the school. When I break away from my office and the peasants who pursue me from every wing of the house, I go to the school; but as it's undergoing alterations the classes are held alongside, in the garden under the apple trees, and it's so overgrown that you can only get there by stooping down. The teacher sits there with the children all around him, nibbling blades of grass and making the lime and the maple leaves crackle. The teacher teaches according to my advice, but even so, not too well and the children feel it. They are fonder of me. And we begin to chat for 3 or 4 hours and nobody is bored. It's impossible to describe these children – they have to be seen. I've never seen the like among children of our own dear class. Just imagine that in two years, in the complete absence of discipline, not a single girl or boy has been punished. There's never any laziness, coarseness, stupid jokes or unseemly language. The school house is now almost completed. The school occupies three large rooms – one pink and two blue. One room, moreover, is a museum. On the shelves round the wall, stones, butterflies, skeletons, grasses, flowers, physics instruments etc are laid out. On Sundays the museum is open to everyone and a German from Jena does experiments. Once a week there's a botany class, and we all go off to the woods to look for flowers, grasses and mushrooms. Four singing classes a week and 6 of drawing and it's all going very well ... The classes are supposed to be from 8 to 12 and from 3 to 6, but they always go on till 2 o'clock because it's impossible to get the children to leave the school –

they ask for more. In the evening it often happens that more than half of them stay and spend the night in the garden, in a hut. At lunch and supper and after supper we – the teachers – confer together. On Saturdays we read our notes to each other and prepare for the following week.

(Christian 1978: vol 1, 149)

In the same letter Tolstoy writes of his plans to publish a journal about the school and about education in general. He saw this as an opportunity to spread his ideas and to start a debate about popular education in Russia. Twelve numbers were published in all, during 1862 and 1863. They contain a remarkable series of essays on educational theory, school organization and teaching methods, alongside vivid accounts of the work of the Yasnaya Polyana school. The journal was accompanied by supplementary booklets full of the children's writing and a variety of teaching materials. To Tolstoy's great disappointment, however, his journal caused little stir and was largely ignored. The failure of the journal was a bitter blow and this, combined with his heavy responsibilities as Arbiter of the Peace, responsible for settling disputes between serfs and their former owners, as well as teacher, estate manager and writer, undermined Tolstoy's health. Late in May 1862 he set off for the Russian Steppes to undergo a health cure. Effectively that was the end of the school as far as Tolstoy was concerned. On his return in July he fell in love with Sonya Behrs and within two months they were married. The effect on the school was devastating as one of Tolstoy's pupils, his favourite Fyedka, was to write in a memoir many years later:

We were disturbed by the news that Lev Nicolayevich was getting married. We knew that the fun we had had with him before would come to an end. After Lev Nicolayevich's marriage our school still continued for a certain time, but it was not at all the same as it had been before. We had Pyotr Vassilyevich, Ivan Ivanovich and Vladimir Alexandrovich for teachers but Lev Nicolayevich himself rarely visited us. And the school began to flag. The pupils were gradually dispersing. Within a few months there were only half of the pupils left, or even less. And a short time saw the removal of half of that half that remained as well. The benches were ever more thinly filled. The last pupils were bored and gloomy. The pupils from other villages and districts left. There were only the Yasnaya Polyana pupils left, and only about ten of these. I do not remember whether our school carried on for as much as a year after Lev Nicolayevich's marriage but I do remember that our school was closed altogether in 1863. And I never found anything so difficult in my life as parting with the Yasnaya Polyana school and with our teacher Lev Nicolayevich.

(Tolstoy 1982: 218)

But marriage was not the only reason for Tolstoy's declining interest. As Morozov's memoir puts it: 'At that period Lev Nicolayevich was writing some big book or other' (1982: 220). The book was *War and Peace*, begun in the autumn of 1862. Tolstoy's disillusionment with writing was over. One year later he would look back at his school in affectionate astonishment:

I've never felt my intellectual powers, and even all my moral powers, so free and so capable of work. And I HAVE work to do. This work is a novel of the 1810s and 1820s, which has been occupying me fully since the autumn. Does this prove weakness of character or strength? I sometimes think both – but I must confess that my views on life, on the *people* and on *society* are now quite different from what they were the last time I saw you. They can be pitied, but it is difficult for me to understand how I could have loved them so deeply. Nevertheless I'm glad that I passed through this school; this last mistress of mine was a great formative influence on me. I love children and teaching, but it's difficult for me to understand myself as I was a year ago. The children come to me in the evenings and bring with them memories for me of the teacher that used to be in me and is there no longer. Now I am a writer with *all* the strength of my soul, and I write and I think as I have never thought or written before.

(Christian 1978: vol 1, 181)

The brevity of Tolstoy's devotion to teaching has persuaded most commentators that his educational essays of the 1860s are more interesting for the light they shed on his own literary development than for their educational originality. Writing about these years in his classic study *Tolstoy in the Sixties*, the Russian formalist critic Boris Eikhenbaum describes the essay 'Who Should Learn to Write from Whom?' as

the most important work by Tolstoy in this period [the early sixties]. It bears only a tenuous relation to pedagogy – the title itself is directed not at teachers but at writers. Here the words 'learn to write' do not mean 'learn reading and writing' but 'learn to compose a literary work' and the word 'we' does not refer to teachers but to writers. The bases for Tolstoy's own artistic method are defined and formulated here. This is not an article on teaching but a literary pamphlet which contains the embryo of future peasant stories and of his treatise on art.

(1982: 65)

But in reading Tolstoy's essay as a critical moment in Tolstoy's return to literature and little else, Eikhenbaum has misjudged it. Tolstoy's essay is far more than a literary pamphlet. By demonstrating that children's stories may legitimately be read as so many versions of the aesthetic – works of art in their own right – Tolstoy seeks to revolutionize our understanding of children's thought, of cognitive development, of the nature of teaching and learning, as well as of literature itself. The essay explores a vast theme: the literary consciousness of childhood, its implications for education and more broadly for thought about culture and its inheritance. It challenges what still passes for conventional wisdom about the transmission of knowledge, the acquisition of literacy, and the induction of children into culture. Though little read and culturally remote, it remains the natural starting point for any discussion of children's narrative thought.

'Who Should Learn to Write from Whom?' is the story of two stories. The first story came about as a collaboration between Tolstoy and his class; the second was the more or less independent work of one particular child. Both of the stories had already been published in the booklets which accompanied Tolstoy's monthly journal, the first of them under the title *He Feeds You with a Spoon and Pokes You in the Eye with the Handle*, the second called *The Life of a Soldier's Wife*. Tolstoy begins his essay by acknowledging that for a long time his pupils seemed to write nothing but trivia: 'According to their inclinations I set them exact, artistic, touching, funny and epic subjects for essays – it did not work' (1982: 223). The problem was simple: 'They did not understand the main point: why write? and what is so good about writing it down? They did not understand art – the beauty of expressing life in words and the absorbing power of that art' (1982: 223).

This is how Tolstoy poses the problem of literacy. Learning to write means learning to compose a literary work. Purpose is everything and the predominant purpose is art. It is interesting to compare the way in which the Russian psychologist Lev Vygotsky describes the development of literacy some 70 years later. Vygotsky had read Tolstoy's educational essays and was one of the few theorists of child development to take them seriously. Noting his disappointment at the triviality of children's writing in Maria Montessori's school in Rome, he argues 'that writing should be meaningful for children, that an intrinsic need should be aroused in them, and that writing should be incorporated into a task that is necessary and relevant for life. Only then can we be certain that it will develop as a really new and complex form of speech (Vygotsky 1968: 118). For Tolstoy, even as he despaired of the future of his own writing, no task could be more necessary or relevant than art.

The revelation of children's artistic sensibility and how to evoke it came about, finally, almost by accident. Tolstoy had been reading at home a book of Russian proverbs. 'For a long time now,' he writes, 'reading Snyegiryov's collection of proverbs has been one of my favourite – not studies – but pleasures. At each proverb I find myself imagining characters from the people, and their clashes, suggested by the meaning of the proverb. Amongst my unrealized dreams I have always imagined a series, not so much of stories as of pictures, written around proverbs' (1982: 223). Like all good teachers, Tolstoy felt compelled to share his enthusiasm with his pupils:

> I brought the book to school. It was the Russian language lesson.
> 'Well then, why doesn't someone write about a proverb?' I said. The best pupils – Fyedka, Syomka and others – pricked up their ears.
> 'How do you mean, about a proverb? Tell us.' The questions came in showers. We came across the proverb 'He feeds you with a spoon and pokes you in the eye with the handle'.
> 'Now imagine,' I said, 'that a peasant took a beggar into his house and then, for reasons of his own, began to reproach him and it ends up with him feeding him with a spoon and poking him in the eye with the handle.'
> 'But how would you write it?' said Fyedka, and all the others who had been about to prick up their ears suddenly turned away, having come to

the conclusion that the task was beyond their powers, and set about their own work which they had begun before.

'Write it yourself,' someone said to me.

They were all busy with their work; I took a pen and an ink well and began to write.

'Well,' I said, 'let's see who will write it best, I will do it too.'

(1982: 223)

After a while Fyedka, who had finished a piece of his own, came up to Tolstoy and started to read over his shoulder. Other children followed and Tolstoy found that he could not continue. He stopped writing and began to read them what he had written. No one liked it. Tolstoy felt ashamed. 'In order to soothe my literary vanity I began to tell them my plan for what was to follow,' he explains (1982: 224). As he did so he recovered his spirits and at the same time the children began to make suggestions of their own about how the story should continue. Before long it was they who were dictating the story while Tolstoy had become more of a scribe than a fellow author.

Tolstoy was immediately impressed by the clarity and precision of the children's judgements and their fidelity to what they understood of experience – Tolstoy calls it their concern for 'artistic truth':

Their demands were so unfortuitous and precise that more than once I began arguing with them and was obliged to give way. I had firmly stuck in my head the demands of correct construction and a right relationship between the meaning of the proverb and the story; they, on the contrary, demanded only artistic truth. I wanted, for instance, to have the peasant who had taken the old man into his home repent of his good deed himself – they considered this to be impossible and created a shrew of a wife.

I said, 'At first the peasant felt sorry for the old man, and afterwards he begrudged him bread.'

Fyedka replied that that would be inconsistent. 'He didn't obey his wife from the very beginning and he won't give in afterwards either.'

'And what sort of man is he according to you,' I asked.

'He's like old Timofei,' said Fyedka, smiling, 'a sort of thin beard and he goes to church and he keeps bees.'

'Kind but obstinate,' I said.

'Yes,' said Fyedka, '*he's* not going to listen to his wife.'

(1982: 224)

Two children stood out from the rest, Syomka for the clarity of his objective images and Fyedka for the power of feeling that underlay his imagery:

It seemed as though Syomka was seeing and describing things which were present before his eyes: the stiff, frozen bark sandals and the mud which flowed from them when they were thawed out, and the dry shells they turned into when the woman threw them into the stove; Fyedka, on the other hand, saw only those details which called forth in him the feeling with which he regarded a particular character. Fyedka saw the snow which had got inside the old man's foot rags and the feeling of

sympathy with which the peasant said 'Lord! What he went about in!'
(Fyedka even demonstrated how the peasant said this, spreading his arms
and shaking his head.)

(1982: 225)

Tolstoy noted the specifically literary quality of the children's writing, especially Fyedka's. 'He wanted to speak by himself – and not to speak in the way
that people tell stories, but as they write, that is to fix the images of his feeling
artistically by means of words' (1982: 226). He refused to let Tolstoy change
his word order and would reject any suggestion that struck him as dis-
proportionate, artificial or superfluous. It was as if he possessed an intuitive
'sense of measure'.

At the end of the day Syomka and Fyedka stayed behind to continue the
story with Tolstoy:

> We worked from seven o'clock till eleven; they felt neither hunger nor
> fatigue, and they even grew cross with me when I stopped writing; they
> took to writing themslves by turn but soon gave it up, it did not work. It
> was only then that Fyedka asked me what my name was. We burst out
> laughing at his not knowing it.
>
> 'I know,' he said, 'what to call you, but what's your household? Like
> we've got the Fokanychevs, the Zyabreks, the Yermilins.'
>
> I told him.
>
> 'And are we going to print it?' he asked.
>
> 'Yes!'
>
> 'Then we ought to put in print by Makarov, Morozov and Tolstoy.'

(1982: 226)

Tolstoy was overwhelmed by what had happened:

> I cannot convey, [he writes,] the feeling of excitement, joy, fear and
> almost repentance which I experienced in the course of that evening. I
> felt that from that day onwards a new world of delights and sufferings
> had opened for him [Fyedka] – the world of art; it seemed as though I had
> been prying into something which no-one ever has the right to see, the
> birth of the mysterious flower of poetry. I felt both fear and joy, like a
> treasure seeker who should see a flower upon a fern; I was joyful because
> suddenly, quite unexpectedly, the philosopher's stone which I had been
> seeking in vain for two years was revealed to me – the art of teaching how
> to express thoughts; I felt fear because that art called forth new demands,
> a whole world of desires which were not consonant with the environ-
> ment in which the pupils lived, as it seemed to me in the first moment.
> There was no mistaking it. It was not chance but conscious creativity.

(1982: 227)

Again and again, throughout the essay, Tolstoy insists that the children's
creativity is no accident. The originality of his insight is nowhere more
apparent. He is the first modern thinker – the first of remarkably few – to have
recognized that children's writing, like other aspects of their art or more
generally of their thought, is neither carefree nor artless but the product of a

conscious intent. 'All this is so far from fortuitous,' he assures us, 'in all these touches we feel such a conscious artistic power' (1982: 227). By way of example, Tolstoy cites an apparently minor point in the finished work. The story is about a peasant who takes in an old man whom his wife has found lying on the doorstep, frozen stiff. The wife is furious when her husband starts to look after the old man instead of sending him away. She hurries round to a neighbour's house to plead with him to talk some sense into her husband. The neighbour is reluctant, being a little frightened of the husband, but eventually he agrees. 'The neighbour put on a woman's fur coat,' the story continues, 'and set off saying "Maybe I'll bring him round somehow and if I can't I'll give him a piece of my mind and be off"' (1982: 250). Tolstoy was surprised that Fyedka should have mentioned that it was a *woman's* fur coat that the neighbour put on:

> I remember that it struck me so much that I asked: 'Why a *woman's* fur coat?' Nobody had led Fyedka up to the idea of saying that the neighbour put a fur coat on.
> He said 'That's right, it's like him.'
> When I asked whether we could say that he put a man's fur coat on he said, 'No, better if it's a woman's.'
>
> (1982: 227)

The more Tolstoy ponders Fyedka's choice, the more it makes sense:

> And this touch is indeed extraordinary. You cannot make out at first why it is a *woman's* fur coat, and yet you feel that this is excellent and that it could not be otherwise. Every word of a work of art, whether it belongs to Goethe or to Fyedka, differs from the non-artistic in that it calls forth a countless multitude of ideas, images and interpretations. The neighbour in a woman's fur coat is bound to be imagined as a puny, narrow-chested peasant, as he obviously ought to be. The woman's fur coat, draped over a bench, the first one he laid his hands on, also conjures up for you the whole life and manners of a peasant on a winter's evening. By way of the fur coat you automatically imagine too the later hour when the peasant is sitting undressed in the light of a wood splinter lamp, and the woman coming in and out to get water and clean out the cattle sheds, and all the outward untidiness of peasant life when not a single person clearly possesses any particular garment, and not a single thing has its own definite place. By that single phrase 'he put on a woman's fur coat' the whole character of the environment in which the action is proceeding is established and that phrase was not uttered by chance, but consciously.
>
> (1982: 228)

We do not need to accept every detail of Tolstoy's interpretation to recognize the validity of his argument. There is a case for saying that Tolstoy's interpretations often tend to weaken the force of the children's linguistic choices. In the end it does not matter. Fyedka's insistence, 'No, better if it's a woman's,' is sufficient evidence in itself of precision and intent.

Tolstoy found it hard at first to make sense of his experience:

It seemed to me so strange that a semi-literate peasant boy should suddenly evince such a conscious artistic power as Goethe, on his sublime
summit of development, could not attain. It seemed to me so strange
and insulting that I, the author of 'Childhood', who had earned a certain
success and recognition for artistic talent from the educated Russian
public, that I, in a matter of art, not only could not instruct or help the
eleven year old Syomka or Fyedka, but I was only just able – and then
only in a happy moment of stimulation – to follow and understand
them. This seemed so strange to me that I could not believe what had
happened the day before.

(1982: 229)

It is tempting to smile at Tolstoy's exaggerations but his hyperbole reflects a
familiar teaching experience. It is impossible to attend to children's creative
thought without recognizing a challenge to one's own. Eikhenbaum and
others have suggested that Tolstoy's teaching experience had its effect on his
own later writing, not only the later peasant stories but even *War and Peace*
itself. Eikhenbaum interprets this as evidence that Tolstoy was less interested
in teaching than in his own literary development. We come closer to the
significance of Tolstoy's experience if we say that in coming to an understanding of children's stories, Tolstoy found himself compelled to reconsider
his own.

Any remaining doubts which Tolstoy might have entertained about the
quality and purposefulness of his pupils' writing were dispelled by a characteristically Tolstoyan sequel. The story remained unfinished at the end of
the first day. On the second and third days the writing continued 'with the
same feeling for artistic truth and measure and the same absorption' (Tolstoy
1982: 230). Then Tolstoy had to go away for a few days and while he was away
a new craze spread round the class for making paper bangers. The precious
manuscript was turned into bangers and when, a day or two later, the children grew tired of making bangers they were all 'gathered up and trium-
phantly thrust into the stoked up stove'. As Tolstoy laments, 'the bangers
phase was at an end but our manuscript had perished with it' (1982: 231).
Tolstoy was in despair. He wanted to start a new story straight away but he
could not overcome his sense of loss until Fyedka and Syomka approached
him and offered to rewrite the original story. 'By yourselves,' Tolstoy growled,
'I'm not going to help any more' (1982: 231).

Tolstoy's description of the rest of that day brings the story of the children's
first story to its dazzling close:

And indeed after the lesson they came to the house between eight and
nine, locked themselves in the study, a fact which afforded me no little
pleasure, laughed for a little while, fell silent and until after eleven, when
I went up to the door, I could only hear them conversing with one
another in quiet voices and the scratching of a pen. Only once they had
an argument as to what had come first and came to me for a ruling: did
he look for the bag before his wife went to the neighbour or afterwards? I
told them that that didn't matter. Between eleven and twelve o'clock I
knocked at their door and went in. Fyedka, in a new white fur coat

trimmed with black, was sitting in the depths of an armchair with one leg crossed upon the other, his shaggy young head propped on his hand and playing with a pair of scissors in the other hand. His large black eyes, shining with an unnatural but serious and adult glitter, were staring somewhere into the distance; his irregular lips, pursed as if he were about to whistle, were obviously in the act of forming a word which, his imagination having hit upon it, he was about to utter. Syomka, standing in front of the large writing table, with a large white fragment of sheepskin on his back (tailors had only just come to the village), with loosened sash and dishevelled head, was writing on the crooked lines, constantly stubbing the pen into the inkwell. I rumpled Syomka's hair and as he looked at me, startled, with puzzled sleepy eyes, his plump high-boned face with its straying hair was so funny that I started to chuckle, but the children did not start laughing. Fyedka, without altering the expression on his face, touched Syomka's sleeve, meaning that he should go on writing:
'Wait a minute, you,' he said to me presently (Fyedka talks to me like that when he is absorbed and excited), and he dictated a bit more.
I took the exercise book from them, and five minutes later when, seated around the little cupboard, they were consuming potatoes and kvass by turns, looking at the silver spoons, which were marvellous in their eyes, they burst out, without knowing why themselves, into ringing childish laughter; the old woman listening to them upstairs also laughed without knowing why.
'What are you laughing for?' said Syomka, 'sit up straight or else you'll be filled up lopsided.'
And as they took off their fur coats and stretched out underneath the writing table to sleep they could not stop their outbursts of childish, peasant, healthy, enchanting laughter. I read through what they had written. It was a new variant of the same thing. Some things were missed out, some new artistic beauties were added. And again the same feeling for beauty, truth and measure.

(1982: 231)

For the remainder of the school year Tolstoy was unable to carry out any further experiments in the teaching of literacy, 'the art of teaching how to express thoughts'. It was not until the summer holidays that a fresh opportunity arose:

Fyedka and some other boys lived with me for part of the summer. Having had their fill of bathing and playing they thought of doing a little work. I proposed to them that they should write a composition and gave them several subjects. I told them a very gripping story about a theft of money, the story of a certain murder, the story of how a molokan was miraculously converted to orthodoxy, and I also proposed that they should write in the form of an autobiography the story of a boy whose poor and dissolute father was sent to be a soldier and to whom the father returned as a reformed and good man.

I said, 'I would write it like this: I remember when I was little, I had a mother, a father and such and such other relations and what they were like. Then I would write that I remember how my father used to go on the spree, my mother was always crying and he used to beat her; then how they sent him to be a soldier, how she wailed and we began to get on still worse, how the father came back and I didn't seem to recognise him, and he asked whether Matryona was alive here – meaning his wife – and how we rejoiced then and started to prosper.' That is all I said to them at first.

(1982: 233)

Fyedka was delighted with the subject and set to work at once. This time he worked on his own and Tolstoy intervened less although it is clear from his account that he made a number of suggestions during the earlier part of the story, interventions which he is quick to dismiss as 'my influence for vulgarity and corruption' (1982: 234). By the time Fyedka reached the climax of the story, with the father's return, he had grown impatient with his teacher's promptings: ' "Don't say anything! I know myself, I know!" he said to me and began to write, and from that point onwards he wrote the whole story to the end at one sitting' (1982: 237).

Tolstoy's account of Fyedka's story takes the form of an interpretation, a reading of the story designed to demonstrate and justify the claims which he has already made for children's literary consciousness in describing the way in which the earlier story was composed. It is the earliest example in European literature of a rare genre, the close reading of a child's literary text. As such it is remarkable no less for its ambition than for its originality. Tolstoy's judgements may at times seem extravagent or overbearing but every disagreement with the particulars of his interpretation forces us back to the text with the effect of uncovering fresh possibilities that only serve to strengthen the general argument. It is a unique moment in the history of educational thought. What Tolstoy had proposed to his pupils was not so much a subject as the epitome of a plot. He challenges Fyedka and the others to bring the story to life on the page. Fyedka's impatience shows that he has recognized and accepted the challenge. In interpreting the story that Fyedka has written Tolstoy is attempting to understand the ways in which Fyedka has made use of the outlined plot to articulate his own distinctive vision. As before, Tolstoy finds himself overwhelmed by the aesthetic and ethical force of that vision, for all its apparent simplicity.

It was Tolstoy who gave the story its title, after Fyedka had completed it: *The Life of a Soldier's Wife*. In effect, it is his first act of interpretation. Eikhenbaum and others have remarked on the elements of folk tale to be found in Fyedka's story. It is interesting, therefore, that Tolstoy's title reverses the pattern of the traditional Russian tale as analysed in Vladimir Propp's famous study, *The Morphology of the Folk Tale* (1968). The title implies that it is not Gordei, the soldier, the hero of the quest, who is to be seen as the protagonist of the tale, as indeed Tolstoy's own outline of the plot implied, but, rather, his wife, Matryona, the narrator's mother who has stayed behind, waiting in expectation and despair. By calling the story *The Life of a Soldier's*

Wife, Tolstoy has drawn attention to the special character of Fyedka's tale. Fyedka, the storyteller, in his guise as narrator, shares the mother's perspective. His is a folk tale told from the standpoint of those who suffer rather than those who act.

This is the first of several occasions when Tolstoy's treatment of Fyedka's story calls to mind another celebrated essay on narrative, Walter Benjamin's essay 'The Storyteller', originally published in 1934 (1968: 83–109). Benjamin's essay is a reflection on the stories of Tolstoy's contemporary, Nikolai Leskov. Benjamin presents Leskov as a traditional storyteller and celebrates the traditional tale as an incomparable but dying art form. Early in the essay he distinguishes two kinds of storyteller: ' " When someone goes on a trip he has something to tell about" goes the German saying and people imagine the storyteller as someone who has come from afar. But they enjoy no less listening to a man who has stayed at home, making an honest living, and who knows the latest tales and traditions' (1968: 84). Fyedka surely belongs among this second group. His story abounds in family tradition and local colour. It is the tale, not of a traveller, an adventurer, but of an onlooker and observer, a child who watches closely and remembers vividly events the significance of which are still in part mysterious.

Tolstoy divides the story into four scenes or chapters and examines each in turn. In the opening scene it is the incidental details that catch his attention, moments of insight which stand out against the formal descriptions of character and setting:

> If there is a certain vulgarity of approach in the opening, in the description of the characters and of the dwelling, then I alone am responsible for it. If I had left him alone I am sure he would have described the same thing unobtrusively in the course of the action, with greater art, without that mannerism of logically arranged descriptions which is accepted amongst us and has become impossible: first the description of the dramatis personae and even their biographies, then a description of the place and milieu and only then the action begins. And strange to relate, all these descriptions, sometimes covering tens of pages, do less to acquaint the reader with the characters than an artistic touch nonchalantly thrown in at a point when the action has already begun, between characters who have not been described at all. Thus in the first chapter just Gordei's one phrase 'That's just what I need' when, shrugging his shoulders, he submits to his fate of being a soldier and merely asks for the meeting not to abandon his son – this phrase does more to acquaint the reader with the character than the description which is repeated several times and was concocted by me, of his dress, person and habit of going to the tavern.
>
> (1982: 234)

The opening scene is full of moments such as these. Take, for example, the first paragraph. Its evocative power is concentrated in just three sentences, each of them an instance of the unobtrusive artistry which so strongly impresses Tolstoy. The prevailing mood of the narrative to come is suggested by a simple comparison: 'I remember, as if in a dream, how my grandmother loved me more than my mother did.' The particular quality of the grandmother's love is captured in a remembered detail: 'When I started running off anywhere she would say "Mind you don't hurt youself, Fyedka".' A single image is enough to bring to life the mother's weakness in the face of her husband's violence: 'She used to weep a few tears and say nothing.'

The end of the scene is heavy with foreboding: 'So we started a poor sort of life, three times worse than when my father was there – nothing to eat, the sheep were sold to buy bread and they sold my pretty little lamb; all we had left was the lop-sided mare and she had broken a leg.' The two scenes that follow present a vivid portrait of a family in decline. Fyedka's account of the birth and christening of the narrator's baby brother is heavy with menace. One of the most striking features of his narrative is the way in which it evokes the imaginative world of a young child, where events are perceived with startling clarity even though their cultural significance is only dimly understood. It is this that gives the description of the baby's christening, as also, later, the sister's wedding, its extraordinary drama: 'We all sat down in our places; the priest arrived and read from a book. The boy was passed over to him and a tub of water was set down. All of a sudden he plunged the boy into the water.' No wonder the watchful elder brother is alarmed. Yet at the end of the ceremony he still does not know his brother's name. It is as if the whole point of the christening has been lost on him. But what exactly is the point of this christening? As Fyedka relates it, it seems more like the pretext for a death than the celebration of new life. No sooner has the mother answered her son's question, 'Ma, what's his name?' with the indifferent reply 'Same as yours' than she brings the christening to a close with the grim plea, 'Lord, when will that brat be dead?'

The shock of the baby's death, following so suddenly, is all the greater for the austerity of its narration and it is this austerity which particularly appeals to Tolstoy:

> I suggested that the boy should have thin legs, I suggested the sentimental detail about old Nefed making the little coffin; but the complaints of the mother expressed in one phrase, 'Lord, when will that brat be dead', put before the reader all the essence of the situation; and after that the night during which the elder brother is aroused by his mother's tears, and her reply to the grandmother's question as to what was the matter with her in the simple words 'My son is dead' and the grandmother getting up and lighting a lamp and washing the little body – all this is his own; all this is so compressed, so simple and so powerful not a single word can be discarded, not a single one changed or added. There are but five lines in all, and in those five lines the whole picture of that mournful night is drawn for the reader, and a picture reflected in the imagination of a six or seven year old boy.
>
> (1982: 234)

The wedding scene brings a temporary lightening of mood. Tolstoy points once again to the precision and power of its details:

All of this description of the wedding is uncommonly good. There are details at which we cannot help being quite bemused, and when we remember that this was written by an eleven year old boy we ask ourselves, 'Could this really not be by chance?' This can be seen by reading between the lines of that condensed and powerful description of a seven year old boy, with clever and attentive little eyes, no taller than the table, whom nobody pays any attention to, but who remembers and notices everything. When he wanted a piece of bread, for instance, he said that he bent his mother down to him. And this is not said by chance, it is said because he can remember his relationship with his mother at that period of his growth and how his relations with his mother were timid in front of other people and close when they were alone together.

(1982: 236)

The wedding forms an interlude in the family's ill fortune, a hopeful space which the narrative, as Tolstoy reads it, personifies in the figure of the sister:

Back in the first chapter he [Fyedka] had characterised the relationship of the sister to the family at a single stroke: 'the only one who worked was my sister and that was not for the family but on her own account – she was buying herself fine clothes and preparing to get married.' And this one stroke is enough to give a complete sketch of the girl, who cannot and indeed does not take part in the joys and sorrows of the family. She has her own legitimate interest, her own sole aim which Providence has placed before her, her future marriage and family.

(1982: 235)

Tolstoy wonders how his fellow writers might interpret this one stroke:

Now our dear friend the writer, especially if he is of the sort that wish to edify the common people by presenting them with examples of morality worthy to be imitated, would certainly have raised the question of the sister's participation in the general hardships and sorrow of the family. He would either make her into a shameful example of indifference or else a model of love and self-sacrifice, and we should have an idea, but no living character of the sister.

(1982: 235)

For Tolstoy the sister's independence is precisely what makes it possible for her to serve

in that woeful period of loneliness for the soldier's wife as a representative of joy and youth and hope. Not for nothing does he say that the only joy they had was when they gave the sister in marriage; not for nothing does he describe the wedding celebrations with such loving detail; not for nothing does he make the mother say after the wedding, 'Now we are ruined and done for.'

(1982: 236)

Just as the christening foreshadowed the infant's death, so now the wedding foreshadows the death of the grandmother. With this final blow the family's despair reaches its lowest depth. Once again Fyedka visualizes the moment of despair in a single image, that of the mother's pallor, an image which broods over the years of poverty that follow: 'When grandmother had been buried my mother came back and I saw that she was so pale. Just the two of us remained, mother and I, and for a long time we lived in poverty.'

'And now six years had passed.' With these words the story leaps forward to its finale, an extraordinary sequence of tableaux representing the return of the hero, his recognition, reform and good fortune, and the family's new and happy life.Tolstoy is understandably astonished. He confesses, 'I have met with nothing like these pages in Russian literature' (1982: 237). Fyedka's resolution of the tale is indeed a tour de force of the youthful imagination, an incomparable instance of the quality which Walter Benjamin discerns in every noteworthy story: 'that chaste compactness which precludes psychological analysis' (1968: 91). Benjamin contrasts storytelling with information:

> Every morning brings us news of the globe, [he writes,] and yet we are poor in noteworthy stories. This is because no event any longer comes to us without already being shot through with explanation ... Actually it is half the art of storytelling to keep a story free from explanation as one reproduces it ... The most extraordinary things, marvellous things, are related with the greatest accuracy, but the psychological connection of the events is not forced on the reader. It is left up to him to interpret things the way he understands them, and thus the narrative achieves an amplitude that information lacks.
>
> (1968: 89)

It is this amplitude that Tolstoy recognizes in Fyedka's narrative, even if in interpreting things the way he understands them he is inclined to force on the reader his own particular explanation of the psychological connection of the events that Fyedka relates. 'In the whole of that encounter,' he insists, 'there is not a single hint that this is touching; it merely relates what went on, but out of all that went on nothing is related except what is essential if the reader is to understand the situation of all the characters' (1982: 237).

Tolstoy points first to the delicacy of the recognition scene which delays the moment of recognition till the revelation of the grandmother's death. 'The soldier said only three phrases in his own home. At first he was still plucking up his courage and said, "How d'ye do." When he had begun to forget the role that he had taken on he said "Is this all the family you've got?" And then everything came out with the words "Where's my mum then?".' So much of the narrative is recapitulated and consolidated here: the grandmother's love of her grandson, her despair at her son's departure, her dying words to her daughter in law, 'If he comes – and God grant it – don't quarrel with him.'

Recognition is followed by evidence of reform which is contained within a further moment of recognition. 'The father is reformed,' writes Tolstoy. 'How many false and clumsy sentences we would have heaped up at this opportunity! But Fyedka simply told how the sister brought vodka and he did not start to drink it ... And consider, if he did not start to drink at a moment like that, then he really had reformed' (1982: 238). Further evidence of the father's reform comes with the almost casual revelation that Gordei has learned to read. 'When we had had supper my sister kissed Father again and went off home. Then Father began to rummage in his pack and Mother and I watched. Then Mother caught sight of a book in it and said, "Learned to read, have you?" Father said, "That I have".'

It was not the book, however, that Gordei was looking for but the fortune. 'Then Father took out a big bundle and gave it to Mother. "What's this?" says Mother. "Money," says Father. My mother was glad and hastened, she put it away safe. Then my mother came back and said, "Where did you get it from?" Father said, "I was an officer and had the army money. I gave it out to the soldiers and there was some left so I took it".' Tolstoy makes heavy weather of this fortune which had been acquired in such a dubious fashion. 'Some of the readers of this story have observed,' he notes, 'that this detail is immoral and that the idea of the exchequer as a milch cow ought to be stamped out and not confirmed in the minds of the common people. But I for my part prize this touch particularly, not to speak of artistic truth' (1982: 238). Almost two pages are spent proving that the apparent dishonesty is true virtue. The story itself, however, is open minded. It offers no judgement but simply presents a fact. For the purposes of the narrative the point is to find a way of linking the hero's return to the family's good fortune. The sturdy realism and ethical ambiguity of Fyedka's solution places it within the finest traditions of the folk tale. This is the artistic truth which Tolstoy finally recognizes, for all his anxiety about the morality of the soldier's action:

> What the author wants is to make his hero happy; his return home to the family should have been enough for happiness, but it was necessary to remove the poverty which had been weighing upon the family for so many years: where could he obtain riches from? From the impersonal public account. If riches are to be given they must be taken from someone – there was no more proper and reasonable way of finding them.
>
> (1982: 240)

Tolstoy is struck by one particular detail in the account of the soldier's good fortune. It is a syntactical point, hard to appreciate in translation but of a kind that will recur many times in succeeding chapters of this book:

> In the very scene where the money is announced, [he explains,] there is a tiny detail, a single word, which seems to strike me afresh every time I read it. It illuminates the whole picture, delineates all the characters and their relationships, and it is but one word, and a word used incorrectly, syntactically wrong – it is the word 'hastened'. A teacher of syntax is bound to say that it is incorrect. 'Hastened' requires a continuation – hastened to do what? the teacher is bound to ask. But here it reads simply 'My mother took the money and hastened, she put it away safe' – and this is splendid. I wish that I might say a word like that, and I wish that teachers who give instruction in language would say or write down a sentence like that.
>
> (1982: 240)

As we will see, the creative use of syntactical errors is a significant feature of children's narrative technique, enlivening their prose, extending their narrative range and confirming their literary intentions. Tolstoy's recognition of the value of Fyedka's faulty syntax is among the most original of his discoveries as he pores over his pupils' stories.

The revelation of the fortune brings Fyedka's story to its natural conclusion but Fyedka adds an extended coda. Tolstoy treats this coda as Fyedka's way of indicating the family's happy future: 'One might think that it is all over; the father has returned, they are not poor any more. But Fyedka was not satisfied with this (those imaginary people had evidently established themselves too vividly in his imagination); he still wanted to imagine a picture of how their way of life changed' (1982: 241). The two scenes that follow are Fyedka's sketch of the new life. There is a further and perhaps more significant aspect of these scenes which Tolstoy ignores. It is remarkable how thoroughly Fyedka's coda recapitulates and transforms the story's beginnings. Already, in the account of the soldier's reform, we catch an echo of the grandmother's sarcastic comment to the elders when Gordei was sent to be a soldier: 'That's just what he wants, to leave his family and his house and not think about anything.' The irony is that it is precisely by leaving his house and family that Gordei has reformed and found his fortune. In a similar way the father's playful pretence to beat his wife for upsetting their son recalls their earlier life together. Then the beatings were all too real and the mother 'used to weep a few tears and say nothing,' while the narrator 'would go running straight up to my grandmother and she would protect me'. Now it is all make believe: 'Mum made out she was crying. And I sat on Dad's knee and was glad.' But the most significant recapitulation of all comes with the story's final sentence: 'Father said, "Yes there's no doubt about it, it's a first rate frame".' In the opening scene the narrator had drawn attention to the weakness of the family house: 'For as far back as I remember our cottage had been in a tumbledown way; we held it up with props.' The new frame, bought, it is worth noting, from a state forester, a 'proper rogue' who has presumably helped himself to the state's wood, symbolizes the family's new strength, which Fyedka has earlier suggested in his father's chopping of firewood on the morning after his return. To end with the new frame itself is the last of the many surprises of this singular tale.

'But what is it we are wanting to say by all this?' Tolstoy asks at the end of his discussion of Fyedka's story:

> What significance has this story, written by one, perhaps exceptional, boy, in a pedagogical context? People will say to us, 'Perhaps you, the teacher, helped him without yourself noticing it, in the composition of this and other stories, and it is too difficult to find the boundary between what is yours and what is original.' People will say to us, 'Assuming that the story *is* good, this is only one of the genres of literature.' They will say to us. 'Fyedka and the other boys whose compositions you have printed are a happy exception.' They will say to us, 'You are a writer yourself. Without realising it you have helped the pupils in ways which cannot be prescribed as a rule for other teachers who are not writers.' They will say

to us, 'It is impossible to deduce any general rule or theory from all this. It is a phenomenon of some interest and nothing more.'

(1982: 243)

There is a wearisome familiarity about these objections. It is not that they are without foundation so much as that they miss the point, as if we cannot bring ourselves to credit the children's achievement. Tolstoy's response is to outline a radical theory of cognitive growth, drawn from his observation and embedded within his descriptions and interpretations. The extravagance of his presentation has persuaded most commentators to dismiss the theory as dogma, rather as critics have responded to the epilogue to *War and Peace*. Here, for example, is how Isaiah Berlin, in a celebrated discussion of Tolstoy's educational thought, sums up his essays:

> They are still fascinating, if only because they contain some of the best descriptions of village life and especially of children, both comical and lyrical, that even [Tolstoy] had ever composed ... His overriding didactic purpose is easily forgotten in the unrivalled insight into the twisting, criss-crossing pattern of the thoughts and feelings of individual children, and the marvellous concreteness and imagination with which their talk and behaviour, and physical nature around them, are described. And side by side with this direct vision of human experience, there run the clear, firm dogmas of a fanatically doctrinaire eighteenth century rationalist – doctrines not fused with the life that he describes, but superimposed upon it, like windows with rigorously symmetrical patterns drawn upon them, unrelated to the world on which they open, and yet achieving a kind of illusory artistic and intellectual unity with it, owing to the unbounded vitality and constructive genius of the writing itself.
>
> (1978: 246)

But the relationship between theory and description is closer than Berlin recognizes. Tolstoy's empirical observation, in all its inimitable detail, has uncovered an unexpected and unexpectedly conscious artistry in the stories composed by his pupils. The persuasive force of his description makes it impossible to ignore his findings. What then do they imply for the way in which we think about children's thought?

Tolstoy's answer is clear. 'The instinct for truth, beauty and goodness,' he concludes, 'is independent of the level of development' (1982: 244). Or to put it another way, creativity is a constant of development. We tend to think of creativity as an achievement of adulthood, the end product of a lengthy process of induction. In that case, we can make little of Fyedka's or Syomka's success. Hence the temptation to treat it as a happy accident or a reflection of the teacher's own creativity or a product of wishful thinking encouraged by reading far too much into the children's stories. As long as this is how we think of creativity we are likely, as Tolstoy sees it, 'to promote mere development and not harmony of development' (1982: 244). We look to the sense that children will make in future as adults and miss the significance of what they have to say in the here and now. Techniques, routines, bodies of knowledge, formal skills become an end in themselves, irrespective of the uses to which they are put. Gratification is always deferred:

> We are so sure of ourselves, [Tolstoy insists,] devoted in so dream like a way to the false ideal of adult perfection, so impatient with the imperfections which are near to us and so firmly convinced of our power to correct them, so little can we understand and value the primitive beauty of the child, that we rush as quickly as we can to exaggerate, to plaster over those imperfections which leap to our eyes, we correct, we train the child ... People develop the child further and further, and draw further and further away from the former primitive image which has been destroyed, and the attainment of the imagined image of adult perfection grows more and more impossible.
>
> (1982: 245)

The mistake is to 'see our ideal ahead when it lies behind us' (1982: 244). We must think of the instincts for truth, beauty and goodness – that is to say the desire for order, measure and form in the worlds of action, ethics and aesthetics – not as a goal but as a given, a potential which we are born with and exercise from our earliest days in the light of what we know, however slender our knowledge may be. This is the meaning, for Tolstoy, of Rousseau's 'great proposition' that 'Man is born perfect ... At birth man represents the model of harmony, truth, beauty and goodness. But every hour of life, every minute of time, increases the spaces, the magnitude and the time of those relationships which were in perfect harmony at the moment of his birth, and every step and every hour threatens to destroy that harmony' (1982: 245). From the child's point of view education is a ceaseless struggle to sustain creativity in the face of experience. Experience is at once a promise and a threat. On the one hand, in the form of everyday knowledge or the more formal knowledge acquired in school, it provides the growing child with 'material with which to complete himself in a harmonious and many-sided manner' (1982: 246). On the other hand, it continually challenges a child's creativity, forcing the child to refigure thought and action in an effort to recapture a pristine harmony that is never secure. This is how Tolstoy formulates the dialectic of development. Its educational implications seem to him transparent. The value of any form of pedagogy should be judged by its capacity not so much to add to the sum of knowledge as to preserve and promote creativity in the use of knowledge. It was Coleridge, rather than Rousseau, who had most elegantly and provocatively formulated Tolstoy's pedagogic goal, in an essay published in his journal *The Friend* in 1818, an essay which Tolstoy almost certainly had never read:

> not to assist in storing the passive mind with the various sorts of knowledge most in request, as if the human soul were a mere repository or banqueting house, but to place it in such relations of circumstance as should gradually excite the germinal power that craves no knowledge but what it can take up into itself, what it can appropriate and reproduce in fruits of its own.
>
> (Coleridge 1969: 472)

Tolstoy's essay may be read as a unique account of Coleridge's 'relations of circumstance' and an irresistible demonstration of his pupils' 'germinal power'.

'Who Shall Learn to Write from Whom? Should the Peasant Children Learn to Write from Us or Should We Learn to Write from Them?' was one of the last of Tolstoy's essays on education. Although he returned to the subject on completing *War and Peace*, publishing *The Abc Book*, his primer and elementary textbook, and engaging in educational controversy, notably on the teaching of reading, he never recaptured the excitement of his previous work. In later years he dismissed his interest in teaching and education as self-indulgent and insignificant. Little attention has been paid to his educational thought in the century and a half since his essays were published, a period which coincides with the history of popular education throughout Europe. Fyedka and Syomka have been forgotten and Tolstoy's account of their stories is recognized more for its title than its content. It is as if, in asking his notoriously rhetorical question, Tolstoy was announcing a revolutionary project that was never to be carried through: to examine the source and complexity of children's creative thought in its narrative dimension and to discover how best to cultivate it. The remaining chapters in this book seek to reactivate Tolstoy's project. Through a series of studies in 'conscious creativity' at different moments of development from infancy to adolescence, I aim to reach a fresh understanding of children's narrative understanding. What can we learn from children's stories about children as storytellers? The question is less dramatic than Tolstoy's but, as we shall see, it raises one by one the selfsame issues.

ORIGINS OF A PRACTICE:
A FIVE YEAR OLD'S
MYTHOLOGY

NINE STORIES*

by Wally, age 5

1.
Once upon a time there was a little lion and he lived alone because his mother and father was dead and one day he went hunting and he saw two lions and they were his mother and father so he took his blanket to their den because it was bigger.

(Paley 1981: 9)

2.
Once there was a man and a mother and two sisters and a brother. First the oldest sister ran away. Then the second sister decided to stay home with the father but he ran away too. So the little brother and the sister were left and she learned how to cook. One day a lion came because she wished for a lion and also they lived in the jungle. He said, 'Can I be your pet?' She said, 'I was just wishing for a lion pet. You can carry us wherever you want.' So they lived happily ever after.

(1981: 12)

3.
Once upon a time a man went out to hunt and his son went with him. He found a lion and the lion killed the boy but the man had two sons and one was still at home. So he shot the lion and he and the other brother ate it for supper and then they went to bed.

(1981: 28)

4.

Once there was a boy hunter. His little sister didn't like him so he ran away. So he found a baby lion. Then he found a girl. 'You can both be my sisters,' he said. Then they met a good fairy and she turned the girl lion into a girl person so he had two real sisters. They lived happily ever after.

(1981: 29)

5.

Once upon a time there was a father and he had four boys. One of them went out to see the woods and a lion killed him. He didn't come back for four days and then the father went out to find him. The father broke his arm and two of the sons carried him back. They took the father to the hospital. He couldn't come home for a year. The last day he died. Then the two boys went back to the forest and a fairy said the other brother was still alive because he was only resting and he just looked dead. So they lived happily ever after.

(1981: 36)

6.

Once there was a little boy and he went out of the house and then the father got home. The father didn't see him so he went out to find the boy. Then the father saw a lion. He started to shoot but the lion became invisible because it was really an invisible witch. Then the witch killed the father and the boy went home and he lived with his mother and sister.

(1981: 46)

7.

Once upon a time there was a little boy and he went out of the house and then the father got home. The father didn't see him and then he went out to find the boy. He thought maybe the boy flew up the moon because the boy was magic. So he went up there but still he didn't find him. He came down and went into the forest and saw a lion. He killed the lion with a gun. Then he found the boy. They went home.

(1981: 65)

8.

There was a boy who lived alone so no-one gave him Christmas presents and so he decided to live in the forest.

(1981: 87)

9.

A little boy lived all alone in a deep forest. When he wanted to know a word he asked lions and tigers and wolves. They told him pretend words because he couldn't speak animal language. One day he saw a lady and man who didn't have a little boy:

'What language do you talk?'
'Animal pretend talk.'

'That's okay because we can teach you people's language. Which one do you want to learn?'
'English.'
'Good, because that's our language. Which words do you want to know?'
'Lion, tiger and wolf.'
'You already know them. You just said them.'
'Then animal pretend talk must be English.'
So they lived happily ever after. But the man and lady knew some words the boy didn't know, so they did have a lot to teach him.

(1981: 120)

Who are these people who dare to reinvent mythology?

(Paley 1990: 4)

Wally, the author of *Nine Stories*, was one of 22 children in a kindergarten class in Chicago whose thought and action over the course of a school year form the subject of Vivian Paley's book *Wally's Stories*. Twenty one of Wally's stories are included in the book but this represents no more than a fraction of the stories that he composed during the year. 'He dictates three of four a week,' Paley tells us, 'never repeating a plot' (1981: 10). Wally's are not the only stories in the book. Many of the other children's stories are also included, alongside taped discussions, conversations with the teacher and Paley's descriptions and interpretations of classroom life. Storytelling was central to the culture of the classroom. Fairy tales were 'read every day at rest time in a darkened room with everyone stretched out on a mat ... It was a good way to do it. We didn't need to look at pictures or look at each other; we listened to the words we would come to know so well and imagined what the characters looked like and what everything meant' (1981: 72). The tales became the subject of endless discussion and were acted out in the classroom over and over again. Picture books were pored over as well as fairy tales and the children also composed stories of their own, dictating them to Paley who acted as scribe and editor. 'My role as scribe is never passive,' she explains, 'whenever possible I enlarge the scope of the story, looking for points that need clarification and asking questions that might lead to new twists in the plot' (1981: 220).

This is how she describes Wally's first attempt to write a story:

The first time I asked Wally if he wanted to write a story he looked surprised. 'You didn't teach me to write yet,' he said.
   'You just tell *me* the story, Wally, I'll write the words.'
   'What should I tell about?'
   'You like dinosaurs. You could tell about dinosaurs.'
   He dictated this story.
   The dinosaur smashed down the city and the people got mad and put him in jail.
   'Is that the end?' I asked. 'Did he get out?'
   He promised he would be good so they let him go home and his mother was waiting.

We acted out the story immediately for one reason – I felt sorry for Wally. He had been on the time-out chair twice that day, and his sadness stayed with me. I wanted to do something nice for him, and I was sure it would please him if we acted out his story. It made Wally very happy, and a flurry of story writing began that continued and grew all year. The boys dictated as many stories as the girls, and we acted out each story the day it was written if we could.

Before we had never acted out these stories. We had dramatised every other kind of printed word – fairy tales, story books, poems, songs – but it had always seemed enough just to write the children's words. Obviously it was not; the words did not sufficiently represent the action, which needed to be shared. For this alone, the children would give up play time, as it was a true extension of play.

(1981: 12)

In her later book, *The Boy Who Would Be a Helicopter*, Paley describes the children's storytelling as 'the academic inheritor of the creative wisdom of play' (1990: 35). The children's classroom play provides the subject matter for most of their stories and dramatization returns the stories to the world out of which they arose but with the crucial difference that play is now guided by the children's own texts. Paley speaks of the stories as scripts and the children as actors. Dialogue is added in performance, more and more of it as the year progresses and the children grow more practised in improvisation. New characters are created and plots are frequently adapted to accommodate the demands and objections of actors and critics. It is as if, in acting out the stories, children participate in the act of storytelling itself, offering their own readings of the text, interpreting the written words, proposing revisions and extensions of the narrative. The distinction between tellers and listeners becomes blurred. Paley suggests that

the dictated segment represents but a moment in a story's life ... Stories that are not acted out are fleeting dreams: private fantasies, disconnected and unexamined. If in the press of a busy day I am tempted to shorten the process by only reading the stories aloud and skipping the dramatisations, the children object. They say, 'But we haven't DONE the story.' It is the same complaint we hear when the clean up bell sounds. 'We didn't get to play in the spaceship yet. We only just builded it.' The unacted story has not been played in; it is an empty structure. The process is incomplete.

(1990: 24)

Paley's insistence on the communal life of the children's stories is supported by many examples yet her conclusion does less than justice, perhaps, to the self-sufficiency of these slender texts. For all the embedding of narrative in play and drama, there is about many of the children's stories a coherence of form and content which makes it appropriate to read them as independent, composed tales, on the borderline of written art. They mark the dawn of a literary consciousness, a child's first leap into the world of the storyteller's imagination.

Wally, as Paley presents him, is a born storyteller. Even when he is sitting on the time-out chair, bored and in disgrace, 'his head dances with images and stories' (1981: 6). Whenever a new piece of equipment is brought into the classroom – a horizontal climbing ladder, a twelve-foot painted circle – Wally has a story for it. Whatever the subject of discussion he seems able to find a way of introducing it into his narratives. Although the hero of his first story was a dinosaur, at Paley's suggestion, it is lions rather than dinosaurs or the ubiquitous superheroes, that for the most part capture his imagination, whether in his stories or in his classroom play. Early in the school year, at piano time, he is 'on the outer edge of the rug, growling. "Don't make that noise Wally," I say. "It's a warning growl." "Not at piano time." "I'm guarding the lions," he whispers. "The growl means I hear a suspicious noise"' (1981: 7). Later he tells Paley that he is going to be a mother lion when he grows up. ' "Why a mother lion?" ' Paley asks him. ' "Because I would have babies and do the mommy work. They stay home and take care of babies. Daddy lions go to work and have to walk fast"' (1981: 7). Wally's 21 stories make up a sustained body of work through which he discovers, invents, explores and examines, with the help of others, a narrative world that is uniquely his own. It is a mythic world, alternately homely and alien, where brothers and sisters, mothers and, more commonly, fathers confront lions, witches and fairies in a struggle for survival, in search of companionship, in the rescue of the lost. The narrative framework is traditional, poised between once upon a time and happy ever after in the manner of the fairy tale that played so compelling a part in the life of the class, but the frame is often stretched or broken and the adventures themselves are full of surprises. Almost every story throws fresh light on this imagined world, introducing new characters, adding to its array of plots, developing the grand themes, extending horizons. Paley describes her kindergarten children as 'these people who dare to reinvent mythology' (1990: 4) and it is far from fanciful to detect in their tales distant echoes and novel transformations of the centuries-old tradition to which Wally and his classmates are being introduced, even as they claim it for their own. Innovation and tradition are the twin poles of Wally's narrative experience as they are of every born storyteller. This chapter sets out to describe his achievement, examining the developing scope of his narrative imagination as displayed in nine of his 21 tales.

Wally wrote the first of his forest tales, as we might call them, directly after he had been shown how to dictate a story and when he was still often in trouble on account of his disruptiveness:

> Once upon a time there was a little lion and he lived alone because his mother and father was dead and one day he went hunting and he saw two lions and they were his mother and father so he took his blanket to their den because it was bigger.

With this, his first independent narrative, Wally announces his fictional world, almost as if he were setting out a programme for the coming year. Its outlines are already clear. The setting is a forest – sometimes called the woods or the jungle. Here is where the action is, the scene of the fateful encounter.

Home is sometimes inside the forest as here, sometimes on its edge. As Wally explains to an importunate classmate later in the year, 'the forest is where the hunter lives'. The cast of characters is made up of a family and lions, plus the occasional witch or fairy and very occasionally some other animal. This first story is the only one in which the family is itself composed of lions. In subsequent stories Wally is careful to distinguish the animal and human kingdoms even if, in the confrontation between humans and animals, the lions may be transformed into people and incorporated within the family unit. Paley speaks of Wally's lions as 'aggressive beasts' but almost as often as not they turn out to be friendly. The action takes the form of a hunt which is often, as it is on this occasion, a quest. The major themes hardly change all year: loneliness and companionship, death and resurrection, loss and recovery, autonomy and dependence.

In this opening story a son, who lives alone, enters the forest not so much in search of prey as of his dead parents. Paley questioned Wally about these parents who come back to life: ' "But weren't the mother and father dead?" I ask. He has a quick answer. "They came alive again because he only thought they were dead. They really went out shopping and he didn't recognize them because they were wearing different clothes" ' (1981: 9). Wally's explanations mean more than they say. In this instance, he confirms his intention to resurrect the dead parents even as he offers an implausibly mundane interpretation of the miraculous event. The forest is a magical world where the lost can be mysteriously found and the dead brought back to life. In almost every case the encounter in the forest brings about a transformation. But the resolution of this first adventure is not quite as we may have anticipated. When Paley had persuaded Wally to revise the ending of his dinosaur story, he had settled for a conventional close: 'He promised to be good so they let him go home and his mother was waiting.' With this, the child is returned to the care, protection and authority of his parents. But now Wally's chosen ending is far less passive. The 'little lion' makes up his own mind to go and live with his parents and for his own reasons: 'so he took his blanket to their den because it was bigger.' The story emphasizes autonomy rather than dependence. The outcome is a matter of choice. It is the first of his innovations. Or perhaps it would be better to say that it is his first independent attempt to locate himself within tradition.

In the transition from dictated narrative to acted script, a new twist is given to Wally's story. ' "Can I be the father in your story?" Fred asks. "Okay" says Wally. "Fred will be the father, Rose is the mother, I'm the little brother and Eddie is the magician." "There's no magician in your story," I remind Wally ... "Yes there is, I just didn't tell you about him" ' (1981: 10). Wally is often prepared to enlarge or revise a story in this way, though not always, as we shall see. Paley interprets this as evidence of the incompleteness of the written text but changes of this kind are better seen as variants on the text rather in the manner in which a folk tale is varied, often substantially, with each retelling. Sometimes Wally's variants are incidental to the plot, as with the introduction of a magician here, which may amount to no more than a recognition on Wally's part that the lion's parents have been magically restored to life. Sometimes, however, the effect of a variant is more dramatic.

When Wally wrote the sixth of these nine stories one of his classmates objected to the part she was asked to play when the story was acted out. 'Kim objected. "I don't want that part!" It was her turn but she refused to be the lion who became an invisible witch. "I'll only be a good witch." "Okay, okay, I'll change it," said Wally. "The lion becomes invisible because it was really the pet lion of a good witch and she didn't want it to get killed. So the father found the boy and they killed a giraffe and ate it for their dinner"' (1981: 46). In both versions the boy who is the hero returns home but in the first version his father is killed in searching for his son. What Wally offers Kim is in effect a different story, robbed of its tragic dimension. Perhaps what these variants signal, more than anything else, is the fertility of the imaginative world out of which Wally draws his tales, where new characters, events or implications can be added at will, turning tragedy to comedy, undercutting a harsh or unacceptable detail, or adding local colour.

As the year progresses and the stories accumulate, Wally grows more confident in the world which he has created. His narrative acquires greater definition and depth. He begins to test its limits and savour its ambiguities. His next story is already a far more circumstantial tale:

> Once there was a man and a mother and two sisters and a brother. First the oldest sister ran away. Then the second sister decided to stay home with the father but he ran away too. So the little brother and the sister were left and she learned how to cook. One day a lion came because she wished for a lion and also they lived in the jungle. He said, 'Can I be your pet?' She said, 'I was just wishing for a lion pet. You can carry us wherever you want.' So they lived happily ever after.

In one respect this story is an exception in Wally's oeuvre. Most of his stories are travellers' tales. The hero sets out on an adventure which, after a period of trial, leads him back home or on to new life elsewhere. But on this occasion the story is about those who remain behind, coping with absence and making the most of whatever fortune brings. There is a parallel with Fyedka's story *The Life of a Soldier's Wife* and once again, and for the only time in Wally's stories, the hero is female although the second sister in Wally's tale is a great deal more adventurous than Matryona, the soldier's wife. The story opens, as Fyedka's did, with the disintegration of a family all of whom but the two youngest run away. It seems that their purpose is escape rather than adventure. In any event they disappear from the narrative; their stories are untold. (We are never told anything about the mother. Wally mentions her and promptly forgets her. Details such as this are quite often ignored in his stories. On this occasion it is plausible to assume that she too fled, perhaps with the older sister.) The father's desertion is especially poignant since it would appear to be on his account that the younger sister has 'decided to stay home'. 'Decided' is the key word. She might have escaped like the others, the story implies. Her staying is a matter of choice, a choice her father spurns. But the girl, whose autonomy has already been indicated, takes charge of the changed circumstances on behalf of her brother and herself: 'so the little brother and the sister were left and she learned how to cook.' That is to say, she learned how to cope, to 'do the mommy work' as Wally would have it. The loss of family is turned into an opportunity.

For all their enterprise, however, sister and brother are unable to reconstitute a family by themselves. Something else is needed, a companion who can take the place of their parents, providing the strength and security that have been so categorically withdrawn. Enter the lion. 'Because she wished for a pet and also they lived in the jungle,' the story tells us. Paley speaks elsewhere of the power of the wish in children's stories but the use of the wish is bound by clear rules, as so many of the children's discussions make clear. So while the lion enters because the sister wishes for a lion, Wally feels it necessary to indicate the plausibility of the wish. Hence the added clause: 'and also they lived in the jungle'. As if we could imagine that there could be anything rash or merely ridiculous in the sister's thought or action. The lions in Wally's first story were themselves the members of a family. By contrast, in this second story the lion asks to be incorporated within the family unit. (It is only in his third story that the lion appears as an enemy.) Wally does not yet know what the word oxymoron means but the sentence 'I was just wishing for a lion pet' is certainly not artless. The sister wishes for a lion as a pet precisely because of its strength, perhaps even because of the fear which it inspires. An aggressive beast is a decided advantage if it is on your side, especially if you have lost your parents. That this is the point of the encounter is made clear by the sentence which follows: 'you can carry us wherever you want'. The reader might expect a pet to carry its owners wherever THEY want. But this particular pet, with all its strength and grandeur, has a very particular function. It is not to be owned; it is to become the children's guardian, replacing the lost father. With the appearance of the lion the family is reconstituted. The children are ready for adventure, their own exploration of the forest, the world into which the rest of the family has disappeared. But it is the lion who will lead the way. Autonomy is thus reconciled with dependence. 'So they lived happily ever after.'

Fairy tale endings, however, are not always as categorical as they appear. The more Wally explores the forest of his invention, the more he finds himself having to confront the ambiguity at the heart of many of his adventures. Happy endings begin to acquire traces of irony:

> Once upon a time there was a father and he had four boys. One of them went out to see the woods and a lion killed him. He didn't come back for four days and then the father went out to find him. The father broke his arm and two of the sons carried him back. They took the father to the hospital. He couldn't come home for a year. The last day he died. Then the two boys went back to the forest and a fairy said the other brother was still alive because he was only resting and he just looked dead. So they lived happily ever after.

Paley comments: 'Wally needed comfort from fairies too. Sometimes, when his own story saddened him, he would bring in a fairy to set things right' (1981: 36). But the fairy's powers are limited. Happy ever after may be the declared outcome but it has its cost and sometimes the sadness of the means seems to outweigh the happiness of the end. Part of the reason for the weight of sadness in this story is that the father is the hero of the tale. It is the only one of Wally's stories in which a father is named as the protagonist. More explicitly than any of his other stories, this is a tale of fathers and sons. By identifying with the father's predicament the story seems to challenge the power of narrative to set things right, even when it restores the dead to life.

A son sets out to explore the unknown, not to hunt but 'to see the woods'. It seems like a first unguarded adventure, undertaken regardless of danger, perhaps uncounselled. He is killed. Four days the father waits, as many days as he has sons, though one of the sons drops out of the story after the opening sentence. Then he sets off in search of his missing son. But he too falls victim to the woods with their multiple perils. Two of his remaining sons carry him back from the forest, apparently leaving their lost brother to his fate unless they already recognize that the boy is dead. The father's needs are paramount. He is taken to the hospital and at this point, in two short, crucial sentences, the narrative reaches a tragic and unanticipated climax. The first sentence, 'He couldn't come home for a year,' suggests that in due time the father will return. The second quickly cancels hope and expectation: 'The last day he died.' What is due is suddenly, shockingly, denied. But the father's sacrifice is not in vain. The two sons return to the forest to be told that their brother is not dead but was only resting. The biblical overtones are irresistible: the dead son is alive again, the lost has been found. A pedantic critic might complain that it takes an unconscionable time for the boys to find out what has happened to their brother but the narrative requires them to wait until the father's sacrifice is complete. The role of the fairy, encountered in the forest, is not to set things right so much as to ensure that the father's sacrifice achieves its purpose. In a similar way the fairy in the fourth of Wally's nine stories makes sure that the boy hunter's declaration, 'You are both my sisters,' achieves its purpose by turning the girl lion into a girl person and thus a real sister. But this time magic is not enough. The son is saved but the father has had to die. His death robs the conventional ending of any trace of light-heartedness. To be lost and to be found is a fundamental matrix of narrative at any age and perhaps in any culture. An early story from the pre-school class described in Paley's book *The Boy Who Would Be a Helicopter* reads simply, 'A little girl is losted. The mother finded her' (1990: 71). Wally's story is evidence of how complex a narrative a child as young as 5, scarcely beginning to write, can compose around this simple core. His tale resists neat categories. It tells us that happiness is hard won and that the fairy tale ending may conceal irretrievable loss.

All year long the forest remains the indispensable setting for Wally's mythic adventures. Nowhere else satisfies so well his narrative demands. It is interesting to watch what happens when once he tries to move a story onto new territory:

Once upon a time there was a little boy and he went out of the house and then his father got home. The father didn't see him and then he went out to find the boy. He thought maybe the boy flew up the moon because the boy was magic. So he went up there but he still didn't find

him. He came down and went in the forest and saw a lion. He killed the
lion with a gun. Then he found the boy. They went home.

Like a number of Wally's experiments in narrative during the year, this particular story had its origins in a class discussion started by one of Wally's
classmates who had maintained one day that you could make a wish on the
man in the moon. The children 'earnestly examined the issues,' as Paley puts
it, and at the end of an intense discussion Wally said, 'That gives me a good
idea for a story' (1981: 65). The story opens with the same two sentences as a
previous story of Wally's (number 6, above), the story that he had radically
revised to satisfy the objections of his classmate Kim. Perhaps Wally felt
dissatisfied with what had happened to his earlier story and wanted to try
again. In any case the magic of the new story is of an entirely different order.
The story led to further discussion, this time initiated by Paley:

> 'Was the father magic too?' I asked. 'No.' 'The reason I asked is that he
> was able to go up to the moon to look for the boy.' 'No, he didn't really
> go up. He only looked up there because he could see the boy's shadow if
> he was there.' Wally explained. 'How about if the boy was hiding in one
> of the holes?' asked Warren. [There had been much debate earlier about
> the possibility of holes on the moon.] 'He wasn't,' said Wally. After all, it
> was his story.
>
> (1981: 65)

Wally's responses to his critics are interesting. Although at times he would
happily rewrite a story to satisfy a would-be actor's objections, he was only
prepared to concede his listeners a modest role in his storytelling, as his reply
to Warren shows. On the other hand, the answer he gives to Paley's question
is more discreet. It is not so much that Paley is the teacher as that the uses of
magic are a matter of great concern to Wally and his classmates. Magic, they
seem to suppose, is exclusive to children and to the creatures of the forest
who help or hinder them. Adults may profit from magic but they do not have
direct access to its power as children do. The adult world is one of rational
calculation; magic is the prerogative of childhood. It is an idea of wide extent,
to be found again, as we will see, in the writing of older children. Wally's
defensive explanation of the father's visit to the moon suggests that he
recognizes the danger that his story may inadvertently have breached a
fundamental rule.

On this occasion there may have been a more pressing reason for Wally to
dispel any thought that the father might have been magic, for it seems that
even the boy's magic is illusory. He is not on the moon after all. Wally's 'good
idea for a story' turns out to be of limited value. The magical flight to the
moon adds colour and a touch of fancy to a familiar tale but in the end it is a
false lead. However powerful a draw to the imagination, the moon is too
distant, too remote from the world where life must be contested. It is out in
the forest, just beyond the boundaries of home, not 'up there', as one of the
children put it in discussion, that the decisive encounter is to be faced and the
issue of life and death resolved. The father turns his gaze back to earth and
enters the forest. The lion is killed and the boy is found; the one event begets

the other. It is the only means of getting home. It seems that Wally is not yet ready to break the self-imposed constraints of his narrative world. The moon that seemed so tempting as the children discussed it, serves as no more than a whimsical aside. Wally briefly inspects it as a site for narration and promptly discards it. This, after all, is not where the action is. Later on, maybe, the moon will come into its own but not yet. For now it is the forest that beckons. It appears to satisfy all of this narrator's needs.

The children's conversation about the moon may not in the end have extended the range of Wally's narrative but there were times when classroom discussion exercised a far more radical influence. That was what happened with Wally's remarkable story about language:

A little boy lived all alone in a deep forest. When he wanted to know a word he asked lions and tigers and wolves. They told him pretend words because he couldn't speak animal language. One day he saw a lady and a man who didn't have a little boy.

'What language do you talk?'
'Animal pretend talk.'
'That's okay because we can teach you people's language. Which one do you want to learn?'
'English.'
'Good, because that's our language. Which words do you want to know?'
'Lion, tiger and wolf.'
'You already know them. You just said them.'
'Then animal pretend talk must be English.'
So they lived happily ever after. But the man and lady knew some words the boy didn't know, so they did have a lot to teach him.

The story was written shortly after Christmas, half-way through Wally's kindergarten year. A few weeks earlier he had written his shortest and bleakest story – Paley calls it 'forlorn':

There was a boy who lived alone so no-one gave him Christmas presents and so he decided to live in the forest.

It is no more than a fragment. Deprived of a family home and its companionship, for which Wally finds the perfect seasonal image, a boy determines to try his luck in the forest. That's that, there is no outcome, no adventure. The story asks a question, 'what next?', and invites its readers to imagine their own adventure. But it seems that Wally was not quite satisfied for now, after the Christmas break, he returns to the very point at which he had left the story and tries again: 'A little boy lived all alone in a deep forest.' Accepting his own invitation he offers us the finest of all his forest tales, a story about language which is in effect the story of a child's search for companionship, a central concern of Wally's stories from the beginning and one which here achieves its most complete expression. Paley's class had been discussing language. A Japanese girl had joined the class and was busily learning English. Her preoccupation led the class into a series of conversations about language in general:

Teacher: Why are there so many languages?
Lisa: Because some people don't know these other languages.
Kim: They can't talk the way we talk.
Eddie: Maybe when people are born they choose the language they want to know and then they go to a special place to learn it. I mean their mother chooses.
Andy: Like a child could tell his mother and father to take him to a place where they can learn French if they are French.
Warren: God gives people all the sounds. Then you can tell if you're in a different place because it sounds different.
Wally: When you're little you try to think of what the name of something is and people tell you.
Eddie: Oh, yeah. Your mother tells you. You come out of her stomach and she talks English to you and she tells you the name for everything.
Deana: If you live in a different country, there's a different language there. Wherever you were born you talk in that language.
Warren: Wherever your mother was born.
Teacher: Your mother was born in China, Warren, but you speak English.
Deana: Because he never lived in China.
Warren: I'm going to go to Chinese school on Saturdays when I'm six.
Eddie: Someone has to teach you. My brother didn't know one word when he was born. Not even my name.
Earl: When I was little I said 'ca-see'.
Rose: What does that mean?
Earl: 'Take me in the car.' Now I know every word.
Rose: Me too.
Teacher: Akemi was born in Japan and she speaks Japanese. How are you learning all these English words now, Akemi?
Akemi: I listen to everybody.

(1981: 116)

Wally speaks only once in the course of this discussion but his intevention is decisive as Paley explains:

> As the children got closer to their own experience they became more logical. 'Why are there so many different languages?' is the sort of abstract question that prompts answers such as Lisa's: 'Because some people don't know these other languages.' Then Wally changed the emphasis of the discussion by describing how a little child learns an object's name. The implied new question – how do you learn a language? – was understood at once. Now the children did not need to guess at meanings, because the subject involved a concrete part of their own development.

(1981: 117)

Wally's comment and the subsequent discussion bear a distinct, if distant, relationship to St Augustine's celebrated account of learning to speak, in his *Confessions*, a passage which Wittgenstein makes the starting point of his own critical reflections on language in *Philosophical Investigations*. Here is what Augustine wrote, followed by a paragraph from Wittgenstein's critique:

> When my elders named some object, and accordingly moved toward something, I saw this and I grasped that the thing was called by the sound they uttered when they meant to point it out. Their intention was shown by their bodily movements, as it were the natural language of all peoples: the expression of the face, the play of the eyes, the movement of other parts of the body, and the tone of voice which expresses our state of mind in seeking, having, rejecting, or avoiding something. Thus, as I heard words repeatedly used in their proper places in various sentences, I gradually learnt to understand what objects they signified, and after I had trained my mouth to form these signs, I used them to express my own desires.
>
> (Wittgenstein 1953: 2)

> Someone coming into a strange country will sometimes learn the language of the inhabitants from ostensive definitions that they give him, and he will often have to *guess* the meaning of these definitions, and will sometimes guess right, sometimes wrong.
>
> And now I think we can say: Augustine describes the learning of human language as if the child came into a strange country and did not understand the language of the country, that is, as if it already had a language, only not this one. Or again: as if the child could already *think*, only not yet speak. And 'think' would here mean something like 'talk to itself'.
>
> (1953: 17)

What Wittgenstein says of St Augustine might equally well, and much more obviously, be said of Wally and his classmates. Indeed the profound silliness of Wally's story depends on just this aspect of the children's Augustinian account of language learning, which had itself been influenced by Akemi's experience as a Japanese speaker trying to learn English. In other respects, however, Wally's understanding of language comes much closer to Wittgenstein's own view, for Wally, like Wittgenstein, insists that language is embedded in a form of life. Already in the children's discussion, the acquisition of language is made to depend on companionship, above all between mother and child. Now, in his story, Wally appropriates all that has been said and transforms the discussion into a narrative in which learning a language is equated with finding a home and thus resolving the loneliness of the hero's predicament. It is Wally's very own story of the wolf child although the child, as so often in Wally's stories, is granted a great deal more autonomy than in the more familiar examples of this tale, or for that matter than in Wittgenstein's account of language learning.

In other stories Wally emphasizes the complicity between the animal and human kingdoms. The lion asks to be a pet and becomes a guardian; the boy hunter invites the baby girl lion to become his sister. But on this occasion he insists on the radical discontinuity between the two kingdoms. The words which the animals tell the boy are 'pretend' words, not part of their own animal language from which the boy is quite simply excluded. There is a wonderful play here on the word 'pretend'. Wally and his classmates, in their play and in their stories, often pretend that animals can talk. But after all it is only a pretence; the real live animals never do talk back. Suppose then it was the other way round. The animals in Wally's story give the boy the very words he might give them: their own names, lion, tiger, wolf. But the effect is the same. The words do not compose a language because they cannot be used to communicate. They signify without being significant. The boy cannot talk with the animals for all that he is able to ask them for words. Between the boy's world and the animal's world there can never be more than the pretence of complicity.

That is the nature of the hero's predicament. Surrounded by animals he remains alone. The animals cannot satisfy his need for companionship. The decisive encounter comes with the appearance of a lady and a man. The significance of that encounter is caught in a single word, the word 'didn't': 'One day he saw a lady and a man who didn't have a little boy.' The negative attribute of the couple marks the defining moment. It is what they lack that draws together the lady and man on the one hand, the boy on the other. Each seeks the companionship of the other, a mother and father, a son. Their meeting is fateful. The conversation that follows, setting aside its charming self-contradiction, turns on the discovery that the boy already knows the words he wishes to know. The animals, it transpires, have taught him 'people's language' after all: 'Then animal pretend talk must be English.' But until this moment it has always been as if he did not know the words he knows and that is because he had no one to talk to, no form of life in which he could participate. Language entails communication, reciprocity, companionship, in short, a culture. In offering to teach him people's language the lady and man – and perhaps it is significant, in view of the weight attached to the mother–child relationship in the children's discussion, that on the adults' first appearance in the story the lady should come first – are offering the boy a home and, with it, humanity. 'So they lived happily ever after. But ...' The 'but' that comes after the conventional formula is characteristic of children's stories. We have already seen how Wally's stories sometimes place in question the finality of the traditional ending. We will come across further examples in the work of older children. Here Wally's point is not to challenge the happy outcome but to insist on the story beyond the story, that is to say on the story's further significance. 'But the man and lady knew some words the boy didn't know so they did have a lot to teach him.' In a way it was everything, for in a human family the words could at last make sense.

It seems appropriate that in a story about words the power of Wally's own words should be so evident. It is tempting to suppose that because of the context in which they were written, the individual words in Wally's stories might be less exact than in Fyedka's story. But in his own way Wally was no less concerned to 'fix the images of his feeling artistically by means of words'. His use of 'pretend', the weight he attaches to 'didn't', the word 'deep' in the opening sentence, absent from his previous story but now necessary in order to emphasize the hero's remoteness from human contact, these are the artful means by which he articulates his narrative vision. It is easy to imagine the children in Wally's class acting out his story, turning into scripted play their thoughts about language and learning. It is hard to suppose that anything might have needed to be added to the written text to enhance its meaning. Of all Wally's stories, this is the most self-sufficient.

In 'Who Should Learn to Write from Whom? Should the Peasant Children Learn to write from Us or Should We Learn to Write from Them?' Tolstoy showed, as we have seen, how to read his pupils' stories as works of art. The stories of Wally may be regarded as so many examples of children's earliest aesthetic practice. They draw on the literary traditions that formed so vital a part of Wally's classroom experience, notably the tradition of the fairy tale. Equally they derive from the children's incessant classroom play which itself reflected the stories which the children heard at home and at school as well as what they watched on television, or picked up from friends and neighbours. Out of this diverse material Wally creates a fictional world which is at once distinctive and deeply serious. It is, from the outset, a highly structured world. The narrative opens at home in an indeterminate time, moves out into the world, usually identified with the forest, and after a series of encounters returns to a home transformed by the forest experience. This underlying structure is firm enough to accommodate a variety of exceptions which gain part of their significance directly from their exceptional status: the encounter that takes place at home rather than in the forest; the return home that marks a loss; the entry into the forest from which there is no return. Within this structure Wally finds room for adventures of many kinds, incorporating triumph and tragedy on the way to endings which are often more ambiguous than they seem.

That Wally is conscious of his craft as a storyteller is clear from the extensions and revisions he makes to his stories and from his responses to his teacher's or his classmates' questions and criticisms. Indeed a developing literary awareness is characteristic of his entire class as they discuss the stories which they write or listen to and turn them back into dramatic play. Among the evidence of conscious artistry it is tempting to place foremost Wally's way with words. His language is extremely simple but he uses it with great care. The most ordinary words – 'didn't', 'but', 'you', 'also', – are made to carry a wealth of meaning. Wally's stories may have only a fraction of the narrative richness of Fyedka's tale but, in their simple, bold outlines, they too may serve as an example, however primitive, of Tolstoy's claim that 'every work of art . . . calls forth a countless multitude of ideas, images and interpretations.' Yet Wally is barely at the start of a storyteller's life. Though he already knows a good deal about storytelling, he still cannot write or read stories independently. What happens as children acquire the rudiments of writing and reading forms the subject of the next chapter.

IMAGE AND TEXT: ENTERING A LITERARY WORLD

THE POORLY MOUSE

by Jessica, age 6

and

THE LITTLE GIRL WHO GOT LOST

by Melissa, age 6

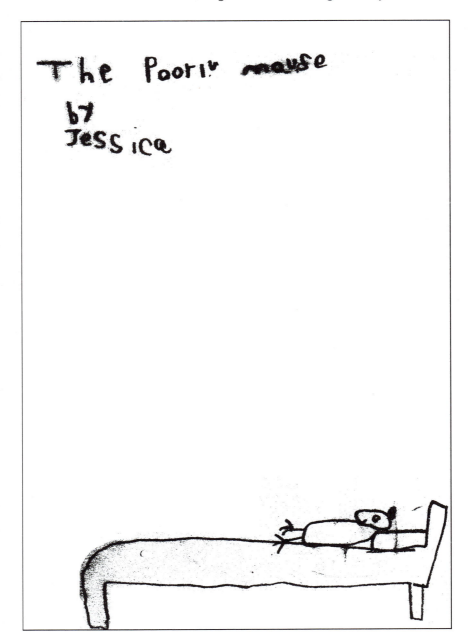

The Poorir mause
by
Jessica

The Poorly mouse

by Jessica

once There was a mouse who
lived near were The wolfs lived
one day a wolf came out of
its home and hurt The mouse.

one day a little girl
was walking in the wood
When she saw
Then she saw the mouse
saw it was ingurd

So She Took it home and
S___ her mum Then Ther both
Took iT To The vet buT The
VeT wes busy

So The litTle girl and her
mum PreTenied TO be
The VeT and Soon GOT The
Mouse beTTer

Even no the mouse was better
The little girl and her
mum still cept it and plaxed
with thay had lots of fun

Then after a while the dad came home from his holiday

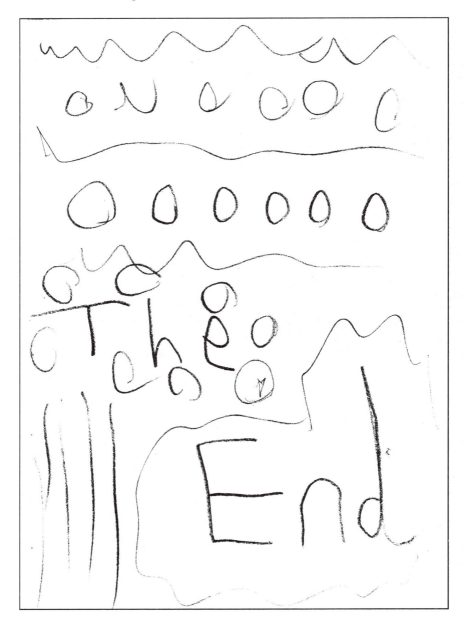

The Litte grel who
got Lost BY Melissa

One day a Little greL came outside and she Deolbeb to do out For a WaIR

But soon the Little grel
vet Lost and She Woonted
her mummy then her
Mummy cane

The Little grel
Was very Happy

and wen we got home We had tea

then it was nily
tim For my bed
.tim

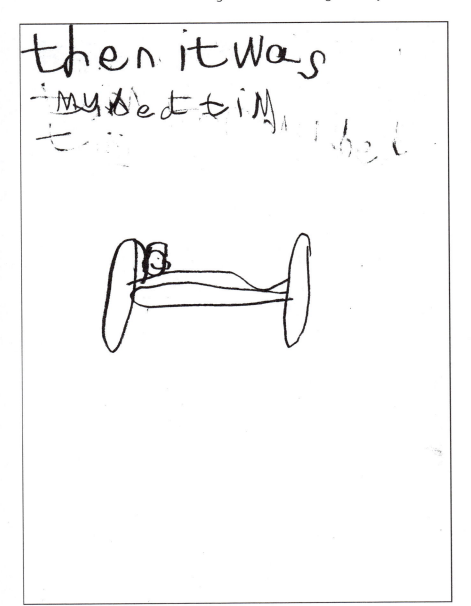

then it was nily
tim For my Mums
and dads bed tim

then it Was 10
minytes untill my
mum sand dads
bed tim

the end

Every life is in search of a narrative. We all seek, willy nilly, to introduce some kind of concord into the everyday discord and dispersal we find about us.
(Kearney 2002: 4)

The scene is Harwell School, a primary school of some 130 children close to the town of Didcot, twelve miles south of Oxford. It is a Friday afternoon towards the end of winter. The children have gathered in the school hall as usual for the end of week assembly. They come clutching stories, poems, pictures, models, reports of experiments, pages of projects, and whatever else they wish, or have been persuaded, to show the rest of the school, evidence of the week's achievement. Jessica and Melissa, young friends barely six years old, have been writing stories. They have written in small handmade booklets prepared by their teacher. She had asked all the children in her class to write a story of their own invention. There was to be no set theme or title. They could write whatever they wished, using words alone or combining words with pictures. They would have plenty of time during the week to complete their stories. Jessica and Melissa had worked side by side, glancing from time to time over each other's stories as they wrote and drew. Now at the Friday assembly, the sharing assembly as it is known, they are preparing to read the finished pieces to the whole school. When their turn comes they walk over to the microphone, prop their books on the music stand and read, clearly and confidently, with no more than an occasional stumble. The audience of children and teachers cannot see the pictures drawn under each few lines of text but they listen closely, smiling at each story's novelty and recognizing the children's pride in their achievement. At the end, unusually, there is a burst of applause. It is a magical moment, as if the world of art has suddenly opened out before us as the two girls read.

The Poorly Mouse and *The Little Girl Who Got Lost* represent a turning point in narrative history. The kindergarten world of *Wally's Stories* has been left behind. Words no longer have to be dictated to a teacher and the fragile independence of the narrative is less readily subject to the demands and objections of listeners and actors. Storytelling will continue to dominate much of Jessica's and Melissa's lives, as is evident in their conversation and play, but now, for the first time, it is the act of writing the story down that takes precedence. Jessica and Melissa have begun to master the rudiments of written language. Their letters are readable, their spelling comprehensible, their sentences coherent even without the aid of conventional punctuation. More significantly, they have come to understand the literariness of narrative and its dependence on the book. But this is literariness of a special kind. The clearest sign of the emergence of a new form of narrative understanding is not so much the written word itself as the children's use of drawing or, more precisely, of that combination of word and image which constitutes the story. These are tales to be studied, not told. They are composed for readers rather than listeners although they may still be shared, as the two girls shared them as they worked, or as their classmates might share them by reading them together, or as the teacher shares a picture book with her class, holding up each page to show the picture as she reads the words. In each of the stories the picture is critical. In truth, the audience in assembly caught only a fraction of the narrative as they listened to the words which were read. Words and pictures are so tightly interwoven in these two tales that the narrative cannot be said to be either written or drawn. It is created only in the exchange of image and text, page by page. The pictures are not to be seen as illustrations to a self-sufficient text. Neither are they alternative narratives, nor a sub-text, nor a pictorial commentary. What is written and what is drawn combine to compose a single tale. As we shall see, it is a form of narrative which Jessica and Melissa, novices though they may be, already have firmly under control.

The significance of drawing in these subtle early narratives has its own familiar history. Both at school and at home, the books that have been read to Jessica and Melissa will mostly have been picture books of one kind or another, as will the books by means of which they have learned to read. Furthermore, drawing will have accompanied the children's narrative play long before they learned to write. By the time they begin to be able to write their stories down for themselves most of the children in Jessica's and Melissa's class will already have become adept at putting their stories into pictorial form. Against this background the exchange between image and text comes naturally to them and gives these early picture stories a formal distinction which adult picture books for children find it hard to match. It is as if, for once, the expertise rests with the novice. *The Poorly Mouse* and *The Little Girl Who Got Lost* are characteristic of the genre. They show how two young children who have just begun to read and write make use of their new-found skill, alongside what they already know of narrative, to 'compose a literary work', as Eikhenbaum put it in describing Tolstoy's essay. This chapter attempts to follow their separate, though linked, narrative concerns and the means by which they contrive to express them, examining each story page by page.

The Poorly Mouse

Title page (see p.46)

The *Oxford English Dictionary* defines 'poorly' as a word which, in its adjectival form, is chiefly used as a predicate. The dictionary cites an example from John Cheever: 'They all agreed that he looked poorly.' Or as Jessica's mother might have written in a note to her teacher: 'Jessica is poorly and won't be at school today.' Jessica's usage is original, a first sign of the verbal inventiveness which pervades her narrative. The drawing at the foot of the page is a visual equivalent of the title. The tiny creature, its head propped on a pillow, lies on a large human bed, suggesting its presence within a human world in the story to come. But this is not an image derived from the story itself. The bed plays no part in the subsequent narrative. Jessica's drawing is simply a picture of what it means to be poorly. The title was chosen before the story was written. When Jessica was asked how the idea came to her she replied that she often wrote about girls and boys so this time she had chosen to write about animals. In the event, the mouse has to share the limelight with the little girl and her mother, but only after the story has been launched. The title names the predicament which the story sets out to resolve.

Page 1 (see p.47)

The opening page introduces a fairy tale: the story of a mouse living in a land of wolves. Wolves are unknown in England except in the fairy tale where they are ubiquitous. *Little Red Riding Hood* and *The Three Little Pigs* are among the most popular of the stories read or told to children long before they come to school while What's the Time Mr Wolf? is a playground game still to be found in primary schools up and down the country, including at Harwell School. With her very first sentence, then, Jessica places her story firmly within an established narrative tradition, the same tradition which Wally exploited in Vivian Paley's kindergarten classroom in Chicago.

The elements of that tradition, as we have already seen, include magic, often employed by those who come to the aid of the hero or heroine, complicity between humans and animals, family conflict and happy endings which may be more ambiguous than the traditional formula implies. Each of these elements finds its place in Jessica's story although her narrative is anything but conventional. Like Wally, she plays with tradition even as she reproduces it. 'Who lived near where the wolves lived': the language is chaste but full of implied menace in the context of the fairy tale. The written text goes on to provide the brute facts: 'one day a wolf came out of his home and hurt the mouse.' To grasp the significance of these apparently bland words, the reader has only to study the drawing underneath. It portrays a bright day in the traditional woods. Between tall trees, delicately outlined in pencil, a fierce sun, its thick, rough disk sprouting jagged rays, shines down on the miniscule mouse. Jessica has taken great trouble to draw the tiny mouse in as considerable detail as she can manage: head, body, legs, eye, ear and flourishing, defining tail. The mouse faces away from the wolf, as if it were enjoying the day, unaware of the peril that lies in wait. Meanwhile, from the edge of the page, the wolf's head emerges. With its upturned muzzle it sniffs the air, surveying the scene. Its sharp teeth are already bared, spiky chevrons as large as the mouse itself. This is what it means for the wolf to come out of its home. The threat is made visible on the page. Image and text complement each other. Together they give unity to this opening page of the story. In one way or another this is equally true of every other page. Each presents its own particular unity. Turning from one page to the next becomes a form of punctuation, incited no doubt by the medium provided by the teacher, the small plain paper booklets which she had handed the children to write their stories in. Jessica does not make use of sentence punctuation, except for a single full stop on this first page. This is a routine which she has still to acquire. But she has found her own way to punctuate her narrative discourse, using each page as a separate segment in her tale.

Page 2 (see p.48)

'One day . . .'. This is the second time that Jessica has used the phrase and the repetition is significant. It may well be the same day on which the wolf came out of its home and hurt the mouse but we have turned the page and started the story again, this time from a human perspective. For all her later insistence on wanting to write about animals for once, Jessica finds herself immediately drawn back to the human world. With this turn we enter the world not so much of the fairy tale as of a family saga: the story of a girl, her mother, the vet and the awesome father. Fairy tale and family saga are interrelated in many of the stories which children tell or are told, as they are within the folk tale tradition as a whole. Angela Carter once remarked that 'a fairy tale is a story where one king goes to another king to borrow a cup of sugar' (1992: xi), and so it is with children's own tales. Wally's stories also incorporated family sagas but everything took place within the ambit of the magical forest. Jessica is more elaborate. The woods are left behind and reappear only at the story's end. From now on the action switches to the world of everyday, but one which will soon be infused with magic. The double opening draws attention to the juxtaposition of folk tale and family life in the story to be told. In an adult writer this might be seen as a self-conscious conceit. Jessica is less knowing but no less deliberate. To anyone reading the words alone it might seem inappropriate for Jessica to speak of a little girl 'walking in the wood' when she has not yet mentioned any wood. But the wood has indeed been mentioned, not in words but in the drawing on the previous page. There could hardly be a clearer demonstration that Jessica conceives her narrative as a unity of image and text. The words themselves are carefully chosen, as they are throughout the story. First the girl sees the mouse, then she notices its injury. The simple succession of the two kinds of recognition shows how clearly the narrator has imagined the scene. It is only after she has caught sight of the mouse, delightedly perhaps, that she realizes with horror that it has been injured, the word 'injured' being Jessica's discriminating variation on 'hurt'. The drawing is equally exact. It has to be read alongside the previous page. The landscape has disappeared so that attention can be focused on the drama of recognition. Once more a figure looks in from the edge of the page as if to dramatize the emergent plot, with its sense of a double beginning. In place of the wolf's head with its bared teeth we find the half figure of a girl, her mouth open in a gasp while in front of her, in the centre of the page, lies the injured mouse on its back, for all the world as if it were dead, a shadow of its former self. Each face signifies the emotion that lies behind the simple words of the text: terror and shock. Together, the two pages define the narrative framework and set out the predicament which the title has named: the tale of a poorly mouse.

Page 3 (see p.49)

The narrative richness of the new page draws the reader into the heart of the plot. Every detail counts. Thus Jessica is careful to insist that it is 'both' the little girl and her mother who take the mouse to the vet and to confirm their collaboration she chooses to draw the mouse on the mother's arm rather than the daughter's. This apparently simple emphasis is full of meaning. It establishes the rapport between mother and daughter, a complicity which binds mother, daughter and animal in a magical embrace from which, as we are to discover, the father, like the vet, is excluded. Mother, child and mouse live in the world of the fairy tale, a liberated world, out of time and beyond care. Vet and father are bound to the appropriate and the orderly, the ordinary world of everyday. 'But the vet was busy . . .' – Jessica might have chosen to place these words on their own separate page. Her decision to include them here is a key to the meaning of the page. The vet's business is the complication, or trouble, that drives the story forward, threatening to frustrate the good intentions of mother and daughter and opening the way for a far more dramatic display of resourcefulness. This page presents the failure of common sense; the vet is too busy to attend to the mouse. The next page substitutes magic. Each page expresses its own thought, the ineffectiveness of the reasonable, the triumph of play. To have placed the vet's business elsewhere would have destroyed the symmetry of the plot. The word 'busy' is placed last on the page for good reason. It marks a critical moment in the story. For children, 'busy' is such a dismissive word, the sign of a world of adult concerns that can find no time or place for children. 'Don't bother me now dear, I'm busy', a parent will say. It is the grace of the mother in Jessica's story that she is not too busy to share her daughter's wish to save the mouse. It is the father's misfortune that he can neither recognize nor share the pleasures of complicity. To see what it means to be busy the reader need only look below the written word to the drawing that pictures it. For the third time a figure views the scene from the edge of the page: a vet inspecting his clients. The girl, her mother and the mouse form a single hopeful group. In front of them a cat waits on top of its basket while its owner approaches the vet. The size of the cat and the prominence of its basket seem to emphasize the insignificance of the tiny mouse. Mother and daughter smile expectantly while the vet looks glum. The words above have forewarned us that these smiles are about to be disappointed, encouraging us to turn the page.

Page 4 (see p.50)

In young children's earliest written narratives, as in Wally's dictated stories, insignificant words are often loaded with meaning. The word 'so' that opens this page is an example. We have reached the scene of transformation. The business of the vet, representing the unavailability of medicine or, in general, of the reasonable world, has opened the way for magic. 'So' is an expression of purest consequence: 'So the little girl and her mum pretended . . .'. The audience of children and teachers, listening to Jessica's story, chuckled at the word 'pretended' but the smiles were as much in recognition of her boldness as of her naïvety. It is the most important word in the entire story, the word around which the story revolves. So much of early childhood is bound up with play and with the pretence that makes of play an imaginative world as rich as the real and vital to any satisfying engagement with the real. In the traditional tale it may take the fairy godmother or the witch to weave the spell that heals the injury but for Jessica all that is required is confidence in the power of pretence itself, a triumph of the narrative imagination in which the wish has become for the moment equivalent to the deed. This confidence is not unilateral. It is the child and her mother who together succeed, as though the very fact of their complicity accomplishes the trick. It is not enough for the child alone to have faith in the power of pretence. Confirmation is sought, not from the creatures of fantasy – witches, godmothers, fairies, genies – but from those who are nearest and dearest. Several weeks after writing her story Jessica was asked what she had in mind when she chose the word 'pretended'. She replied that, well, the mum was a doctor so she was used to treating people. Her reply recalls the plausibility that Wally often sought when questioned about his more surprising effects and may reflect, as Wally's responses seem to reflect, a certain defensiveness in the face of questions asked by readers, especially if the readers happen to be teachers. Or perhaps, like Wally, Jessica is anxious to establish the plausibility of magic. In any case her reply indirectly confirms the power of make-believe. It is suffi-cient to act like a vet to achieve the wished-for event, though of course it helps if you have a medical background. The drawing pictures the magical scene. The mouse lies prostrate between mother and child as on an operating table. But there are no instruments to be seen. While the child looks straight ahead, pleading with outstretched arms, her mother faces the mouse. She has sat down on the floor, bringing herself to her daughter's level in a gesture of solidarity. She holds out a nurturing arm to the injured creature. Next moment, as we know from the text above, the mouse will be on its feet again. Our eyes are already straying to the facing page.

Page 5 (see p.51)

The drawing on this page forms a pair with the drawing on the previous page. Although it is placed below the text, as is every drawing in the story, it anticipates the written words by portraying the fulfilment of the magic of pretence. We have just learned that the little girl and her mum soon got the mouse better and here is the visible proof. The mouse stands upright, flour-ishing its tail and gazing at the reader in triumph while mother and daughter turn to face it, each of them standing now and smiling, admiring the mouse and proud of their own success. Meanwhile, the text above has already moved the story on, hinting, however lightly, that there may be trouble ahead. When Jessica read her story on tape, some time after reading it in assembly, she read the second word as 'though' rather than 'now'. Whichever reading is preferred, a trace of ambiguity enters the story at this point. It is signalled by the opening word 'even' and further by the word 'kept'. In keeping the mouse, even after its recovery, there is the hint of a suggestion that mother and child may be infringing the boundary of the permissible. The magical achievement celebrated in the drawing is about to unravel. Jessica is not, after all, content with the triumph of pretence. Her narrative vision is more complex. There is another side to this story which must now be given its due. Nevertheless, as the placing of the drawing implies, the overwhelming feeling at this point in the tale is one of mutual delight. We have entered a time that is out of time. The magic of make-believe has released the three friends into a world in which, for a while, nothing obstructs their common pleasure in play. Momentarily they are free of the constraints of reality. 'They had lots of fun.'

Page 6 (see p.52)

The accident of turning the page accentuates the dramatic force of the word 'then' which now unexpectedly, for all the faint unease of the previous page, introduces a fresh twist to Jessica's plot. Two times are inscribed here, the time of event, marked by 'then' and the time of duration, marked by the phrase 'after a while'. The juxtaposition is considered rather than casual. Mother and child have been liberated into a magical world of play as if all time were theirs. But it cannot or must not last. Now the father returns to bring play to an end. By calling him 'the dad' Jessica emphasizes the archetypal character of this father but the significance of the bare definite article lies more in the need to preserve the bond that exists throughout the story, up to this moment, between mother and child. If she had written 'the little girl's dad' she would too readily have separated mother and daughter, although, as the picture warns us, that separation is imminent. She might have avoided the problem by naming the father but this is a story without names. To that extent all the characters in the story are archetypal. It is ironic that it should be the father who returns from holiday. The real holiday has been the magical holiday of mother, child and mouse, that imaginative complicity from which the father has been excluded. Perhaps that is Jessica's point. Although the father is returning from a holiday, it is those who have stayed at home who have enjoyed, in his absence, the more significant freedom. In answer to a question, all that Jessica would say, some weeks later, was that the family usually went on holiday together but this time the father had chosen to go by himself. Neither holiday, it seems, can last. With the father's return reality intrudes upon magic, separating once more the worlds of the animal and the human. The fairy tale world is about to turn back on itself with a waving of hands and a last scribbled line. Below the simple, fateful words, the drawing, in its starkness, confirms this sense of an end to magic and to play. It is in marked contrast with the drawing that precedes it. Father and mother confront each other across an empty space. The father's head is spiky and hard, like the fierce sun on the opening page. The mother's mouth is open in what might be either a shout of welcome or a cry of alarm. Their hands are firmly by their sides. The child and the mouse alike have disappeared. The adults confront each other alone.

Page 7 (see p.53)

The ending of the story is deeply ambiguous. For the first and only time the mouse is identified by gender, a poignant touch at the parting of the ways. We cannot know what awaits him in 'his old home' but we cannot but remember that he lived 'near where the wolves lived'. In conversation, Jessica said that the mouse might find a new home further away from the wolves but she didn't sound convinced. The father dislikes animals yet he can speak to the mouse apologetically. Perhaps his words, 'sorry you have to leave', express something of the inevitability of an end to magic. This is the only drawing that includes speech. Like many of her classmates, including her friend Melissa, Jessica incorporates into her story, without difficulty, the conventions of the comic strip. But the father's words are not only an occasion for demonstrating the writer's command of the speech bubble. The words are also necessary if we are to understand the complexity of the father's feelings. We can see from their diverse gestures the responses of mother, daughter and father to the mouse's departure but without the spoken words we could not be sure of the father's apologetic tone. The words add a subtlety which is as yet beyond Jessica's visual scope. This final drawing is a curtain call, a farewell to the reader as much as to the mouse, as the line drawn across the page immediately below the last words seems to imply. All four actors face the reader, announcing variously their sentiments. The father's hands stay by his side; only his words evoke apology. The girl waves her hand which has grown almost as large as her face. The mother waves too, only more sedately, her hand still, as everywhere else, a button. She has changed her skirt for trousers, perhaps to indicate the difference in the relationship between mother and child now that the father has returned. In front of them the mouse looks out at the reader from the bumpy path, the uneven line, that will lead him back to the perilous wood. His departure is double edged. There is danger in the woods but he will no longer be 'kept'. His own world beckons. Animal and humans alike move on, into another story, an uncertain future. 'It's happy and sad', was as much as Jessica would later say.

The Little Girl Who Got Lost

Melissa and Jessica were friends and classmates who composed their stories side by side in the classroom. It is not surprising, therefore, to find that the two stories have much in common. Both are written in the plain paper booklets which their teacher had handed them, although by accident Melissa's booklet contained four more pages, which turns out to be of some significance for the story she has to tell, as we will see. Both incorporate text and image on each separate page, the image invariably placed below the text. There is the same complex interplay between image and word and the same use of the page to punctuate the narrative in the absence of conventional punctuation. Each story features a little girl and each opens with the girl walking out on her own. Each concerns a simple nuclear family: child, mother and father. Yet their common features, however striking, seem insignificant when set alongside the two young writers' contrasting visions. The narrative imagination follows a new direction in Melissa's tale. The common means which Jessica and Melissa employ as they begin to explore a literary world serve very different ends.

Title page (see p.57)

At first sight the title seems misleading. The story of the little girl who got lost is no more than the prelude to a larger adventure, an extended and heartfelt celebration of family life. Yet the title is central to the tale. Like the title of Jessica's story, it names the predicament which the story has to resolve. Getting lost is the consequence of an act which ignores the reality of the child's dependence on her family. That dependence is never challenged, as it is in various ways in *The Poorly Mouse*. On the contrary, it is recognized as the necessary support for the child's growing autonomy and the point of the story is to reaffirm family solidarity. Getting lost is the rupture which Melissa's tale sets out to heal. The picture personifies this rupture. The image of a small girl facing the reader and crying out at us, 'I want my mum', represents the heroine whose first person voice will eventually move from the speech bubble to become the voice of the narrator herself. But it is only at the point of resolution, two-thirds of the way through the story, that this transition can be managed.

Page 1 (see p.58)

Unlike *The Poorly Mouse, The Little Girl Who Got Lost* is exclusively a family story. Melissa has no need of the fairy tale frame within which Jessica chose to set her story of the power and peril of make-believe. Her concerns are centred around the world of everyday. The only trace of magic comes on the second page and it serves a very different purpose. Melissa's story opens on the equivalent of Jessica's second page; the first five words of the two pages are identical: 'One day a little girl ...'. Here at the beginning the heroine asserts her independence. The vocabulary is deceptively simple. The words 'came outside' draw attention to the girl's leaving home. In the outside world, the world beyond home, she is apparently free to decide for herself, following her own inclinations. 'I love walking,' she says to herself as she steps boldly out, justifying her decision by the smile on her face, the spoken thought and the determined stride. Throughout the story the legs and feet of the figures that Melissa draws express this delight in walking. These huge feet and the marching gait have nothing in common with Jessica's static poses. There is a physicality about the characters, a sense of movement, which Jessica never attempts but which Melissa requires in order to demonstrate the significance of walking in her story. Walking is no less than adventure itself.

Page 2 (see p.59)

No sooner is the adventure announced than it is over. Crisis and resolution follow in a single sentence. 'Why so soon?' the reader wonders. The answer is implicit in the sequel. This is to be no more than the opening drama in a more elaborate plot. Circumstantial details are irrelevant; all that matters is the child's recognition, almost at once, that she has attempted too much, like the baby who tries to walk across a room, takes a few steps and suddenly realizes that she is stranded. It seems that Melissa cannot bear to leave her heroine in suspense for a moment longer than she needs to. Help is sought and there it is to hand. Once more the wish is enough; it is the one hint of the magic of the fairy tale in Melissa's story, the faintest echo of Jessica's play with the word 'pretended'. The absence of a full stop after the word 'then' is intriguing. Although Melissa's story contains no full stops, she is as careful as Jessica in her own form of punctuation, making use of the movement from page to page to separate her sentences one from another. Every other time that the word 'then' appears in the story, it opens a page, no fewer than seven times in all. On this occasion, however, the effect which Melissa requires is of the immediacy of aid once sought. The absence of a break between the words 'mummy' and 'then' precisely suits her purpose. This is not to say that Melissa has self-consciously chosen to ignore the full stop at this point in her story. It is to note that the variation in her placing of the word 'then' indicates a subtlety in the use of written language which it is easy to ignore. Suppose a teacher were to persuade her to place a full stop between the words 'mummy' and 'then'; the meaning of the page would be significantly altered. The drawing redoubles the effect created by the unpunctuated text. Child and mother stride confidently towards each other, all smiles. The girl shouts in recognition, as if she has just realized that she needs her mum when, lo and behold, there she is before her. Melissa drew the speech bubble twice. She explained that she could not fit the word 'mum' into the first bubble that she had drawn. She drew it again but nearer to the figure of the mother, almost like a label. With its long, tongue-like, ribbon, extending from the girl's mouth, the speech bubble becomes the visual sign of recognition, a symbol of identity, closing the space between mother and child. The two figures are drawn as one, partners in a dance of recognition and relief.

Page 3 (see p.60)

The reunion of mother and child brings the opening adventure to its predictable end. The curtain closes on the first act of the family drama. The lettering grows larger in recognition of a successful conclusion and for the first time the pencilled figure of the little girl directly faces the reader, beaming. The bold feet have disappeared and attention is focused on the child's expressive hands, with their extravagent fingers, opened out in a gesture of acknowledgement and delight. The adventure is safely over. Rescued by her mother, the girl is free to be herself once more, but free only under the protection of her family as we are about to learn.

Page 4 (see p.61)

'Then one day the whole family went out for a walk ...'. The language recapitulates the opening page, thereby drawing attention to the transformation that has taken place. It is the same walk but no longer undertaken alone; the unity is now that of a collective: 'the whole family'. The emphasis placed on the word 'whole' is a clue to the meaning of this page. Every detail evokes family solidarity, none more so than the word 'sticked'. It is arguably the most important word in the story, equivalent in its power to the word 'pretended' in Jessica's tale. Even its grammatical irregularity is an advantage inasmuch as it confirms the deliberateness of Melissa's usage while at the same time alerting the adult reader to the force of this particular word in this particular context. The little girl is free to be herself only when she is inseparable from her family. Melissa's drawing, in its extraordinary confidence and vivacity, dramatizes and acclaims solidarity. Mother and child no longer confront each other as on page 2. The three figures march in line as one, identical smiles on their faces, identical postures, one foot forward, arms by their sides. Except for the father's spiky hair – Jessica and Melissa are as one on this detail – it would be hard to tell them apart. There is no difference in the relative sizes of the three figures, in marked contrast to the figures in *The Poorly Mouse*. Melissa wishes to emphasize the oneness of family life while Jessica is more attentive to its diversity. When Melissa was asked which of the figures was the girl she replied, 'the one in the middle because she's sticking to her mum and dad.' The child is dependent on her parents yet her dependence does not diminish her standing as one among three equal figures within the family unit.

Page 5 (see p.62)

On the second page of the story the word 'then' was placed breathlessly in the middle of the page, emphasizing the immediacy of aid and defusing anxiety on the part of either the characters in the story or the reader. But now the turning of the page need occasion no alarm so that the word can maintain its familiar place at the head of the new page. We turn the page to find the family returning in the same order and with identical expressions and gestures. The smiles that signified delight in a new adventure have become smiles of satisfaction at its happy outcome. The drawing is an almost exact mirror image of the previous page. It is a brilliant narrative stroke but one for which Melissa offered a somewhat roundabout explanation. She said it was just that when she turned the page she could see through the paper that the father was on the other side of the page, so that was where she chose to draw him. Her explanation seemed to imply that the reversal of figures in her drawing was as much accidental as intentional. But accidents of this kind are organized. They gain their significance from the narrative context in which they are placed. Melissa's story is especially rich in such details. It is part of the appeal of her story and at the same time a consequence of the care with which she wrote and drew.

Page 6 (see p.63)

'And when we came home we had tea.' What are we to make of this sudden, dramatic switch to the first person, a change which is sustained throughout the closing pages of Melissa's story? When she recorded the story on tape later in the year, Melissa at first read 'they' and then corrected herself. She would not admit that she had deliberately chosen to write 'we' rather than 'they' but the unanticipated shift, whether or not it is symptomatic of a young child's insecurity in the use of person in written language, becomes a central element in the narrative. It would not be possible to regularize the use of person on this and the succeeding pages without damage to Melissa's thought. If 'we' became 'they' and 'my' became 'her' the aura so carefully established in these pages would be erased. The word 'we' is triumphant, a sign that the narrative has at last reached its goal. Now that the terror of the first, unaccompanied adventure has been exorcized by recasting it as a family outing, the narrator is finally able to enter her own tale in imagination, becoming herself 'the little girl'. She may have thought of herself as the heroine all along but it is only now that she is free to admit it. Once achieved, it is this movement into the first person, the identification of the girl with the narrator, that leads the way into the long, slow epilogue, the winding down of the day, of the story, of time itself. It is characteristic of teachers to wish to encourage children, even in their earliest writing, to be consistent in the use of person. But this is to assume that any irregularity is necessarily pointless or at best no more than a confusion. Melissa's story shows the mistake to be the teacher's rather than the child's. As Melissa grows older and more experienced as a writer there will be time enough for didacticism, but it is not here and now. Her literary imagination would only be blunted by adult pressure to conform to as yet irrelevant norms. In Tolstoy's terms, to insist would be to mistake development for harmony. Significantly, the first person is introduced in its plural form. It is as a member of a family, alongside mum and dad, that the narrator can identify herself as the principal character in her tale. All three of them are drawn at the table, the girl and her father already seated, the mother bringing in the tea. Melissa was asked if the food on the table was biscuits. No, she replied, it was beans: she always drew fish and chips and beans, she said, when she was drawing tea. Tea: the appropriate end to an afternoon's walk. But there are still five pages of the booklet to fill. Does the available space explain, then, Melissa's curious, repetitive ending, as beautiful as it is strange? In part it may, since, as we have seen, Melissa's teacher had inadvertently given her a booklet containing four extra pages. But that is hardly a sufficient explanation. It would be more accurate to say that once again an accident of circumstance has provided Melissa with an added opportunity. She uses it to compose a five-page epilogue which closes the story down frame by frame, creating the effect of a quiet and solemn ritual, in elegant contrast to the excitement of getting lost, finding mum and setting out a second time as a united family. It is a symphonic conclusion in which the music slowly dies away in a sequence of soft, repeated chords.

Pages 7–11 (see pp.64–69)

When Melissa read these pages in assembly, her audience began to smile and then, softly, for a moment, broke into laughter. Afterwards she told her teacher, somewhat irritably, that she could not see why they should have laughed. She was right, of course, except that this was no mocking laughter but an expression of amused delight at Melissa's naïve yet controlled sense of an ending. Succession is the key to these pages: the succession of beds, now empty, now occupied; the successive appearances of particular phrases and words – 'then it was time', 'nearly time', 'bedtime'. When at last we reach the words 'the end', written on their own separate page unaccompanied by drawing, we know that the tale is told. Whatever comes next can only be another time, a different story. Melissa seems well aware of the ritualistic character of her closing pages. Identical beds are drawn four times, the sentences repeat themselves over and over again while time is intoned on every page with the regularity of a clock chiming the hours. The repetitive flow is broken only once, on the penultimate page: 'Then it was ten minutes until my mum's and dad's bedtime.' This was the point at which Melissa's audience had broken into gentle laughter. Its pedantry accentuates the prolonged ending. But this page brings a vital pause to the ebbing narrative, giving the narrator one last opportunity to picture the intimacy of family life which the story has set out to explore. In its unobtrusive way it is Melissa's equivalent to the closing scenes of Fyedka's narrative, as Tolstoy interprets them. The narrative force of the page is concentrated in the drawing. Mother and father sit side by side on armchairs in front of the television set. They are no longer distinguishable; they have no need to be. On a shelf above and behind them a lamp glows while a clock ticks off those last ten minutes, one by one. It is the end of the day though not of the little girl's day for she is already asleep, safe in the knowledge that mum and dad are downstairs watching TV. So many times are invoked here: the time of the clock, the time of day, the time for bed, the time to draw the story to a close. It almost seems that here at the end of her tale Melissa is brooding on the nature of time itself, her final trick in a narrative that never ceases to delight in its own semantic play. We are close to a fundamental theme, the bond between the nature of time and the structure of narrative. It is a theme to which we will return in the final chapter of this book.

The Poorly Mouse and *The Little Girl Who Got Lost* represent the literary imagination in its opening phase. The two stories have much in common as has already been suggested. They are products of a shared literary tradition with which their young authors are already familiar and which includes the fairy tale, the family adventure, the animal story, the early reader, the picture book and the comic strip. But Jessica and Melissa are no more inclined than Wally to reproduce tradition as given. Their approach to literature is playful and experimental. Jessica encloses a drama of family conflict within the framework of a fairy tale. Melissa transforms the conventional plot of a lost child found into an ode to family solidarity. Both children exploit the narrative power of drawing to animate the written word. Their playfulness is a matter of choice goaded by necessity. At the same time as they appropriate tradition for their own particular purposes they are obliged to accomodate tradition to the limitations of their present experience, whether of literature or of life. Their achievement depends on their success in turning constraints into opportunities. Thus, in the absence of an extensive literary vocabulary individual words such as 'busy', 'pretended', 'sticked', or 'poorly' evoke a special resonance. Even the meanest words are loaded with meaning, as they were in the stories dictated by Wally: 'so', 'then', 'both', 'we', 'whole'. The absence of punctuation is countered by the use of the page to segment the discourse. Above all, the interplay of word and image becomes a way of extending the range and depth of the narrative. Each medium supplies what the other seems to lack. Where words fail the authors, images come to their aid, in depicting the beauty and terror of the wood or the exhilaration of walking. When drawing is inadequate to convey a particular thought or a shade of emotion, a speech bubble suffices. Throughout the stories words and images collaborate in moving the narrative forward.

Aside from these formal similarities, the two stories explore common

themes: the nature of authority, autonomy and dependence, family relationships, the power of pretence, conflict and companionship, the nature of
time. Narrative is the privileged means by which Jessica and Melissa speculate
on central concerns of their lives, privileged inasmuch as it offers them
immediate and disciplined access to the heart of cultural practice. The stories
do not aim to raise their concerns directly. But as each plot develops, so the
narrative winds its way through the problems and puzzles of experience,
turning questions over, exploring implications, establishing relationships,
complicating issues, alternately offering and cancelling possibilities, now
acknowledging and now subverting the order of things. Yet behind the
common themes we find contrasted visions. Jessica's and Melissa's stories
look out on the world from opposing perspectives. We can appreciate that
best by noting the different ways in which they treat the question of homecoming, a theme which also links the two tales to the world of Wally's stories
and to *The Life of a Soldier's Wife.*

The Poorly Mouse casts a cold eye on homecoming. Jessica's tale is concerned
with the elaboration of difference, between the human world and the animal
world, parent and child, mother and father, magic and reality, the world of
play and the world of care. Her story acknowledges with innocent delight the
communion of mother, child and creature but treats it as a magical interlude
in a world which separates rather than unites. Fun is cut short by the
homecoming of the father, in marked contrast to the concluding scenes of
The Life of a Soldier's Wife. His return breaks the spell and restores the order of
the everyday, leaving both the characters in the story and the reader with a
sense of loss and regret. On the final page each of the protagonists is isolated,
facing the world and the reader alone. Only the father speaks words of
apology but the drawing permits us to intuit the different modes of regret, the
girl waving goodbye with a huge hand, the mother more tentative in her
leave taking, the mouse already on his way. His homecoming too is fraught
with danger. The wolf is still to be faced, back there in the world of the fairy
tale. 'Happy and sad' was how Jessica described her ending. The resolution is
hesitant, unsentimental, the very opposite of starry eyed. The author of *The
Little Girl Who Got Lost* does not share her friend's scepticism. Melissa's story is
as categorical as *The Poorly Mouse* is ambiguous. Rather than elaborating difference it insists on unity. Home is its central value and the moment of
homecoming is the moment that crowns adventure with success and defines
the narrative. The sign of this conjuncture is the sudden movement into the
first person by means of which the narrator identifies herself not only with
the heroine but, by choosing the first person plural, with the family of which
the heroine is a member, equal though dependent. The picture of the family
at tea round the table seals the story. What follows is an afterthought, a deep
sigh of satisfaction prolonging the return, indefinitely it begins to seem, in
order to confirm that all is well and that this is the way it should be.

In an essay entitled *The Narrative Construal of Reality* Jerome Bruner (1996:
130–49) draws attention to the 'implied canonicity' that underlies every well-
formed narrative. 'To be worth telling' Bruner writes, 'a narrative must run
counter to expectancy, must break a canonical script or deviate from legitimacy' (1996: 139). Legitimacy and deviance are the issues at stake on almost

every page of *The Poorly Mouse*. The story challenges the legitimacy of the everyday world only to find legitimacy restored at the close, however uneasily. By contrast *The Little Girl Who Got Lost* is a celebration of legitimacy. Deviance is reduced to a minor role as the prelude to legitimate adventure. But Melissa's story breaks the canonical script in a different way. The vivacity and novelty of its narrative means cast a new light on the value and pleasure of family life. Bruner suggests that 'through language and literary invention, narrative seeks to hold its audience by making the ordinary strange again' (1996: 140). Melissa's story, no less than Jessica's, does just that with its marching feet, its recapitulated walk and its calm, clear portrait of family happiness at the end of the day. Implied canonicity is only one of nine 'universals of narrative' described by Bruner in his essay. Others stand out equally clearly in these earliest of written narratives. Both stories exploit what Bruner calls 'a structure of committed time', distinguishing between the time of the clock and the unfolding of crucial events. Both are examples of the 'generic particularity' which makes a good story at once typical and original. Both place intentionality at the heart of the action. Both incite a variety of interlocking readings, which Bruner defines as 'narrative's hermeneutic compulsion'. The substantial presence of so many features of well-formed narrative in the work of children so young, and their evident skill in putting these features to good use, takes us back to Tolstoy's account of creative development. *The Poorly Mouse* and *The Little Girl Who Got Lost* show that the characteristic principles and purposes underlying written narrative are well in place already, here at the start. The history of narrative begins to look less like a long, slow induction into a dimly understood way of life and thought than the successive exploration of territory with which children are already, from their earliest schooldays, familiar. But familiarity is always incomplete. Each successive exploration makes the ordinary strange again. Experience, as Tolstoy reminds us, is at once a promise and a threat which constantly upsets the balance between constraint and opportunity on which children's narrative achievement depends. At each new moment of development a fresh balance has to be struck, a narrative world remade.

ENCODING THE MARVELLOUS: NARRATIVE THOUGHT AT NINE YEARS OLD

SIX TALES

by Lydia, age 8–9

The fire Alarm

by lydia

chapter 1.   1.

On mondays on my way to School, I Saw some Sweets in the corner of a bus-Stop. I went to See if the SweetS had papers on. I looked into the bag, there were 5 Sweets in the bag.

2.

I had good luck, they all had papers on. I was just about to eat my first one, when I heard a fire-Alarm. It was coming ((my)) way. I suddenly looked at My watch. I was late for School. I Started to run to School.

chapter 2.   3.

on the way to school, running,
I saw a fire engine on it's
way to School. I ran after it.
When I got to School,
The fire darm was going off.
It was so laud that it hurt
my ears I saw my class
lining up.

4.

I ran to line up.

5.

I Saw Some fire coming out of the dining hall. Then I Saw Some fire men running in to the Hall. They had a long pipe. One fireman pushed a Knob on the end of the pipe. Water Started to come Out.

5.

After One hour the fire
went out.

chapter 3.   7.

that day at school we had
more or less a better time.
The next day I was
walking to School. I went
down the Street near the
corner shop. I Stopped to go
in-side the corner Shop.
This time I had bad
luck.

8.The Shop waS Shut. AS
I was walking away
I heard a fire engine,
it was going the way to
School. But this time I had
not got my watch on. But
I started to run After it.
It went down the road to
my School.

1

It got to the school gates, when suddenly it swerved round the corner.

School gates

THE PUPPIES

One day on Monday I went for a walk down the street. Suddenly something jumped up at me. It was a dog. Somehow it tried to make me follow her. It was a she. I started to follow her. She went down an alley way. And I still followed her. It got darker and darker. And I still followed her. She stopped. and in front of me and 'her' was a box. An ordinary box. The dog opened the box. And inside the box were three puppies. I lifted one up. It was nice, and sweet. I ran home and told my mum about it. But she did not believe me. So I got some milk from the fridge and got a saucer. Then I took it down the alley way again. I found the dog lying next to her puppies. I poured some of the milk into the saucer. All of a sudden the puppies and their mother ran to drink the milk. I thought to myself I had done my good deed for the day.

THE MAGIC STONE

One day I was walking down my garden path when I saw a stone. It looked red. I wiped my eyes and then looked again. It was blue and as I watched it turned pink. I ran inside to show my mum. But when I opened my hand it was grey and white again. But no matter how many times I told my mum that it did turn red then blue then pink my mum did not believe me. That night I put my stone under my pillow. But just when I was going to put it under my pillow it turned green and then it turned yellow. That night I could not sleep because something was moving underneath my pillow. Then I remembered the stone. I said to myself it must be magic. The next morning before I got out of bed and had breakfast, I looked under my pillow for my stone. It was not there. Then I heard my mum calling me down. But before I went down I looked under my bed and everywhere. But I could not find it. There was nothing to do. So I was just about to go downstairs when I saw the door was already open. Then I heard some singing. It came from behind the door. So I looked behind the door and there was my stone. It sounded like it was singing. And while it was singing it was the colour black with red spots all over. I quickly grabbed it with my fist, then ran downstairs to my mum. I showed it to my mum, I said it was magic. For the second time it was the colour grey and white. And this time my mum went mad. She said 'It's that school you go to that is making you like this. It puts silly ideas in a young person like you.' And she sent me to my bedroom. Then I heard some more singing. I looked out of my window. The sound was coming from the bin. I went outside and around the corner to the bin. I bent down and I looked into the bin. There was my stone. I picked it up and put it in my pocket. I was just about to go inside when I saw a beam of light coming out of my pocket. Then I saw the stone had burned a hole in my pocket. Then it rolled out onto the ground. I thought it must have not liked it in my pocket. It was brighter than ever yellow. That explains the yellow beams that were coming out of it. It sounded like it was going to explode. I ran down the street with it in my hand. It started to tick. It started jumping in my hand. I dropped it accidentally on the ground. I bent down to the ground, ready to pick it up. It suddenly vanished and then appeared again. But it appeared again on the ground. I picked it up again and ran on. I was thinking of going to the street's dump. It suddenly vanished again, then appeared again on the ground. From then on it kept vanishing and appearing all the way to the dump at the bottom of the street. I at last got there. I threw down the stone on to the floor of the dump, then it disappeared completely. That was that, it had gone completely. I looked all over the dump yard. After one whole hour I gave up. I started walking home. On the way home I stopped at my friend's home. Her name was Joanna. I told her all about it. But I told her to keep it a secret. So she said 'yes'. So I said 'goodbye' to my friend Joanna. And then ran home. When I got home to my mum she sent me to bed and told me off very very badly. Because I went out without telling her about it and why I went out. I ran upstairs and jumped into bed. Then lay down. I felt so unhappy. No one believed me. My friend Joanna did not believe me so much as well as my mum. My mum was getting worried about me. She thought I was daydreaming and that I was not very well. But I was not daydreaming. And I am not ill at all. I was getting mad with everyone. Even my best friend Joanna. I did not know what to do. So I fell asleep. Something was under my pillow. It woke me up. I lifted up my pillow and under the pillow was my stone. It was the colour green with blue spots. I said to myself 'When it had vanished it had not quite gone after all. It had just vanished and appeared again in somewhere else like all the way to the dump.' I was more happier now than before. Now I had my stone back. Then I heard someone at the window. They were tapping on it. I opened it. It was silly old Joanna. She said 'I was thinking about the story you told me and I think it is true.' I said 'That's great. Try telling that to my mum. She would not ever believe us.' I asked Joanna if she would like to see my magic stone. She said 'Yes! I would love to.' So I showed it to her. It was the colour red with yellow bright spots. It looked very very pretty. At that time my mum came in. And she saw the stone. Now it was the colour purple with reddish coloured spots. Mum said she was very sorry. Then I felt very very proud of my stone. Then the stone went bright red. I thought to myself it must be blushing. Then it was put in a museum.

THE SPARKLING STAR

One night I was in bed and I thought that it was a little bit hot. So I ran over to the window and opened it. In flew a star that was sparkling. I stood back and just looked. Then I started to stare very badly. Then the room went dark again and the room was the same. Because when the star flew in it just lit up the room. But now the star looked strange up against my spotty and stripy wallpaper. It was also multi-coloured, it had every colour of the rainbow. The star was glittering and sparkling worse than ever. It looked just like a very very precious jewel or diamond. I walked closer to the star. Suddenly it changed multi-coloured like my wallpaper. Then it started to flicker different colours. Now it blended in very very well. It looked like it was overheating. It flickered in time with saying Help Help Help. I thought it must be like a fish. Because a fish cannot go on land for very long or it will die, and a star has to stay high in the sky. But if it is on ground it will die. I was a little scared. But I closed my eyes and picked up the star and threw it out of the window.

I FOUND IT IN MY BOWL OF CEREAL

One day I was eating a bowl of cereal when I looked and saw something in my cereal. It was a bit of chewing gum. It was the colour pink. I picked it up and put it into my mouth and it was stawberry flavour. It was yum. Whenever I eat something I always swallow it even if it is some bubble gum. You get all of the flavour out that way. So I swallowed it. For a moment I had a tummy ache. I then felt as if I was being blown up into a balloon. I looked at myself I was blowing up and I started to float. !OH NO! the window was open and I was heading straight for it. I tried to hold onto the edge of the window. But it did not do any good at all. I just hurt my finger. As soon as I got outside I got higher and higher and suddenly I was sitting on top of a cloud. I sat down and I started to cry. Then a little cloud went flying towards me, it was going to crash into me. I jumped up and I started to go higher and even higher. I was going so high that I was going up into space. I could stand it no more. I tried to stop myself. I still did not get anywhere. I was so fed up I did not want to be alive any more. So I tried to choke myself and suddenly I felt something in my mouth. I took it out and I saw it was the chewing gum. I threw it into space and as soon as it was out of my mouth I suddenly popped and – shooooooow – I was falling down and down. Boomth I had landed. I looked around and I saw that I was sitting on a cloud – shooooooow – I had fallen straight through the cloud and I was falling again. Boomth I had landed again. This time when I looked around I saw that I was on a double decker bus! I also had a ticket in my hand. Suddenly I saw my house through the window. I pressed the special button and gave the driver the ticket. I got off and went inside. My mum was up now and she said 'Did you have a nice time at the cinema?' I said 'What cinema?' 'Why' my mum said, 'of course the cinema that you went to today to watch the film called *The Girl Who Blew up Like A Balloon.*' Then I said 'Oh yer, now I remember.' I thought to myself 'I don't remember.'
The end

THE TALKING TREE

Once upon a time there was a little boy and he went for a walk in a forest and after a while it started to get a bit dark. So he started to find his way back but after an hour he started to feel a bit frightened. Because he thought that he was lost. He sat under a tree and started to cry. He thought that he would never find his way home or see his relatives or his friends at school or his cat Will-Will. Suddenly he thought of an idea and this was it. He would find a very very tall tree and climb as high as he could and then see if he could see his home or anything for that matter. He started to climb the tree that he had found. But as he was half way up someone or something said 'ouch'. Then it said 'Please, oh please, do not climb up me but if you want to see something or someone I will lift you up to see.' Then he shouted out 'Who are you or what are you?' Then the voice said 'I am the tree that you are climbing up.' He said 'Sorry if I was hurting you.' Then the voice said 'That's all right.' Then he started to climb down and on the way he told the tree what had happened and at last he had

climbed down to the ground. Then he asked the tree if it had a name. It said 'Yes. My name is Joanna'. Then he said 'And my name is Ross.' So Joanna said to Ross 'Do you want me to lift you up now?' Ross said 'Yes please.' So the tree called Joanna lifted up the little boy called Ross. So Joanna bent down one of her branches and Ross jumped on and holded tight. The branch started to move. Ross went up and up and up. Ross did not dare to look down so he closed his eyes. Suddenly he felt something moving. He opened his eyes, the tree was shaking, someone was trying to cut the tree down. Ross shouted down to the man who was trying to cut the tree down 'Stop it please, do not hurt my friend Joanna' but he did not hear Ross. Suddenly – crash, bang, wallop – the tree had fallen down and Ross had fallen onto the ground too. Ross stood up, he dusted his self up, then in the distance he could see the woodcutter walking off. So Ross started running after him. When Ross caught up with him he said 'Will you take me home to my house?' The woodcutter said 'Yes'. So they went through the forest and to Ross's home. When they got to the boy's home Ross's mummy and daddy were very very pleased to see him. And everyone lived happily ever after.
The end.

But after all of that no one, [even the woodcutter] did not believe him.
The end.

[NB Throughout these stories by Lydia, spelling has been regularized but punctuation has been left as in the original.]

From an innerspace of marvels composed of the palpable and the imagined, the artist molds a compelling dialectic. She gives us a luminous, magical world where the marvellous is encoded in the real. Tomas Ybarra Frausto
(Lomas Garza 1991: 37)

During her ninth year, her fourth as a pupil at Harwell School, Lydia wrote more than 20 stories. The stories vary in length from a few lines to several pages. Most of them are fictional, a few autobiographical. All but three are written in the first person. Several of the stories are illustrated but only one of them can be considered to be a picture story in the manner of *The Poorly Mouse* or *The Little Girl Who Got Lost*. Usually Lydia would make neat copies of her stories, correcting the spelling and punctuation and incorporating minor revisions agreed in discussion with her teacher, myself, not always for the better. Lydia wrote alongside her friends in the class, sharing ideas from time to time as she worked. Occasionally she would take a story home to finish but most of the writing was done in school. One or two stories were never completed, a few were never revised. Lydia was among the eldest in a class of 32 seven- to nine-year-old children taught partly by myself and partly by a colleague. At the start of the year mathematics was her favourite subject – 'it was the best thing at school', as she puts it in one of her earliest stories. But by the middle of the year she was telling a visiting County Councillor over lunch that writing was her favourite school activity.

The present chapter presents Lydia's work as a nine year old's year-long journey through the landscape of narrative, 'the kingdom of the as if,' as Paul Ricoeur describes it at the start of his monumental study *Time and Narrative* (1984: 64). Lydia's journey may give the appearance of an organized adventure, the product of a single-minded intention, but it was not so. There were many unpredictable turnings, shifts of focus that sometimes seemed casual and sometimes deliberate. Only with hindsight is it possible to discern the narrative thread and determine its purpose. What follows is the story of Lydia's stories. My aim is to describe the various interests that govern Lydia's narrative thought, their development and refinement as the year progresses and the stories accumulate, the persistence of certain themes and the struggle with certain ideas, the overriding concern with narrative form and narrative identity. I want to pick out the meaning of Lydia's narrative practice.

On a first reading Lydia's opening story conveys little sense of what is to come. It was written on the first day of a new school year. The class sat on the classroom's corner carpet, swapping stories of their earliest memories. The discussion was lively, everyone wanted a say. Later, the children were asked to write a story with the title *I Remember*. Lydia's story was typical of the response, a brief record of a fragment of memory, roughly set in context:

> *I remember*
> When I was about 3 years old. My mum, my dad, Kate, Alex and me went down to my grandma's home, in Ashford in Kent. She lives at no. 73, Torrington Road. When we got there we were very hungry. We started to eat and have dinner. My grandma had a cat called Nicky. When I sat up to eat my dinner, suddenly Nicky the cat jumped up and scratched me. It hurt a lot. Then a week later we went home.

The significance of this slender autobiographical fragment became apparent only in retrospect. It lay in the character of the recorded experience itself, a disconcerting moment set in the midst of daily life, a moment that defies expectation and thereby sets in motion a train of events or brings a story to its climax or closure. It is a theme to be repeated again and again in Lydia's stories and it is signalled here, for the first time, by her use of the word 'suddenly'. At first Lydia had written 'I sat up to eat my dinner when Nicky the cat jumped up and scratched me.' Later she rearranged the sentence, introducing the word 'suddenly'. It was to become a favourite word. It occurs in over half of her tales, often two or three times. It marks the occasion for narrative, the crisis that provokes, sustains or resolves adventure. This early memory, slight and sparse as it may seem, is the seed out of which the most extravagant of Lydia's later tales will grow.

Lydia's next story was on a theme of her own choice. Entitled *One More Day of School*, it is an account of a typical school day with its familiar routines and occasional distractions. Lydia seems to be attempting to come to terms with her new class environment and, incidentally, to let her teacher know something of her likes and dislikes. Maths is 'the best thing at school', Fluff, the hamster, is 'very very nice', writing a story about 'our houses' (though no such topic had been set) is 'very very boring'. There is little incident to report. The high point of the day is being allowed to stay in at playtime with her friend Joanna and play with Fluff. It is the one novelty, offering at least the possibility of excitement.

Two weeks later, in another story of her own choosing, Lydia returned to the subject of school, but this time to very different effect. She told me in advance that she had a particular story in mind to write. It was to be called *The Fire Alarm* (Six Tales, 1). The division of the story into three chapters was part of Lydia's original intention but it was only after the story was finished that she decided to rewrite it in the form of a picture book, adding illustrations page by page. These illustrations are different in form from those of Jessica or Melissa. They are not integral to the narrative but afterthoughts, illustrating and emphasizing particular elements in the story: the sweets in the corner of the bus stop, the fire engine, the class lining up, the burning school, the corner shop, the fire engine swerving round the corner. The fire engine, the sweets and the burning school are richly coloured: everything else is black and white.

With this strange and striking tale Lydia's narrative world begins to take shape and it becomes possible to sense the scope of her narrative ambition. The story is set in a familiar world yet it is not exactly Harwell. The gates of the real Harwell School are not on a corner and although the village has both a bus stop and a village shop neither is as Lydia describes it. Only the illustrated school, with its unusual roof, is modelled on the real thing. More significantly, the I of the narrative cannot be identified with Lydia herself, although she shares many characteristics with the real Lydia. Part of the appeal of the story depends upon the way in which Lydia begins to create for herself a narrative identity, the Lydia of her imagination, living in an imaginary village not unlike Harwell itself. (In none of her fictional stories is the village ever given a name.) The imagined Lydia is an intriguing and complicated character. She is well brought up, even a little prim; she makes sure the sweets are properly wrapped up before she deigns to eat one; she is afraid of being late for school; she runs into line the moment she arrives. Yet she is nonetheless adventurous. She is happy to eat the dropped sweets and delighted by the fire which, as she notes with characteristic understatement, means that 'that day we had more or less a better time'. The following day she looks forward to a repetition of her good fortune, only to be cheated at the last moment. Above all, she is attentive and aware. She notices the sweets lying in a corner of the bus stop; how the fireman pushes a knob on the end of the hose to release the water; how the fire engine swerves as it reaches the school gates. It is out of such everyday attentiveness that Lydia conjures even the most fantastic of her narratives.

The theme of the tale is the waywardness of fortune. Good luck is followed by ill, don't expect history to repeat itself. Lydia constructs her narrative carefully in order to emphasize its argument. It is a mirrored tale. Each element in the first half of the story finds its parallel in the second half, each time with a negative twist. The shop is shut, the narrator has forgotten her watch and, just as, despite everything, the fire engine approaches the school it swerves aside. The predominant image is that of the corner: the corner of the bus stop, the corner shop, the corner round which the fire engine swerves. It is interesting that Lydia should choose to place the conclusion to the first half of the narrative at the beginning of her third chapter rather than at the end of her second. The effect is to tie the two halves of the story together, avoiding any impression of caesura. The story itself here turns a corner.

Behind the theme of good luck and ill we sense a larger concern. The story deals with order and disorder, the contariness of life, the suspicion of forces beyond the control of the mind however observant, a hint of magic. Is it the picking up of the sweets, drawn in brilliant colour in the corner of the bus stop on the opening page of the story, that causes the day's excitement : the alarm, 'so loud that it hurt my ears', the bright red fire engine with its flashing blue light, the burning dining hall? What is the significance of the watch which the narrator has forgotten to put on the second time round? Roland Barthes has written of 'the confusion of consecution and consequence' as a mainspring of narrative (Sontag 1983: 266). The mystery and magic of Lydia's story are closely bound up with this confusion. When I first read the story I was disconcerted by the ending. I remember asking Lydia if there was more to come. But she was clear that this was how she wanted her tale to end. It was an effect that she was never to repeat yet the curtness of the final sentence now seems to me to be indispensable. For once the word 'suddenly' is used to close an adventure rather than to set it in motion, as so often in Lydia's stories. The story breaks off in mid-flow: 'It got to the school gates when suddenly it swerved round the corner.' Lydia's illustration, with the fire engine drawn coming down the page, hard against the corner of the road, captures all the drama of the swerve. The suddenness of the surprise ending sums up the story. Life is untrusworthy, inconsistent, unexpected. Be on your guard.

Read in the light of all that followed, *The Fire Alarm* seems to announce a programme, or outline a scenario. The magic that lies just behind the everyday, the sense of an alternative world, the unexpected wonder, these are the preoccupations that haunt Lydia throughout the year. It is as if, in this one story, by way of her newly created narrator, Lydia has set herself a puzzle, the ramifications of which will occupy her in each successive story as the year unfolds. It was a month before Lydia returned to the narrative world which had opened up in *The Fire Alarm*. In the meantime, she had written a second autobiographical fragment which appears, incidentally, to confirm her new design. The class had been asked to describe a frightening experience in their lives. Lydia chose the occasion of a recent family outing to the fair in a nearby town:

I was frightened

One day I said to my mum and dad that a fair was in Abingdon. So I asked if I was allowed to go. I was allowed to go. I was so happy that I ran to find Kate and Alex. At last the night came. Mum and Dad, Kate, Alex and me all went to the fair that night. When we had parked, I ran into the fairground. And I ran straight to a house. But it was not any ordinary home, it was a special home. It kept moving to one side, then to the other side. I asked my mum if we could go in it. She said 'yes'. So me, Kate and Alex gave in the money and went in the door. There were funny noises. That was when I started to feel frightened. There were some stairs.

I went up them. So did Kate and Alex. When we got to the top, we had to walk along a long lane. Then there were some more stairs. We went down them. I was just about to turn a corner when a loud scream came from ahead. I went running straight back up the stairs again. Then I went down the stairs and I ran through and out of the door. Then I went back to get Kate and Alex. Then I ran to my Mum and Dad. Then I had a candy floss.

The story may be slight enough but the experience which Lydia chooses to describe is significant. The house that was no ordinary house but an unstable affair of corridors, stairs, noises, screams, is an appropriate image of so much that will concern her as a storyteller as the year proceeds. Once again a corner marks the critical moment of the adventure, almost as if it were the borderline between two levels of experience. Instability lies at the centre of Lydia's narrative world. But the instability is not necessarily frightening or out of control. It may also be a source of independence and moral strength, as Lydia's next story reveals.

The Puppies (Six Tales, 2) was written in response to a reading of one of Tolstoy's stories for children, a story entitled *The Kitten* (Tolstoy 1965: 5–9). *The Kitten* is the story of a brother and sister who have a cat that is lost and subsequently found in a barn with a litter of kittens. The two children are allowed by their mother to keep one of the kittens. One day they take it to the meadow to play with but get distracted and forget all about it. Suddenly they hear a huntsman calling to his dogs and turn round to catch sight of the two dogs about to leap on the kitten. The boy falls on the kitten to protect it just as a hunter gallops up and chases the dogs away. The children take the kitten home and never bring it to the meadow with them again.

Tolstoy's story is a cautionary tale, a gentle warning to children told by a sympathetic adult – the voice of experience. Lydia's story preserves the moralizing conclusion but in every other respect confronts Tolstoy's with its contrary – a child-centred narrative in which innocence has the upper hand. Even the moral is quietly triumphant rather than shamefaced. Maybe the simplicity and directness of Tolstoy's style, so characteristic of his children's stories, had its effect on Lydia. At any rate her story is written with notable precision. Its curt sentences and the use of repetition give the story an impetus that deepens the sense of mystery as the child follows the dog down the alleyway to the box. 'An ordinary box.' The three-word verbless sentence alerts the reader to the possibility of surprise. This box, as we might suspect, is less ordinary than it appears. We are reminded of the house that was 'not any ordinary home' in the earlier fairground reminiscence. The ordinary uncovers the extraordinary, the world of romance in which an animal may become, momentarily, closer to a child than her own mother.

'I ran home and told my mum about it. She did not believe me.' With these words a new figure enters Lydia's narrative world. The disbelieving mother will become a familiar character in Lydia's subsequent stories, posing an adult's challenge to the child's imaginative world. What is the source of her disbelief? Is it the implausibility of the dog's communication with the girl or might it be a more general mistrust of the tales that children tell, a suspicion of narrative itself? In later stories Lydia will reflect more deeply on questions such as these. For the present her narrator announces the mother's disbelief almost casually. It is merely the occasion for a display of her own ingenuity and self-sufficiency: 'She did not believe me so I got some milk from the fridge. And got a saucer. Then I took it down the alleyway again.' Adult scorn is no more than a momentary distraction. It has no power to divert the narrator from her purpose or to shake her confidence in her rapport with the animal kingdom. This confidence is a novel element in Lydia's narrative identity. In *The Fire Alarm*, the world disclosed beyond the everyday took her by surprise and appeared to be beyond her control. In *The Puppies*, the dog that 'suddenly jumped up' also came as a surprise but this time she is in full control of the disclosed world. She knows what to do, her mother notwithstanding, and moves swiftly and securely to accomplish her goal. The 'good deed' is hers, owing nothing to the world of experience. She is left to her own solitary, unguided counsel: 'I thought to myself I had done my good deed for the day.'

After *The Puppies*, Lydia returned to the autobiographical mode in two stories written immediately before and after her ninth birthday: *When I Went to Bed* and *Christmas*. In their quiet assurance, the two stories show how far Lydia had already travelled as a storyteller by the end of the Autumn Term. Both stories explore the scope of a child's autonomy within the limits of family life, a theme touched on in Jessica's and Melissa's picture stories but here given a more subtle treatment as we might expect. The same image recurs in each story, the 'little crack' through which the child narrator perceives a hidden world without being observed. Lydia has begun to pay attention to the relationship of the narrator to her readers. In the first of the stories she is careful to explain in an aside in present tense how she came to be mistaken in supposing her mother to be heading her way: 'I heard my mum coming to my bedroom. But my mum's and dad's room is opposite to my bedroom and my mum went straight into her bedroom to get something.' In the second story, she makes sure the reader identifies her correctly: 'I saw three bags of presents on the sofa. On one of them was the name Alex and on one of the others was the name Kate and on the last one was the name Lydia. (My name).' Yet, for all their control, one has the sense that Lydia is marking time, consolidating before a new advance. The moment was to come soon after the start of a new term the following January.

Lydia came back to school excited by her Christmas presents. Her two favourites, described in a short piece she wrote on the first day of the new term, reflected alternate aspects of her personality. One was a bicycle on which she had been out for a ride in the dark with her dad to show off its 'special lights'. The other was a grotesque plastic head with an eye which you could pull out of its socket. 'And it can make four different noises. The hair smells as well,' Lydia added. She drew the head alongside her writing and later she brought it to school to show her friends. It lived up to its reputation and was much admired. One week later she began to work on a new story. From the start she knew it would be a longer piece than any she had yet written. It was to be called *The Magic Stone* (Six Tales, 3).

The Magic Stone took three weeks to complete. Lydia began her story with great enthusiasm but by the end of the second week she was running into difficulties. She could not see how to extract the narrator from her adventure; she had no sense of an ending. She discussed the problem with me, once or twice, and eventually the outline of a resolution began to take shape. It was I, her reader and teacher, who gave her the idea of placing the stone in a museum, a wretched idea, as we shall see, since the final sentence undermines the entire narrative. I am not sure that Lydia ever much liked it but she went along with it for want of anything else. From the amount of time she spent on it, her anxiety as to where it was going, her inability to end it – a struggle evident in the story itself – it would seem that Lydia recognized that the story marked a significant advance in her narrative practice. It gathers up the various elements introduced in previous stories, elements of setting, theme, voice and identity, and binds them into an extended and sustained narrative, reaching out to a complexity which she had never before attempted. The story marks a turning point in Lydia's year, the moment at which her narrative thought acquires its definitive shape. Perhaps it is significant that this was the very moment at which she told a visiting dignitary that writing was her favourite activity in school. *The Magic Stone* is the story that determines her identity as a storyteller.

Like *The Fire Alarm* and *The Puppies*, the story opens in the familiar world of everyday, the here and now rather than the distant 'once upon a time'. 'One day I was walking down my garden path when I saw a stone.' Observation is almost always the point of entry into Lydia's fictions, but observation, as ever, prepares us for surprise. 'It looked red.' The colour may not seem particularly surprising but it is sufficiently unusual to cause the narrator to wipe her eyes and look again. As she does so, the colour changes and changes once more as she picks the stone up and runs inside to show her mum. The urge to reveal her discovery to her mum repeats the plot of *The Puppies* and once again her mum rejects it but this time the narrator chooses to dwell on the mother's rejection where before it was no more than a momentary distraction. The question ignored in the earlier story – what is the source of the mother's disbelief? – now becomes a determining factor in the plot. After all, the mother has good reason to mistrust her daughter's story, for the stone that lies in the daughter's hand is just an ordinary stone, grey and white. It is not simply that the mother refuses to see what the child sees; she cannot see it. Magic itself conspires against her. Why? Because, as the story will show, the mother lacks the imaginative eye, the capacity for vision. 'All that we see is Vision,' wrote William Blake among the texts surrounding his late engraving of the Laocoon, 'from Generated Organs gone as soon as come, Permanent in The Imagination, Considered as Nothing by the Natural Man' (Keynes 1976: 31).

Vision is central to the thought of Lydia's story. The mother is Blake's natural man, incapable of seeing beyond the everyday: 'No matter how many times I told my mum that it did turn red, then blue, then pink, my mum did not believe me.' Telling, in this context, is ineffective. A child's stories are so much child's play, at best a charming fancy, at worst profoundly irritating, as we are soon to learn. To the adult mind fiction is no more than fantasy, Lydia's narrator seems to be saying. Magic, representing here the realm of the imagination, the possibility of worlds beyond the familiar, is the prerogative of childhood. Or to put it the other way round, magic refuses to let the adult world into its secrets.

Rebuffed by her mother, if not by the stone itself in declining to confirm its powers, the narrator nevertheless keeps faith with her vision, holding on to the stone which, by the time she places it under her pillow, has become 'my' stone. In the privacy of the child's own world, the stone once more changes colour but it is only when it moves under the pillow that the narrator is convinced of its magic. Before it moved it was a phenomenon. Once it moves it becomes a living thing: 'I said to myself it must be magic.' The sentence comes at the bottom of the first handwritten page, which is as far as Lydia wrote on the first day. Down the left-hand margin of the page she has drawn five coloured disks, red, blue, pink, green and yellow, the stone's magical colours. The only colour that is missing is the grey and white of the stone as it appeared to mum. It is as if only the world of the imagination merits colour or display.

The disappearence and rediscovery of the stone the following morning confirms its magic but introduces a new element, the capriciousness of magic, perhaps of the imagination itself. The stone will not be tamed. It is more than a living thing, it has a 'mind of its own', to borrow a phrase from a later story, and will lead the narrator a merry dance before the tale is told. For the moment, however, she grabs the singing stone, now 'black with red spots all over', as we can see in another marginal drawing on the second page of the manuscript, and hurries off to mum again. The previous night she had convinced herself. Now surely her mother would see too. Throughout the story the narrator is never content with her own private vision. She wants others to share it, to make it public. Without confirmation, how can she be sure of herself and her vision? It is a question which haunts almost every story that Lydia was later to write. But confirmation is witheld. 'For the second time it was the colour grey and white' – we may note in passing Lydia's character-istically careful phrasing – 'and this time my mum went mad. She said "it's that school you go to that is making you like this. It puts silly ideas in a young person like you".' At first sight, it might seem surprising that Lydia should choose to have her narrator identify school with the world of imagination. In her early story, *One More Day of School*, school seemed to represent routine rather than magic while in *The Fire Alarm* it was the burning of the school itself that signalled 'more or less a better time'. Yet it is at school that she writes her stories and those stories that represent her own imagination at its most explicit. School, then, becomes the point of access to a world beyond the everyday, a repository for fantasy, the play of the imagination, rather than a training ground for utility. For the mother – that is to say the fictional mother of Lydia's narrative – fantasy equals falsehood, the world of 'silly ideas'. For the child, fantasy is a means to the truth of things; the stone is magic, the stone is real.

There is a certain ambiguity in magic, nevertheless, a sense that it is not altogether to be trusted and in the scene that follows the confrontation between mother and child it is the unreliablity of the imagination that commands attention. Consigned to the bin, the rubbish bin of 'silly ideas', the stone is recovered by the narrator to whom it beckons and pocketed. But once rescued it refuses to be so readily possessed. In the margin of her third page Lydia has drawn the pocket, torn in half by a stone-shaped beam of light and below the pocket the stone already rolling out. The subsequent chase from the house to the dump throws the narrative into hectic confusion. Why should the narrator rescue the stone from the bin only to take it down to the dump? Is it because the stone is apparently turning into a bomb? But why then does she pick it up once she has dropped it? And why is it teasing her with its alternate disappearance and reappearance? It seems the narrator wishes to be rid of the stone while continuing to desire it. She is at once fascinated and fearful. Finally she throws the stone down 'on to the floor of the dump', apparently in disgust, only to spend 'one whole hour' searching for it. Yet for all her perplexity at the stone's mischievous behaviour, the narrator never loses faith in the reality of her vision, even now that the stone has 'disappeared completely'. As before, her instinct is to take others into her confidence. This time, however, it is her friend Joanna rather than her mum for by now she knows that only another child has the capacity to believe and that belief, of such a kind, is best kept secret from adults.

The mother's anger, on her daughter's return, is a masterpiece of irony. The child is told off 'because I went out without telling her about it' where previously she had been told off precisely because she did tell. It seems that telling has become the overwhelming problem. But it is at just this point in her tale that Lydia achieves her most daring effect. For a moment the narrator's sympathies are reversed and she begins to see things from her mother's point of view. 'My mother was getting worried about me. She thought I was daydreaming and that I was not very well.' The unexpected switch from the child's perspective to the mother's implies a recognition that the adult viewpoint must be given its due, a recognition which the confusion of the chase has rendered more plausible. It is as well, it seems, to acknowledge the dangers of an unrestrained imagination. But the moment passes and to mark its passing the narrator bursts into the present tense. The disruption of perspective is followed by the disruption of time. 'But I was not daydreaming and I am not ill at all.' This extraordinary sentence is the climax of the tale. In an impassioned reaffirmation of her belief in magic or, as I have interpreted it, in vision, the narrator all at once steps out of her narrative to confront the reader directly. The magic stone is no daydream but reality, no fantasy but solid truth, and as if to prove the point the stone now reappears under the pillow where the narrator has fallen asleep in despair and awakens her. Lydia has drawn it once more in the margin of her text – a green disk with large blue spots. The stone thus rescues the narrator's imagination or, rather, it confirms a recovery that has already taken place in the narrator's mind. As before, as always in her narratives, Lydia's narrator immediately reflects on her experience. 'I said to myself "When it had vanished it had not quite gone after all. It had just vanished and appeared again in somewhere else like all the way to the dump".'

It was at this point in her story that Lydia approached me to ask how I thought the story might end. In a sense, the tale was already told. The decisive encounter had taken place, not in the forest of Wally's imagination, nor in the sudden arrival of a fateful figure, as in *The Poorly Mouse*, but within the mind of the narrator herself. Her cry 'I am not ill at all' passes the test that enables her to find again her magic stone. All that remains is to extract the several characters from their adventure. Until the final sentence the ending, however contrived, largely through my own somewhat clumsy intervention, preserves the spirit of the tale. First Joanna is brought forward, 'silly old Joanna'. The word 'silly', it is worth remembering, carries a rather special resonance in this story. It was, after all, the word which the narrator's mum used to describe the ideas put into her daughter's head at school. Joanna has come to say that she believes what her friend has told her, despite the narrator's earlier doubts. Because she believes she is asked if she would like to see the stone. The appearance of the stone to another person is the confirmation which the narrator has been seeking throughout her adventure, confirmation in the public nature of her vision. To mark the moment, Lydia for the first time brings her illustration in from the margin and places it in the middle of the page, bold and twice the size of previous illustrations, directly under the words 'It looked very very pretty.' Her intention cannot be doubted. A smaller, uncoloured disk, in the margin of the page, has been rubbed out. The large red circle covered in yellow bright spots dominates the page.

It is now the mother's turn to reappear but her arrival is very different from Joanna's. Joanna came to acknowledge her belief in the magic stone. The mother, by contrast, arrives at the very moment when the stone is shining before Joanna in its full glory. She just happens to catch sight of the stone rather than being shown it. She encounters the child's magic only by accident. Because she sees it she believes and apologizes. The stone resumes the colour it had at the start of the story when the narrator caught sight of it on the garden path. Lydia has drawn it, a deep red, below her last line, right at the bottom of the eighth page of her manuscript. Alongside it, she has written her final sentence: 'Then it was put in a museum.' Even now, years later, I cannot read the words without embarrassment. But perhaps they are, after all, no more than an unfortunate aside.

The Magic Stone represents a considerable achievement. After a series of trials, Lydia has finally discovered her subject and invented a narrative style that does it justice. The use of the first person allows her to forge a narrative identity that is at once engaged and detached, deeply implicated in the action but free to reflect on it from different temporal perspectives and to assume alternative voices. She has devised a form of plot which encourages her to exploit her love of speculation without distracting from the flow of the narrative. She manages to combine close observation of the natural, familiar world with disclosure of the fantastic. She is a realist entranced by magic, a visionary who is not afraid to question the status of her imaginary world. The stories that Lydia goes on to write may be read as so many variations around this central theme. The story gave her great confidence. She was as proud of her story as her narrator was of the magic stone. It was typed out, illustrated a second time, and displayed among other children's stories, poems and paintings in the village church on Education Sunday, where it was much admired. Few of her later stories gave her as much trouble to write. Her writing gains in fluency and assurance as she returns over and over again to the visionary world she has created to examine its complexity and explore its further possibilities.

In the interval between *The Magic Stone* and her next story Lydia composed a short poem for Valentine's Day which, in its incomparable style, demonstrates her new confidence. There was to be a Valentine Disco in the school hall and Lydia's class were writing poems and stories to mark the occasion:

Valentines
On the day
before Valentines,
posh people are excited.
For they know that they will
get a card or two.
Then that the boys
will ask for a kiss.

On Valentine's day
all, well most of,
the boys will go
mad. They will
send lots and lots of cards
to the same person
over and over again.
Because they are in
love.

Then finally ask
for a kiss.
That's how it goes.

The voice is ironic but ambiguous, by turn ingenuous or cynical according to the tone imparted by a reader reciting the poem. In either case, the poem is evidence of Lydia's developing identity as a writer. She stands a little to the side of the action, clear sighted though quizzical, sure of her own authority : 'That's how it goes.' Her destiny is to be the participant observer, at once stranger and friend. It is an identity which, no longer ironic, achieves its fullest expression in the story that followed a week or two later, *The Sparkling Star* (Six Tales, 4).

The Sparkling Star was perhaps Lydia's finest story of the year. Of all her stories, this is the one which most completely represents her narrative thought. Composed within a few weeks of *The Magic Stone*, the new story revisits the imaginative world of the earlier and longer narrative with the assurance of a writer who knows precisely what she wants to say. It is a story in which every word seems indispensable, as Tolstoy argued it must be in a work of art. The disbelieving mother has disappeared, along with the uncertainty that forces the narrator to seek confirmation of her magical discovery from others, adults or peers, and at times even to question the reality of her vision. She no longer needs to wipe her eyes and look again. She never doubts what she sees but only looks harder: 'I stood back and just looked. Then I began to stare very badly.' Startled by the star's erratic flickering, she nevertheless comprehends its need of her and moves decisively to answer the star's call. This time she makes no attempt to pocket or possess the magical object, for all that it appears 'like a very very precious pearl or diamond'. She picks it up only to release it into the sky out of which it flew. In the freedom of the final gesture it is tempting to read an implicit rebuke to the ending of *The Magic Stone*, confined to its museum. There is once again an unwitting echo of William Blake:

> He who binds to himself a joy
> Does the winged life destroy;
> But he who kisses the joy as it flies
> Lives in eternity's sun rise

(1966: 179)

In its epiphanic precision, *The Sparkling Star* is the most philosophical as well as the most poetic of Lydia's stories. It dwells on the quality of looking. Throughout the tale the looking intensifies, until the moment when the narrator must stop looking in order to act: 'I closed my eyes and picked up the star and threw it out of the window.' In the introduction to his *Theory of Colours*, Goethe wrote: 'For merely looking at an object cannot be of any use to us. All looking goes over into an observing, all observing into a reflecting, all reflecting into a connecting and so one can say that with every attentive look we cast into the world, we are already theorising' (1970: xi). Lydia's tale reads like a poetic demonstration of Goethe's method. The more closely the narrator attends to the star that has flown in through the window, the more she notices, and the more she notices, the more she reflects, and the more she reflects, the more she connects until finally she grasps the significance of the event and can determine the appropriate response. Restlessness pervades the narrative. Throughout the story the narrator remains on her feet, stepping back to look, walking closer, pausing in thought before picking up the star and throwing it out of the window. She records every detail of the star's incessant movement, from the moment it enters the room in a burst of light, through its shifting colours and contrasts, to its final coded flickering, and while she stands and stares at it, she never stops puzzling it out. It looks strange at first, up against the wall, coloured like a rainbow, sparkling like a jewel. Later it appears to blend in, to become as one with the spotty and stripy wallpaper. But the effort to blend exhausts it. The star overheats and its fevered pulse, which recalls the ticking of the magic stone when it seemed about to explode, becomes a cry for help. This is the moment at which the story reaches its climax and, remarkably, Lydia chooses once more to mark the climax by breaking out of the time frame of her narrative, in order to reflect, in present tense, on the significance of the star's appeal: 'Because a fish cannot go on land for very long or it will die, and a star has to stay high in the sky. But if it is on ground it will die.' The present tense indicates the theory which incorporates all that the narrator has seen. Unlike the equivalent moment in *The Magic Stone* this climax is not so much a part of the narrative itself, a bursting of the present into the past, as a meditation in present time of the past's meaning. It is an extraordinary touch in an extraordinary story.

The Magic Stone describes a child's privileged access to the visionary world, parental incomprehension and the capriciousness of magic itself. *The Sparkling Star* ignores adult scepticism in order to focus on the quality of visionary experience. The contrast between the ticking of the stone, which the narrator reads as a threat, and the pulse of the star, which she interprets as an appeal, signals the divergence between the two stories in their approach to magic. Capriciousness is no longer an issue and in its absence the child's possessiveness has also disappeared. Or perhaps it is the absence of possessiveness that has removed the need for caprice. The theme of the tale is the delicacy of the confrontation between the child and the visionary world. The narrator is granted a moment of illumination but illumination, it seems, can never be more than momentary. To recognize the vision is to acknowledge at once its closeness to us and its overwhelming difference. Like the fish whose beauty cannot survive out of the water, the star belongs to a world that is irredeemably other. The best we can hope for, the story tells us, is the visitation, the fleeting communion of worlds, a moment of insight, a touch of magic.

Around the time that Lydia was writing *The Sparkling Star*, her class had been listening to a Lincolnshire folk tale called *The Buried Moon* (Jacobs 1968: 211–14). The story tells of a journey to earth, made by the moon, disguised in a black hooded cloak, to discover for herself why there is such witchery in the marshes when she does not shine. She is caught by bogles and evil spirits and buried under a stone beside a giant snag where she remains until the villagers, alarmed at the moon's disappearance from the sky and advised by an aged fortune teller, go searching for her through the marshes. When finally they reach the pool where the moon lies buried, they struggle to raise the coffin-like stone:

> And afterwards, [the story concludes,] they said that for one tiddy minute they saw a strange and beautiful face looking up at them glad-like out of the black water; but the Light came so quick and so white and shining, that they stept back mazed with it, and the very next minute, when they could see again, there was the full Moon in the sky, bright and beautiful and kind as ever, shining and smiling down at them, and making the bogs and paths as clear as day, and stealing into the very corners, as though she'd have driven the darkness and the Bogles clean away if she could.
>
> (1968: 214)

I doubt whether this story had any direct influence on the composition of *The Sparkling Star* but in their treatment of the sympathy and separateness of heavenly body and humankind the two stories run in parallel. *The Buried Moon* represents the ancient literary tradition from which a story such as Lydia's is ultimately derived. Yet the contrast between their respective endings is interesting. The villagers are blinded by the light that shines up at them out of the marsh and the next moment there is the full moon back in her element in the night sky. Lydia is more direct, her narrator more aware and in control. Knowing exactly what she is up to, she closes her eyes. The vision is at an end. The worlds must once again be separated.

The Sparkling Star was written in a single burst of inspiration. It was never revised and although a neat copy was begun it was never finished. The manuscript takes up two pages and includes a pencil drawing of the star dropping through the window to the bottom of the stripy and spotty wallpaper. The window is half open and four more large stars are drawn in the framed sky. To one side of the wallpaper, opposite the fallen star, sits a television set, its indoor aerial drawn like the bow of a ribbon on top of the set. Although Lydia's spelling is characteristically wayward the story is carefully punctuated. Both times she introduces a clause with the word 'because' she punctuates it as a separate sentence, as she frequently does in other stories also. Here the separation is particularly appropriate since she is anxious to distinguish sharply between event – 'Then the room went dark again and the room was the same' – and explanation – 'Because when the star flew in it just lit up the room' – or between a thought – 'I thought it must be like a fish' – and the reasoning behind it – 'Because a fish cannot go on land for very long or it will die, and a star has to stay high in the sky. But if it is on ground it will die.' To have punctuated these passages otherwise would have been to distort their meaning. Throughout the story, words and word order are carefully calculated. 'In flew a star that was sparkling,' Lydia writes, so as to dramatize the initial event. The pejorative words 'badly' and 'worse' point up the disconcerting effect of the star's light. 'Suddenly', 'then' and 'now' follow each other at the opening of successive sentences as the star's kaleidoscopic changes hurry the story along. Then, at the climax, for the space of three sentences, one of them the longest in the story, the forward movement is suspended as the narrator reflects on the meaning of her tale. Explanations over, the story sweeps to its conclusion in a flurry of simple clauses. The ending recalls *The Fire Alarm* in its suddenness but the effect is more deliberate. There is no sense of breaking the story off in full flow. No sentence could legitimately follow the final line.

In retrospect, *The Sparkling Star* might seem to mark the high point of Lydia's narrative exploration of magic but it was by no means her last word on the subject. Her next story, *Dilly the Daffodil*, describes the rescue of a clump of daffodils, dying in the grass beside an old canal for want of water. The story lacks the power and precision of its predecessor but continues the theme of communion between the world of nature and the world of childhood while reintroducing the narrator's mother as the unwitting recipient of a magical gift. Then, in the final week of the spring term, came a sudden change of direction with a story disarmingly entitled *It Happened on My Street*. In a frightening extension of the capriciousness of the magic stone, the new story imagines an altogether unsympathetic and wayward magic which threatens rather than appeals, the vision of a world beyond human control or influence, a world by which the narrator might herself be possessed. Halfway through the summer term Lydia returned to the theme in a story to which *It Happened on My Street* appears to be a prelude. It was to prove the most surreal of all her tales, as hinted in its eccentric title: *I Found It in My Bowl of Cereal* (Six Tales, 5).

I Found It in My Bowl of Cereal was the first of Lydia's summer term stories to be written in the first person. At the start of term she had chosen, for the first time, to use the third person for her stories. Her opening story was a comic version of *Little Red Riding Hood*, in contemporary mode, and she followed it with an extravagent fairy tale of her own invention, *When Mrs Thatcher Went Double*. For all their ingenuity, neither story seemed to satisfy Lydia. She had difficulty finishing them and was loathe to revise either of them. It seemed that she still needed the first person to find a narrative voice that would meet the requirements of her fiction. At any rate her new story, which in tone has much in common with the two fairy tales, pleased her and she typed out a corrected version at home, taking the opportunity to revise just one sentence at the end of the tale.

'One day I was eating a bowl of cereal when I looked and saw something in my cereal. It was a bit of chewing gum. It was the colour pink. I picked it up and put it into my mouth and it was strawberry flavour. It was yum.' By now Lydia's beginnings have become almost formulaic. As the story's title has already hinted, the mundane will prove to be the point of entry into the magical, that alternative reality which lies just behind or beyond the every-day. Mention of the colour of the chewing gum provides a further clue. Colour is associated with magic throughout Lydia's narratives, as it was in her early story *The Fire Alarm* and again, most notably, in *The Magic Stone*. Alongside the manuscript, as if she is doodling in the margin of the text as she imagines the adventure ahead, Lydia has drawn the bowl of cereal with the pink chewing gum in the middle of the flakes, and below it an empty grey spoon, a pink rectangle representing the piece of gum and another grey spoon, this time with a fragment of pink in the middle. The action that triggers the magic is the swallowing of the gum but Lydia chooses to delay it by interposing an explanatory aside in the present tense: 'Whenever I eat something I always swallow it even if it is some bubble gum. You get all of the flavour out that way. So I swallowed it.' The aside serves two purposes. It dramatizes the fateful moment by witholding it, and it draws attention to the character of the narrator. Hypothesis, test and speculation are the very conditions of her existence; experience is, as ever, her method. There is an echo of *The Sparkling Star* but on that occasion the present tense was used to reflect on the significance of a story just told whereas now its role is to prepare us for the story to come.

What follows is in effect an ironic reversal of the earlier story, told in a quizzical, tragi-comic manner. In *The Sparkling Star* it was the star that found its way into the earthly world and had to be helped back into space, its own sphere 'high in the sky'. Now it is the narrator's turn to be drawn out of her proper sphere. But this time there is no helping hand to speed her return, no communion of worlds. The magical world has become indifferent, even alien. To return calls for rebellion rather than complicity. From the outset, as she watches herself blowing up into a balloon, the narrator resists the pull of magic: 'I tried to hold onto the edge of the window but it did not do any good. I just hurt my finger.' Drawn into space, the other world, against her will, she bursts into tears but the clouds offer no aid and she is unable to prevent herself from drifting ever further from the world she knows. 'I was so fed up I did not want to be alive any more.' The despair has a certain mocking quality suggestive of the fairground, appropriately enough since this is an altogether anarchic tale, on the borderline between nightmare and farce. But the attempt to choke herself turns out to be the narrator's salvation, releasing the magic gum. It is as if in preferring death to magic she frees herself from magic's power. A choice has been made, in favour of the real world, and it is the choice that saves her. The chewing gum is thrown back into the space that is its element while the child can be returned, 'boomth' by 'boomth', to earth.

The story's anarchic surrealism is nowhere more apparent than in the narrator's discovery that she is sitting in a double-decker bus with a ticket in her hand. Why a double-decker bus, an altogether unfamiliar sight in a village such as Harwell? Perhaps it is no more than a roguish detail in an extravagent tale. But the detail may also have a larger significance. The double-decker bus reminds us of the superimposition of worlds, the world out of which the narrator has fallen through an act of sublime resistance, and the world to which she returns, a ticket in her hand, in place of the discarded gum, like a passport back to a world she was in fear of losing altogether. And yet the story's ambiguous ending prevents the reader from interpreting the tale as no more than a nightmare, a sign that the narrator has finally rid herself of her devotion to magic. Lydia had already toyed with the idea of an ambiguous ending in her story *It Happened on My Street* where the final sentence, 'I said to myself "I must have been dreaming"' hints at an alternative possibility. Now she pushes the ambiguity further. 'My mum was up now,' the narrator reports, as if it had only been a short while since she had been sitting at the breakfast table eating her bowl of cereal. But the mother's words imply that the day is as good as over. Which is the true account? The question remains open right to the last. 'My mum was up now and she said "Did you have a nice time at the cinema?" I said "What cinema?" "Why" my mum said "of course the cinema that you went to today to watch the film called *The Girl Who Blew up Like a Balloon*." Then I said "oh yer, now I remember." I thought to myself "I don't remember".' The memory that is cancelled no sooner than it is acknowledged reawakens the conflict between mother and child that dominated the narrative of *The Magic Stone*. For the mother the tale that has been told could never be other than a Hollywood fantasy. The child sees it otherwise. Magic may no longer be sympathetic yet it remains an open possibility. 'I was not daydreaming and I am not ill at all' the narrator protested at the climax of *The Magic Stone*. She is no longer so sure. Yet there may still be more to be said, more to be experienced, than her mother recognizes. She is not yet ready to give up the hold of magic over her imagination. So it is that Lydia prepares the ground for her last great adventure of the year, the tale of *The Talking Tree* (Six Tales, 6).

The Talking Tree is unique in Lydia's *oeuvre*. Earlier in the term, as we have seen, she had experimented with third-person narratives but had appeared dissatisfied with the results. Now, after the success of *I Found It in My Bowl of Cereal*, she returns to the third person one more time, as if finally to prove herself in a new genre. The story is set within the traditional framework of the fairy tale. For the first and only time Lydia opens her narrative with the conventional formula 'once upon a time' and closes it with 'happily ever after', although, as we shall see, she immediately discounts the time-honoured ending. We are no longer in the here and now of the everyday but in a time that is out of time, the time of Wally's adventures as reconstructed in a nine year old's imagination. The narrative voice is less immediate and less self-conscious. An elegiac note enters Lydia's language, a gentle deliberation composed out of a pared-down vocabulary and a simplified style: 'He thought that he would never find his way home and see his relatives or his friends at home or his cat Will-Will.' She seems to be writing with a distinct audience in mind, the young listeners to whom the narrator might be reading her strange tale. Her sentences, with their repetitive rhythms and the slow piling on of detail, suggest the sing-song cadences of the bedtime story: 'Once upon a time there was a little boy and he went for a walk in a forest and after a while it started to get a bit dark.'

But if the genre is familiar, the tone muted, the language spare, the significance of the tale that Lydia has to tell is far from straightforward. Her story marks the final stage of a year-long examination of magic and reality. The tension between these two realms of being has been at the centre of her narrative thought throughout the year. Here in her first successful attempt at a third-person narrative, the deceptively naïve story of a little boy lost, she pushes that tension to a limit.

Readers of the story are often disconcerted by the ease with which the death of the tree is passed over. It seems that once the tree has been cut down despite his protest, the boy follows the woodcutter without so much as a backward glance at his fallen friend, reaching home safely to live with his parents 'happily ever after'. But this is to ignore the story's double ending, underlined by the repetition of the words 'the end'. Once again, as in Lydia's previous story, the afterword is no mere aside. Its function is to challenge the reader to investigate the narrative further, uncovering its double meaning. The story appears to be about Ross, the little boy who is lost and found, a successor to Melissa's little girl who got lost. However, the title of the story suggests that we should attend at least as closely to the fate of the tree. The tree is presented to us as the child's magical helper. It talks, it has a name, and therefore it is at one with the boy, a candidate for friendship, an ally in the quest. The exchange of names is the sign of complicity between the two protagonists. And yet the tree's help is entirely ineffective. Ross is already halfway up the trunk, on his way to see what he can see, when the tree calls out to him in distress and before it can lift him back up to the top, while his eyes are still closed, the tree is cut down. It is the woodcutter, not the tree, who shows Ross the way home. The tree's usefulness is merely to have been cut down.

What then does the story mean? We might try to interpret the entire adventure in the light of common sense. A boy is lost in the forest. He sits down under a tree and starts to cry. Then it occurs to him that if he climbed up the tree he might be able to spot his home. While he is putting his idea into practice, along comes a woodcutter and cuts down the very tree he is climbing. Seizing his good fortune, the boy runs after the woodcutter who takes him home. It is a triumph of sound sense and good luck. Fortune follows the brave; who needs magic? The tale of the talking tree is a charming but irrelevant invention, a figment of the boy's overstretched imagination. So it may seem. But the double ending refuses common sense, insisting that magic is still the issue, as the title of the tale has implied. It is true that no one believes the boy's story, neither his parents nor the utilitarian woodcutter. It is sufficient for them that all has ended happily. But the narrator thinks otherwise. Her extraordinary final sentence, with its irresistible double negative, as potent in meaning as it is faulty in grammar, discounts the happy ending and directs us back to the reality of magic, to the story that neither the adults nor even maybe Ross himself can credit: the story of a tree that talks, has a name, becomes the child's accomplice and for its pains is killed. Wasn't this, believe it or not, the true story?

The apparent futililty of the magic of the talking tree underlines the tension that lies at the heart of the tale. At one level the death of the tree may be read as an act of sacrifice which saves the lost child, as if the tree summons the woodcutter to his fateful task. At another level the child's return to earth marks the end of magic in favour of common sense. 'Suddenly – crash, bang, wallop – the tree had fallen down and Ross had fallen to the ground too. Ross stood up, he dusted his self up, then in the distance he could see the wood-cutter walking off. So Ross started running after him.' The story sets the reader a puzzle. What happened here? What are we to make of magic? How are we to configure the relationship between the fantastic and the mundane? All year long these have been the questions that have fired Lydia's imagination. Here, in what was to be her last but one story of the year, she confronts them for the first time in the literary form in which she will first have encountered them herself, the young child's bedtime fairy tale. Walter Benjamin describes the fairy tale in the following terms:

> The wisest thing – so the fairy taught mankind in olden times, and teaches children to this day – is to meet the forces of the mythical world with cunning and with high spirits ... The liberating magic which the fairy tale has at its disposal does not bring nature into play in a mythical way, but points to its complicity with liberated man. A mature man feels this complicity only occasionally, that is, when he is happy; but the child first meets it in fairy tales, and it makes him happy.
>
> (1968: 102)

Of all Lydia's stories, *The Talking Tree* comes closest to the spirit of the fairy tale as Benjamin describes it. The myth which her stories confront with such high-spirited cunning is the myth of adult authority. In story after story that authority is challenged, sometimes with a light heart, occasionally with passion, but most of all in a spirit of inquiry. For Lydia is a cautious visionary, at times sceptical, at times simply frightened. Her final story of the year, written a fortnight later, transforms magic into an unqualified nightmare from which the narrator has to be rescued by the very parents whose authority she has so often contested. The reality of magic remains, for her, a mystery, right to the end. The more she insists on the truth of her vision, the more she puzzles over its uncertainty. This tension is the creative matrix of her narrative thought, generating one story after another, pushing her work forward, from the sweets in the corner of the bus stop to the puppies in the box at the end of the alley way; from the magic stone to the sparkling star; from the chewing gum in the bowl of cereal to the talking tree, cut down and ignored yet still not quite forgotten.

At the beginning of this chapter, I referred to Paul Ricoeur's description of narrative as 'the kingdom of the as if'. Ricoeur's metaphor is peculiarly apt for Lydia's *oeuvre*. Over the course of her ninth year, the invention and discovery of a possible world has become, as it was for Jessica and Melissa, a form of philosophical and ethical inquiry, by way of which she can explore the nature and limits of authority and independence, the pull of imagination against the constraints of the familiar world, the variety of truths, the status of narrative itself. This is the meaning of her practice. To follow her progress as a story-teller is to trace the intricacies of a speculative journey which thrives on its own inventiveness as story follows story and thought piles on thought. By the close of the year the issues have become clearer, the questions more acute, the presentation more vivid, but nothing has been resolved, nor should it be. The puzzle remains. There is no end to this particular journey or rather, there is only the double ending of Lydia's idiosyncratic fairy tale:

And everyone lived happily ever after.
The end.
but after all of that no one, [even the woodcutter] did not believe him.
The end.

APPROPRIATING TRICKSTER: THE STORY OF LAURA AND THE WORKSHOP

UPSETTER FINDS THE FOUR LEAF CLOVER CIRCUIT

by Laura, age 9

One day Upsetter was walking along a narrow footpath when it suddenly ended in a vast area of field. Although Upsetter didn't know it, it was the clover circuit. Many people don't know about it but they're only the little ones who can't be told yet because they won't understand. But the bigger ones were told and were also told about its powers and warned about its dangers. But because no one liked Upsetter nobody told him about the clover circuit. Now over the past 5000 years one clover has grown each year.

And now, in the centre of the field was (as the clover people call him) the four leaf clover-king. There he sat proud & wise on his four leaf clover.

As Upsetter approached, the King winced his eyes against the sun.

Then when Upsetter was about 1 metre away from the King, (the King by now was standing up, staring gob smacked at Upsetter).

''WHO ARE YOU?!'

'WHAT DO YOU WANT?!'

'I COMMAND YOU TELL ME?!'

boomed the King.

Upsetter jumped, he never thought that tiny creature with a silly little crown on his head could be so loud.

'Ppppplease sssir IIII didn't mean to intrude.' Stammered Upsetter.

'Please forgive me and I'll go.'

'No' said the King calmly.

Upsetter was amazed, here he was panicking like HELL! yes like HELL! whilst **CLOVERFEATURES** just sits there looking bored.

By now Upsetter was rushing around in a frantic panic trying to confuse the King so he could get away. But the King could mind read so he just sat there feeling even more bored than ever. In the end Upsetter was so tired he just flopped down on the floor in front of the King who by now was dozing off, but he managed to say something that sounded like 'just put him in the dungeons'.

So Upsetter was taken to the dungeons.

Now oh dear oh dear I've forgotten to mention his parents, and to think I've had all this time to explain, so before I go on with the story I shall tell you about his mother & father.

Now then, Upsetter's mother was a very fat jolly woman with a squidgy backside, and a chubby face.

But his father on the other hand was a tall thin stern man, who was always moaning and groaning, but worst of all he was always asking very complicated questions. Now do you get the picture?, good, now we can continue with the story. Now then where was I . . . oh yes I remember, we were at the part where poor old Upsetter (or should I say poor young! Upsetter) was thrown into the dungeons where he had a wooden bench to sleep on, with a blanket to keep him warm.

[Here Laura includes a drawing of Upsetter standing in the dungeon looking at the bed and saying 'Wow'.]

Oh and by the way they did have dungeons big enough for a human.

Upsetter just sat on the bench, leaned back against the wall and shut his eyes. Soon he fell asleep, and believe you me, did he snore loudly. Every time he breathed in, his blanket was sucked up into his nostrils, and then when he breathed out again, his blanket was blown out of his nose with a load of !BOGY ON IT!

When Upsetter woke up it was dark and he wondered if his mother and father would be worrying about him.

And so they were, his mother whose name was Jill was rushing around with her big fat bulgy boobs which I forgot to mention earlier on in the story, were flying about all over the place.

But his father was as usual asking lots of hard questions, like: 'where did you see him last,' and 'you should have been there with him, I told you it wouldn't be safe letting him go on that walk on his own.'

And his mother trying to think of an answer for both questions at the same time was tearing out her hair and going cross eyed.

Meanwhile in the dungeons Upsetter had discovered a loose stone and pushed. To his astonishment it gave way quite easily. So he tried another one, and that gave way too, so he tried another, and another, until he had made a hole big enough for him to climb through, and because his cell was on the end of the row he didn't find himself standing in another cell when he climbed through, but found himself facing the doorway out. He jumped into the air, turned a somersault and with a big thud landed on his bottom.

Ow! said Upsetter. He stood up and rubbed his bottom. He thought as all scared children do, that the door would be open because no one was as smart as him. But when he tried to open the door it was locked. Suddenly to his horror he heard footsteps coming along a corridor. He was so scared that he started to ram himself against the door.

Just then he noticed a key by his foot. He picked it up, and tried it in the lock, (the footsteps by now were getting rather close). Upsetter turned the key in the lock, the door swung open, and Upsetter ran like !**Hell**!, out of the door. When the clover guard reached the cells, Upsetter had disappeared and left the door wide open!

The guard had an escape trumpet, which he blew whenever a prisoner escapes (every guard had an escape trumpet).

Now then the guard, since Upsetter had got away, had to blow his trumpet. The blare of the guard's trumpet reached another guard who sounded his trumpet and the blare of his trumpet reached another guard who sounded his trumpet, and so on.

By now, about 10,000 guards were chasing Upsetter. Suddenly he noticed two rockets, one was big enough for a human, but the other one was way too small for him. He stopped, and stared for a moment, but then he remembered, that he had to get away from the clover guards.

He jumped into the big rocket, and found that someone had papered instructions all over the walls of the rocket. 'Whoever did this must a right Wally' chuckled Upsetter. 'But since I HAVE! to GET AWAY! from the clover guards, I may as well follow the advice.' (Upsetter didn't even know how to fly the rocket so it's just as well he had the instructions.) He was looking for a red button with the word !LAUNCH! on it, when the clover guards appeared on top of the hill. By now it was definitely early morning, and not late at night.

When he found the button he was looking for he thumped it with his fist. Almost immediately afterwards, the rocket lurched into the air, with a jolt, that sent Upsetter flying across the room.

The clover guards were furious, they ran down the hill yelling and cursing him, saying words that nobody would ever want to print, so I won't print them either. When they got to the bottom of the hill Upsetter's rocket was only about 6 metres from the ground so they all tumbled into the small rocket, and one of them punched the !LAUNCH! button. Now the clover guards were chasing Upsetter all over the

!UNIVERSE!

Suddenly Upsetter's rocket's engine started to chug, it was conking out! Just then Upsetter fell backwards out of the pilot's sat, his rocket had landed. 'Thank god!' said Upsetter. But when he stepped outside, he was surprised to find that he was where he had started out, (by the way I didn't mean from scratch, where he first got away from the dungeons). He stood puzzled, for a moment or two, and then he realized what had happened, he had been chased by the clover guards, right round the !UNIVERSE, in a circle.

So before the clover guards' rocket was even in sight, Upsetter was well out of the way of the clover circuit.

When he got home, his mother saw him out the window and screamed (with fright) because, although Upsetter didn't know it, he'd actually been away for seven years. There had been a big change in the family, his mother was now as thin as a pencil, and his father was as fat and round as a football.

But when they realized it was really him, they took him in, fed him up and lived happily ever after.

(But they never ever again, let him go on another walk by himself.)

> *We always inhabit a story that others have shaped but we also always participate in the shaping.*
>
> (Hyde 1998: 278)

It was Richard Speed, arts and craft adviser to schools in Oxfordshire, who introduced us to David Cox. We had already run a series of arts workshops under Richard's guidance and we were ready for another. Richard was enthusiastic. 'I've got just the right person for Harwell' he explained when I phoned him for advice. David was an artist who lived just outside the county of Oxfordshire, near the town of Bradford on Avon. He worked mostly in cardboard, wood and paper, making animated figures, masks, puppets, rattles, shakers. But he was also a storyteller and when he visited schools as an artist in residence, he liked to combine craft work and storytelling within a single project. Richard knew we loved stories and storytelling. That was why he was so sure that we would enjoy working with David.

Soon afterwards Richard brought David to Harwell for a preliminary visit during which David explained his ideas. The project would revolve around a West African trickster story, recreated by David for his own use. He called it an Upsetter Story. On the opening day of a three-day workshop he would begin by telling the story. Afterwards he would show the children some of his models, demonstrate how they were made, and explain his intentions for the days ahead. Everyone, teachers as well as children, would make rattles, shakers, masks and figurines to be used during a dramatized performance of the opening story at the end of the project, on the third day. The children – there would be 85 children taking part in all – would be divided into mixed-age groups and the teachers would work alongside them, helping as necessary but also making models themselves. David and Richard would oversee the activity, making sure that the children were kept aware of the theme and encouraging integrity of design in construction and decoration. We would use cardboard, withies or willow sticks, coloured newsprint, beads and thin strips of plastic. The colour range would be restricted and the models would be decorated exclusively by means of the coloured newsprint. The use of pencils, pens, paints and crayons, would be discouraged. From time to time everyone would gather together in the school hall to review progress, show work, ask questions and discuss the final performance, for which a number of children would need to be chosen to play the leading parts, miming their roles as David retold the story. During these larger gatherings David would tell further Upsetter stories and encourage the children to tell their own stories. On the afternoon of the third day we would all reassemble for the final performance, bringing with us the models which we had made, ready for use. After the play was over David would tell one last trickster tale and the workshop would end.

The story David chose to open the workshop was called *The Story of Number Eleven*. This is how he described it in a letter written shortly after his visit:

A mother and father have five sons and five daughters. These children are greedy and ungrateful. Tucked on the end is a special child called Number 11. With his magical and intuitive insights, Number 11 guides the children through a series of traps, where they come to no harm –

traps which have been set up by their parents to teach them a lesson. The King and Queen are finally appealed to and in a rage they send the children to the land of Grandma and Grandpa Bogey, which is the land of the dead. They are ordered to return home with the golden treasures of these terrifying two. The children are scared but are encouraged and cajoled on the way by Number 11. They leave the land of their birth and come to a strange, spooky place. After a long and tiring journey they arrive at the village of Grandma and Grandpa. At first they are welcomed but things soon begin to go awry as the children display their usual rudeness, greediness and bad temper. Number 11 saves the day with a number of ingenious and hilarious tricks. The children return home with their treasures. They have, however, received such a fright that they are cured of their bad habits. The story ends with a twist for Number 11. Grandma and Grandpa Bogey plot revenge. 'We're going to come and get you, all of you, one of these days, but not you Number 11, you're just too much trouble, we never want to see you again.' And so, the story tells us, Number 11 is still around, even today. Maybe you've seen him. Maybe he's just going out of the door.

For all the advance preparations, on the opening day of the workshop, two months later, no one, neither children nor teachers, knew quite what to expect. Children from all three classes taking part sat with their teachers in the school hall, awaiting David's arrival. Suddenly there he stood in the doorway, wearing a dragon's head mask. He stalked over to a chair, turning his head this way and that, snatching at the children sitting closest as he went. Then he sat down, took off his mask, introduced himself and prepared to begin his story. But before he began, he walked over to a girl sitting crosslegged in the front row, held out his hand and offered her the end of an imaginary ball of string. He had chosen wisely, if accidentally. Vicki, the girl in question, turned out to be an exceptionally trusting accomplice. Step by step, moment by moment, he persuaded her, still clutching the imaginary string, to walk to the doorway from the hall into the school car park, open it, step outside, pretend to get into a taxi, travel to the nearest railway station, board a train for Heathrow Airport, take a plane to Moscow, Tokyo, San Francisco, New York, London, return to Harwell by train and taxi, re-enter the hall and walk back through the smiling, intrigued children to where he stood, in front of everyone, pretending to hold the other end of the string. At each stage of the imaginary journey he would ask her if she was still holding the string. Every time she unhesitatingly answered yes. Finally he took from her the end of the string which she had been holding, thanked her, and reminded her to gather up the string when the workshop was over. Then he looked up at the audience and said with a smile, 'so now we have wrapped the whole world in our story'. The story then began, in words which one of the children would later use in a story of her own: 'Once upon a time (longer ago than a piece of string) . . .' The spell was cast.

From this moment on, the workshop proceeded much as David had planned. The greater part of each day was given over to craft work. The children made rattles, shakers, and figurines out of cardboard and withy sticks, beads and dried beans, decorating them with strips of coloured paper cut out from newspapers and magazines. A few of the older children made football rattles also while others helped to construct large masks for use in the final play. Older children worked with younger children, and teachers sat alongside, organizing, assisting, observing and making their own rattles and figures. Every so often David, an unassuming presence amid the bustle, would ask everyone to return to the hall to check on progress, exchange ideas and show off finished models but most of all to listen to new stories from his repertoire of Upsetter tales. By the end of three days, after the story of Number 11 had been retold for the last time, to the accompaniment of masks and rattles and miming, Upsetter had become a familiar figure, and not just among the children. As one of them put it in a letter to David, 'I loved the Upsetter stories. When I got home I told my mum and dad the stories. I do hope you come again and tell some more stories. I think my mum enjoyed the stories even more than I did.'

Many other children wrote letters to David after the workshop was over, thanking him for coming. They were enthusiastic:

> Dear David, [wrote Isabella,] I really enjoyed the three days, I thought it was interesting how you could make exciting patterns out of just black, white, red and yellow. The best thing I made was the big belly I think. [This was the name that David had given to one of the types of rattle he had asked the children to make.] I enjoyed the Upsetter stories and Number 11 and I thought it was very clever that you didn't lose your temper with us, how do you do it? I really do wish I could rewind the tape back and do it all over again because it was so much fun.

Isabella's letter hints at the significance of David's personality in the success of the workshop. He neither looked like a teacher nor behaved like a teacher. He was soft spoken, reticent, gentle. He told stories as if to a circle of young friends at home, by the fireside. Not once did he insist on his own authority, for all the evident beauty and originality of the models he brought along to show us. His emphasis was all upon collaboration, between younger and older children, teachers and pupils. Beatrice spoke for many when she wrote: 'I think I especially enjoyed the fact that we were all working together.'

Many children named Number 11 as their favourite story and one or two recalled the ball of string. 'Dear David,' wrote Hayley, 'I'm writing to thank you for coming to Harwell School on Tuesday 10th, Wednesday 11th, Thursday 12th of May and to tell you that Vicky still hasn't collected the ball of string ...' Several children included with their letters stories of their own or sent stories instead of letters. Most of these stories presented Upsetter in an unflattering light. For Jane, he was an altogether foolish trickster. Her story opens and closes much as David's did but Upsetter is treated less sympathetically;

The Upsetter and the Magic Ring Stone.
Once upon a time (longer ago than a piece of string) there was a myth or legend about a magic ring stone. It was very, very magical, if it changes purple and you say the password money falls from the sky (so legend has

it). One day Upsetter heard of this. He thought here's my chance to become rich! so he went around keeping an eye open. He didn't find anything so he thought here's my chance to be Sherlock Holmes. He looked at every lady's ring. One day it was the opening of the Channel Tunnel, he saw the Queen, she had an amethyst ring on. Upsetter saw it out the corner of his eye. He crawled through the fat people's legs, sprang over the short people and squeezed through the thin people. At last he reached the Queen. He said to her, 'my dear 61 year old, oh I mean 16 year old queen, can I help cut the red ribbon?' 'Oh of course,' the Queen replied. So he helped and as he did he pulled the ring stone out of the Queen's ring. Now the password, could it be peanut butter sandwiches, nope, no money falling, chocolate cheese cake or lemonade, I don't know. All I know is Upsetter is still trying to find that password today. You may find him some day.

For Tom, Upsetter is an angry and envious child.

Upsetter

One day Upsetter was walking home from school when he heard a party was going on and HE was not invited. He was so angry that he decided to play one of his tricks. So he shouted over the fence, 'Someone is giving away £200,000,000.' 'What!' said all the children and jumped over the fence and ran off. 'Good,' said Upsetter, and jumped over the fence and smashed everything.

But of all the stories that followed the workshop Laura's was the most ambitious. She was, from the first, uninterested in writing David a letter. She wanted to send him a story and she knew just what she wanted to write. Nine-year-old Laura and two of her friends spent much of the next two or three weeks working on their stories. They assured me that these were going to be really long stories and seemed to compete with each other as to whose would turn out to be the most sustained and complex tale. By the time the stories were finished the rest of the class's letters and stories had already been posted, and we were preparing for an exhibition of all that we had made, in a local museum.

When David finally received Laura's story he wrote back enthusiastically:

As for *Upsetter Finds the Four Leaf Clover Circuit*, by Laura, well ... what can I say? It will go into my special collection of stories. It has just the right combination of panic, fear, fun and wonder for a true Upsetter Story. It's like a strange little dream. I love it!!! The other stories were super too. Please, Please, Please ... keep on making and writing.

In the rest of this chapter I want to examine the way in which Laura draws a narrative out of a particular cultural experience. Her story appropriates both a tradition and an event. The tradition is that of the trickster tale, as represented by David Cox's Upsetter stories, reinforced no doubt by other stories which Laura had listened to or read for herself in the past. The event is the workshop itself which colours Laura's narrative like the strips of newsprint that coloured the children's rattles, masks and figures. Looking back, three characteristics of David's workshop stand out from the rest: the prevalence of storytelling, revolving around the figure of the trickster; the emphasis on the process of making or forming; and the disruption of the school's familiar procedures. For a fleeting three days, children and their teachers entered a new kind of world. Routines were abandoned, lines of authority blurred. The familiar classrooms vanished as children changed places, older children worked alongside their younger brothers and sisters, teachers struggled to match their pupils' achievements.This topsy turvy world lies at the heart of Laura's story. In detail after detail her narrative recognizes and exploits the intimate bond between the figure of the trickster and the character of David's workshop. She was more shrewd than she may have supposed in preferring to send David her story rather than write him a letter. It would be hard to imagine a more dramatic way of acknowledging her debt to his three-day residence at Harwell School.

The first thing that strikes a reader of Laura's tale is its insistent narrative voice. That voice can be heard already in the story's opening lines, with their knowing asides – '(as the clover people call him)', '(the King by now was standing up, staring gob smacked at Upsetter)' –; the brash colloquialisms – 'gob smacked', 'like HELL! yes like HELL!' – ; the use of handwriting for dramatic effect, as in the King's boomed words or the coloured capitals of the derisory nickname CLOVERFEATURES. Yet notable as they are, these indications of a vivacious narrative presence scarcely prepare us for what is to come. The first scene ends quietly, with the king dozing off and Upsetter being taken to the dungeons, at which point the reader is startled by the narrator's unexpected intervention: 'Now oh dear oh dear I've forgotten to mention his parents and to think I've had all this time to explain, so before I go on with the story I shall tell you about his mother and father.' A colleague, to whom I had shown Laura's story, wondered whether, under the influence of David's workshop, she might have thought of her story as a tale to be told rather than as a text to be read. But Laura denied this and with good reason. Over and over again her story makes play with its written form. The use of brackets is one sign of this, as is the dramatic use of upper case lettering. Laura delights in making narration visible on the page, finding visual equivalents for tones of voice, whether the booming of the king, the flamboyant indecency of the narrator or the whispered correction – '(or should I say poor young! Upsetter)'. At one point she even includes what looks like a deliberate visual joke, following up her question 'Now do you get the picture?' with a drawing, the only drawing in the entire manuscript, though, with characteristic guile, it pictures the scene that follows the question rather than the scene that provokes it. Significantly she even envisages her story's eventual publication: 'The clover guards were furious, they ran down the hill yelling and cursing him, saying words that nobody would ever want to print so I won't print them either.' It is the reader rather than the listener in whom the narrator confides, the reader whom she delights to tease, provoke, humour, instruct, surprise.

Soon after I had read Laura's story for the first time I asked her why she had chosen to interrupt the narrative after Upsetter was taken to the dungeons. Her explanation was straightforward, if not banal. This was where she had stopped writing on the first day, she replied. When she took up the story again she realized that she would need to include Upsetter's parents in the tale. Here was a way of doing so without rewriting the opening, which she was reluctant to attempt. Convincing as it may be, Laura's explanation is incomplete. For, whatever its origin, the effect of her choice is to reshape the narrative, incorporating the narrator, the reader and the circumstances in which the story is told, into elements of the plot. It is as if at this moment a new story begins, the story of telling the story of Upsetter, a story that turns out to be central to Laura's dual conception of the trickster.

Narrator and reader alike are the creatures of Laura's literary imagination. It is not just the storyteller whom she invents, as Lydia did: a figure somewhat like herself yet not quite herself, bolder perhaps and certainly more sure of herself. (Laura wouldn't read out her story in assembly although she allowed me to read it.) The reader too is invented, the imaginary witness of the narrator's playfulness. As the story proceeds it seems as if Laura identifies herself at different times with both writer and reader. The narrative bristles with incidental remarks that suggest the presence of attentive readers, readers such as Katy and Lucy, Laura's two friends who sat beside her as she wrote, exchanging ideas and showing each other what they were writing; readers who might at any moment question the reliability of the plot or of its narration, forcing the narrator to explain an apparent implausibility or acknowledge a verbal ambiguity. Every so often the narrator will interrupt the flow of narrative with a 'by the way', 'or should I say', to lay to rest any possible objection to the matter or manner of her tale. Laura's story may not have been envisaged as a tale to be told but it is imaginatively embedded within a company of tellers and listeners, a world full of echoes of the storytelling to which Laura herself had been such a recent witness. The digression that opens with the words 'Now oh dear, oh dear I've forgotten to mention his parents,' introduces us to a circle of listeners caught in the narrator's spell, at one in their commitment to the tale. The shifting pronouns, 'I', 'you', 'we', mark a common engagement: 'Now do you get the picture? good, now we can continue with the story. Now then where was I ... Oh yes, I remember, we were at the part where poor old Upsetter (or should I say poor young Upsetter) was thrown into the dungeons ...' Behind the lines we sense the audience settling down once more as the narrator returns to her tale. The digression is over but from this point on it colours every moment in the story. So it is that Laura recreates the magic of David's storytelling within the story that she has written for him. The imagined readers hang on the narrator's every word, enhancing her authority. The narrator in turn loses no opportunity to remind them that this is her tale and she can't be easily faulted: 'Oh and by the way they did have dungeons big enough for a human.'

Authority lies at the heart of the story. It is evident not only in the numerous asides but in the pedantic concern for detail. 'By now it was definitely early morning, and not late at night,' we are told, at the moment when the clover guards chasing Upsetter appear on top of the hill, as if the narrator fears we might think she had forgotten that 'when Upsetter woke up it was dark'. Earlier the exact position of Upsetter's cell in the row of cells is noted, in order to explain his situation more precisely: 'and because his cell was on the end of the row he didn't find himself standing in another cell when he climbed through, but found himself facing the doorway out.' Years and guards are quantified, distances calculated: 'about one metre away from the King', 'about 6 metres from the ground'. When Upsetter finally climbs out of the rocket and finds himself back where he started, his exact position must once again be clarified: 'But when he stepped outside he was surprised to find that he was where he had started out (by the way I didn't mean from scratch, where he first got away from the dungeons).'

The narrator enhances her authority by distancing herself from the world of childhood. Of Upsetter, she writes that 'he thought as all scared children do, that the door would be open because no one was as smart as him.' She knows better, she is beyond such childish fears. She knows about the clover circuit too, unlike 'the little ones who can't be told yet because they won't understand' or Upsetter, 'poor young! Upsetter', whom nobody has told because nobody likes him, or even 'the bigger ones' who 'were told and were also told about its powers and warned about its dangers' but lack the narrator's fuller understanding, an understanding which she keeps to herself throughout the story, forcing readers to interpret it as they will. But though she is more than a scared child she is far from being a feckless adult. Her most irreverent satire is directed not so much at the child Upsetter who, in his excitement at escaping from the dungeons 'jumped up into the air, turned a somersault and with a big thud landed on his bottom' as at his ill-matched parents, his mother, Jill, that 'very fat jolly woman with a squidgy backside and a chubby face' and his unnamed father 'who was always moaning and groaning, but worst of all he was always asking very complicated questions'. It takes a child to caricature parents so slyly.

Wherein lies the authority of this narrator, who can look on the worlds of children and parents with such even-handed amusement? It lies in the act of storytelling itself. The story is what commands attention and the story is what the storyteller knows best, as Laura's digression reminds us. Challenge her as you will, she'll always find an answer. But behind the figure of the knowing narrator, whom we encounter in every bracketed aside, every byway in the plot, lurks another, the figure of the trickster. Trickster and storyteller are as one in Laura's tale. The storyteller's craft is synonymous with the trickster's cunning. David Cox's workshop has presented her with a model series of tales, the *Upsetter Stories* as David described them. Now she appropriates the genre, but not simply by telling her own Upsetter story. She goes further, imagining a new kind of tale, the story of a trickster as told by a trickster, a tale with two heroes, Upsetter himself and the girl who tells his story. From the moment the narrator enters the story the suspicion arises that she too is a trickster, a second Upsetter, more commanding than her counterpart. The reader is welcomed but gently teased; the forgotten parents are introduced only to be mocked. Meanwhile, the ground is prepared for the explosive scene that follows.

The fourth page of Laura's manuscript ends with a drawing of 'a surprised Upsetter' staring at his dungeon cell, complete with its 'wooden bench' covered by a 'blanket' and its 'barred window,' each object labelled. 'Wow', he exclaims, and underneath, as if the drawing has brought to mind a plausible objection, comes the narrator's reassurance: 'Oh and by the way they did have dungeons big enough for a human.' Above the next page, Laura has written the words 'funny page!', just in case her readers, more especially if they are teachers, might not get the point. It is time for the narrator to display the trickster's comic gifts, cheerfully risking offence to a prim adult reader's sense of decorum while delighting her more youthful, or less stuffy readers with a pageful of gratuitous childish vulgarity. Her first victim is Upsetter himself, her own counterpart now to be upstaged. No sooner is he asleep in his cell than he is snoring. 'And believe you me, did he snore loudly,' the narrator adds with a grin. We may well believe her while wondering why it should matter. But now comes the point. 'Every time he breathed in, his blanket was sucked up into his nostrils, and then when he breathed out again, his blanket was blown out of his nose with a load of !BOGY ON IT!' Compared with the obscenity of many a folk tale trickster, Laura's verbal impropriety is mild enough but the effect is similar. Trickster is the expert in the indelicate, the indecent, the impolite. Laura takes her chance and gives her narrator licence to break the rules of polite discourse. Placing the words 'bogy on it' in capital letters and surrounding them with exclamation marks is Laura's way of drawing attention to the indelicacy, just as, earlier in the story, she used the same device to emphasize her use of the word 'hell'. Readers of these lines occasionally complain of their irrelevance, but while they may be irrelevant to the plot they are essential to the story. They confirm what the attentive reader may already have recognized. They establish the narrator's credentials, determining her role within the story. We are reading a double tale, the story of Upsetter and the story of the storyteller whose capacity to upset the order of things is no less conspicuous.

Having lampooned her hero, the narrator turns her attention to his parents. Their quaint, contrasted looks and personalities make them a laughing stock, both father and mother, although it is the mother who is caricatured the more mercilessly. 'When Upsetter woke up it was dark and he wondered if his mother and father would be worrying about him. And so they were, his mother whose name was Jill was rushing around with her big fat bulgy boobs which I forgot to mention earlier on in the story, were flying about all over the place.' The crazy syntax of this galloping sentence, barely under control, mimics the frantic mother, sharpening the narrator's mischievous glee. Ridicule is one of the trickster's favourite weapons and Laura's storyteller turned trickster employs it mercilessly. On this, her 'funny page', she merrily conjures up a family of grotesques: the snotty-nosed boy, the scatter-brained, dishevelled mother, the father with his hard, useless questions. Family life could scarcely look more ridiculous at this critical moment in the story. Yet it is family life, as we learn in due course, that the tale will at the end ingeniously reconstruct.

At certain moments in the story it seems as if the narrator is the hero of her own story, the one true trickster, but to claim so much would be to mis-represent the tale she has to tell. The scared child and the knowing storyteller represent alternate aspects of the trickster and it takes the two of them to bring the story to its rightful end. If the storyteller embodies the trickster's cunning intelligence, Upsetter portrays his witless opportunism. The story opens on the boundary between two worlds, the 'narrow footpath' that ends in 'a vast area of field', the four leaf clover circuit. Upsetter is set before the reader as a marginal figure, the child whom no one likes. No one has told him about the 'powers' and 'dangers' of the clover circuit. He blunders into it accidentally, unaware of the consequences. Much as he might like to ridicule the 'tiny creature with a silly little crown on his head', old CLOVER-FEATURES, all he can do is to panic. It is Upsetter rather than the King who is confused, 'a surprised Upsetter' left standing by his dungeon bed in childish ignorance. But it is at this moment of apparent defeat that his trickster's skills begin to emerge. Upsetter's gift is his ability, despite his fear and his ignorance, to seize the advantage, making use of every opportunity that presents itself, however improbably. He may be the scared child who mistakenly supposes that no one is as smart as himself, but luck is on his side. As he rams himself in fright against the door of the dungeon he just happens to notice 'a key by his foot'. Coincidence saves him again when he reaches the rocket that is 'big enough for a human' and discovers that its walls are papered with instructions: ' "Whoever did this must be a real Wally" chuckled Upsetter. "But since I HAVE! to GET AWAY! from the clover guards I may as well follow the advice".' Coincidence is a device by way of which Laura moves the adventure forward, but it is also the clue to Upsetter's distinctive craftiness. Unschooled in the narrator's cunning, he has the happy knack of outsmarting his adversaries by a combination of good fortune and quick thinking. The dungeon stones turn out to be loose, to his surprise, so he makes his way out of his cell. A key happens to be on the floor so he escapes through the door, though he compromises his escape by leaving it 'wide open'. The papered instructions save him in the rocket: '(Upsetter didn't even know how to fly the rocket so it's just as well he had the instructions).' Puzzled to find himself, after the chase, back where he started, he quickly steps out of the clover circuit and makes his way home. Each time he is taken by surprise but it is surprise that incites him to action.

From the moment Upsetter wakes up in the dungeon, wondering if his parents are worrying about him, and discovers a loose stone in the dungeon wall, the story takes on the character of a chase in a silent film, or an animated cartoon. Upsetter is the irrepressible hero, always threatened but never more than momentarily daunted. The 'frantic panic' which so signally failed to impress the clover king, now comes into its own. Upsetter runs 'like !Hell!' from one predicament to another, pursued by 10,000 miniature clover guards blowing their trumpets and 'yelling and cursing' in unprintable language. He is always about to be caught but always a step ahead, aided by the coincidences conveniently supplied by a helpful narrator. Providence is the narrator's prerogative and her hero chuckles and takes advantage. So armed, he can return home in unexpected triumph to his reconstructed parents, his unacknowledged task complete. Walter Benjamin (1968: 102), in the passage from *The Storyteller* quoted in the last chapter, suggests that the courage characteristic of the fairy tale is dialectically divided between two poles, cunning on the one hand and high spirits on the other. In effect, Laura has chosen to represent these two poles in the form of two protagonists, the cunning narrator and the high-spirited Upsetter. It takes the two of them together, sage and simpleton, to bring her tale to its appropriate end.

The Clover Circuit, by way of which the adventure achieves its goal, remains mysterious throughout. Its formidable powers and dangers are never specified. It is a kingdom of insect-sized people with huge voices, advanced enough in knowledge to be able to circle the universe yet oddly incompetent, leaving loose bricks in dungeon walls, keys lying on the floor, instructions papering the walls of rockets designed, it seems, for intruding humans. The clover people seem almost to want Upsetter to make fools of them, for all their riotous pursuit. In this respect also, Laura's narrative recalls the conventions of the animated cartoon. But while the Clover Circuit itself may be mysterious, the consequences of entering it are unmistakeable and revolutionary. The journey 'right round the UNIVERSE in a circle' turns Upsetter's world upside down, restoring him to a family transformed. It was not for nothing that David Cox chose to call his trickster figure Upsetter. The power of the name is nowhere more apparent than in the ending of Laura's story. It is not just the proprieties of the adult world that Laura's Janus-faced trickster upsets. No less than a cultural revolution is the goal of Upsetter's journey or, if not the goal, at any rate the outcome. The circle of the universe reverses the order of things.

Upsetter enters the Clover Circuit unwittingly. He trespasses onto forbidden land, the back of beyond, a territory that recalls the world of Grandpa and Grandma Bogey that David had set before the children on the opening day of his workshop. The Italian historian Carlo Ginzburg, in the conclusion to his fascinating study of the folkloric origins of the Witches' Sabbath, describes the theme of 'going into the beyond, returning from the beyond' as an 'elementary narrative nucleus [which] has accompanied humanity for thousands of years' (1990: 307). Inspired by David's workshop, Laura's narrative plays with this theme in a way that is all her own. The adventure which Upsetter embarks on is not of his own choosing and it remains beyond his comprehension right up until the final lines of the story. When he steps out of the rocket at the end of the chase, he is surprised to find himself back where he started from: 'He stood puzzled for a moment or two, and then he realized what had happened, he had been chased by the clover guards right round the !UNIVERSE, in a circle.' Even then he fails to understand the significance of the circular chase. It is only once he leaves the Clover Circuit and finds his way home that the meaning of his journey becomes apparent: 'When he got home, his mother saw him out the window and screamed (with fright) because, although Upsetter didn't know it, he'd actually been away for seven years. There had been a big change in the family, his mother was now as thin as a pencil, and his father was as fat and round as a football.'

At the end of the letter which he wrote back to the children after receiving their letters and stories, David added a postscript. 'A little girl called Morgan,' he wrote, 'has just come to our house as her mum hasn't got home yet. She is 6 years old. I've just read her *Upsetter Finds the Four Leaf Clover Circuit*. She just sat there with her mouth open. She liked the bit where mother got thin and father fat best.' I think that Morgan's delight in the reversal of mother and father here at the end of the tale may be read as a sign that she recognizes in this comic exchange of appearances Laura's ultimate narrative trick. Upsetter's unanticipated circling of the Universe, pursued by the clover guards, has resolved his family's predicament and brought about a happy ending. The change of appearances stands for a change of heart. In his story *The Life of a Soldier's Wife*, Fyedka's hero, Gordei, returns home a changed man and transforms his family's life. By contrast Upsetter returns home to a family that is already mysteriously transformed. Upsetter himself remains the same child who left home the day before. Meanwhile, for his parents, seven years have passed, a magical number which symbolizes the revolution that Upsetter's journey has accomplished, though without his knowledge. Before the journey began his mother was 'a very fat jolly woman with a squidgy backside and a chubby face', as incompetent in thought and action as her uncontrolled body implied with its 'big fat bulgy boobs ... flying about all over the place'. By contrast his father was 'thin, stern' and disagreeable, for ever 'moaning and groaning' and questioning. Between the two of them the child Upsetter, whom 'no one liked', stood no chance. Now their roles are reversed or, rather, they have each acquired the virtues of each other's weaknesses of character. The mother is 'thin as a pencil', that is to say thoughtful and articulate, while the father has become playful, 'as fat and round as a football'. It is as if, in journeying through the Clover Circuit, Upsetter has, by a serendipitous combination of accident and sagacity, disenchanted his parents. A happy ending is thereby assured, as of course Upsetter's counterpart, the wily narrator, had always known.

Readers of Laura's story sometimes complain that the chase around the Universe, which appears to be the climax of Upsetter's adventure, is no sooner begun than it is over. There is some evidence that Laura was growing tired of her tale at this point. She had been writing for some three weeks and was, she told me more than once, anxious to finish. I may also have implied myself, as teachers do, that it was time she brought the story to an end. But we can now see that this curtailing of the chase makes sense in terms of the narrative design. The significance of the chase is symbolic rather than episodic. Its function in the story is to mark the revolutionary impact of the trickster's adventure. David Cox had introduced his storytelling with a symbolic encircling of the world. Laura seizes on this idea and reinterprets it. For David the symbolic circle was a way of emphasizing the oneness of storytelling, where each tale is part of every tale. For Laura it means that the journey into the beyond and back is a journey that transforms, remaking the world through the power of narrative.

Once Upsetter steps out of the Clover Circuit the story is over, the family reinvented, and they can all live happily ever after. But what are we to make of the final parenthesis: '(But they never ever again, let him go on a walk by himself)'? At face value it seems to suggest the moral to a fable. There is an echo of Melissa's tale of the little girl who got lost, a warning to parents and children alike to stick together. But the brackets introduce a hint, at least, of irony. The narrator may have lowered her voice to whisper to her readers, taking them into her confidence in order to undermine the moral so forcefully stated. The unusual placing of the comma suggests a further lowering of the voice. The narrator, when all said and done, is herself a trickster. Can we really believe her tricks are finished? Upsetter may have put things right this time but there will surely be other times when his erratic adventurousness, abetted by a narrator's cunning, will be required once more. The story ends with a wink. 'Don't be fooled,' the narrator tells us, 'there's more to come.' Other times, other stories; trickster's work is never done.

In his book *Trickster Makes This World*, a study of trickster mythology and its place in a history of the imagination, Lewis Hyde describes the trickster as

> a character living on the cusp of reflective consciousness. Trickster embodies reflection coming into being; in him we see both the need for reflective consciousness [without it he suffers] and the rewards of that consciousness [with it he exploits the world] ... We see trickster waking to symbolic life or becoming aware of his own imagination and its powers.
>
> (1998: 56)

Laura's story marks a significant moment in the history of narrative: the moment when a child's narrative consciousness turns in on itself. Her story displays a self-consciousness that goes well beyond anything that we have seen in the stories of Wally, Jessica, Melissa or even Lydia. This self-consciousness finds expression in her fascination with the processes of thinking and making involved in writing a story: with the narrator's power to disguise as well as to reveal, to play with her readers' expectations and anxieties, to place herself inside the tale she tells. But the story is also itself a tale about self-consciousness as Hyde defines it, about how it comes into being and about its rewards. The two halves of Trickster stand on either side of the cusp of reflective consciousness. Upsetter becomes aware of the significance of his adventure only at its end, as he confronts his converted parents and discovers that he has been away for seven years. The narrator, by contrast, is in control of her adventure from start to finish, the one figure who knows all about the powers and dangers of the Clover Circuit. The journey on which she takes her hero is a journey of discovery through which every participant in the story, narrator, reader, hero, is made aware of the power of the imagination to transform life, to reconstruct culture. The disenchanted parents are the narrative proof and Upsetter's reward.

Elsewhere in his book, Hyde speaks of a trickster story as 'a teaching story, meant to remind its audience that the symbolic world into which each of us is born and which, in one sense, has created us, is, in another sense, our own creation ... We always inhabit a story that others have shaped, but we also always participate in the shaping' (1998: 278). Laura's story may be read as a unique demonstration of Hyde's argument. The story begins with David Cox's workshop, a topsy turvy affair as we have seen, devoted to making and thinking about making and suffused with trickster tales. Laura's own story derives from the trickster tradition as David relayed it through the stories of Upsetter. It is one more trickster tale. But Laura, like all the children whose stories we have been examining, is not content to reproduce tradition as given. Inspired by the unorthodox context of the three-day workshop, she creates her own eccentric and inimitable variation, a new twist to tradition.

Assimilation and reconstruction come together as she writes, with unerring self-confidence, the tale of the Clover Circuit. It is a singular achievement.

6

INTO THE BEYOND: IMAGINATION AND REALITY

THREE TALES OF THE IMAGINATION

by Rebecca, ages 11 and 16

DODECAHEDRON

A scream broke the silence of the quiet village Minah, next to the docks. Sebastian sat upright in his bed. That was the second scream he had heard that week. 'Where do the screams come from?' he asked himself. Then his thoughts were disturbed by a wailing noise which then stopped, and the curious metal noises began, as usual, sounding like the tin miners in an old tin mine hundreds of years ago. No one else heard these noises, Sebastian had found that out long before now. But still the noises tormented him every night, giving him such determination to find out what they were. But he always told himself, 'Wait till morning,' and in the morning he thought he was only dreaming. But this night was different. He simply had to see what was making those noises. He got out of bed and got dressed. He went downstairs and packed a small breakfast for himself. Then he stole up the stairs and opened the old window on the landing. He climbed out of the window onto the old ivy below. Sebastian carefully clambered down to the wet grass in the yard. He scrambled up and over the old rickety fence at the bottom of the garden and landed on the cobbled lane that led out of the streets and down to the docks. Sebastian took the path it showed and walked down to the water's edge. It was quiet, apart from the occasional ripple on the icy cold waters. Strangely, the metal sounds seemed to have got louder as the boy got nearer the docks. Now, as he got into a rowing boat, the noises seemed even lifelike in his head. They drew him in, closer and closer to the middle of the harbour. Suddenly, the water's occasional ripple became more like a constant wave, and the clouds above darkened and joined together. The water rocked, tossing Sebastian's boat round and round. A loud crack of thunder and a torrent of rain brought angry villagers outside, cursing the weathercock which spun in a blur on the very peak of the farmhouse's roof. Then, they heard a cry for help, and they turned towards the docks, only to see a small boy struggling in the dark water, drenched by the rain and the spray from the icy water. Ladies frowned in thought to see who the boy was, while the men argued who was to save Sebastian. The farmer shook his fists at the boy, for it was his boat Sebastian had taken. Then, a whirlpool sucked the startled boy down, and all was quiet. The villagers looked on, and as for Sebastian's parents, they did nothing, for they were in heaven, long since dead. Sebastian had been pulled down below the surface so suddenly he hadn't had time to take a breath, and was now rapidly running out of air. Sebastian noticed a strange transformation in the water. It got cleaner and cleaner as he got further down, and gradually all the plants and mud disappeared, and he was floating in a black nothing and could breathe freely once more. In his frantic struggle on the surface Sebastian had forgotten his hunger. But now he was desperately hungry. He reached for his breakfast pack, but it wasn't there. Nor were his clothes, slaves' ragged torn dismal clothes were there instead. Sebastian gasped as he saw what was in front of him. A huge Dodecahedron frame was there. It was partly covered with metal. Hammering it on were people, men, women, girls, and boys, as old as 90, as young as 2. 'So that's where the noise was coming from,' said Sebastian, in awe. A girl moaned. She was almost half starved, like a skeleton. A big man whose head was a rhino's roughly shook her and whipped her. The girl screamed. Sebastian understood everything, from the metal noises to the wailing. He was to become a slave, to build a new world. He was in a daze, and knew nothing except to build the planet and that he would return to Earth when the dark moon came. And in a hundred years time it did.

GIRL TODAY, HARE TOMORROW

Saturday, June the 13th. The time was 7.00pm. Rachel Slatter was going to be in a play called Alice. She got in the car with her father. He started the engine of their big Citroen Family Estate. It shuddered. 'Got everything?' said Mr Slatter. 'All my costume is in the hall apart from my ears,' Rachel replied stiffly. She was a bit nervous. 'Right' said her dad. He let the Citroen roll slowly down the drive. He swung it round, and drove to the junction. Then he sped past the White Hart and up the Grove Road. He accelerated all the way up to Rowstock. They went round the roundabout and headed for Wantage. They were nearly at Wantage when the car started hiccuping. 'She's got the hiccups again,' said Mr Slatter. Suddenly a great spurt of steam came up from the car bonnet. He stopped the car in a layby. He got out and opened the bonnet. 'What is it?' Rachel cried. 'I can't be late.' She fingered her felt ears nervously. 'It's not much,' said her father. 'But I'll have to phone up Pete to tow us back.' 'Where's a telephone?' Rachel said. 'I can't see one.' 'There'll be one in Ardington,' Mr Slatter replied. 'But Ardington's 4 miles back!' Rachel shouted. 'And I've got a play to put on.' Her father thought for a moment. Five minutes later he had gone to find a telephone. Rachel began to walk to Wantage. She put on her felt ears. She sucked a travelling sweet hungrily. 'I wonder if they'll miss me,' Rachel thought. 'After all, I am only the March Hare.' Her nose began to itch. She twitched it. Her hands and feet tingled slightly, probably with cold. Rachel was still hungry. She picked some grass, and chewed it thoughtfully. Her glassy eyes shone with the moon reflection. Her furry paws glistened with the dew of evening. Far away Mr Slatter returned. In the light of the moon, he saw a hare jumping away on the grassy bank. It leaped over the hedge and scampered on the corn field. Mr Slatter shook his head and smiled. 'As mad as a march hare,' he thought.

JANE'S DREAM

I became still; and watched the shadows thrown by candle light flickering against the panelled walls. There was a feeling of anticipation and waiting, and every sound I heard was magnified. The disconsolate moan of the wind outside amplified to cries in my ears. A great booming passed inside my head and I expected to see a grandfather clock as I turned to look down the long passage. There was nothing but the walls themselves with iron candle braces fixed to them, holding the long tapering candles with their wavering flame; and I realised the sound was just my heart beating, – reluctantly, it seemed: so slow was the rhythm.

There was a movement at my side. I turned again – my actions exaggerated and heavy – it was an age before I could look down and see Pilot, my master's dog, padding slowly past me. Wolflike he was, and the huge jet shadow he cast across the floor and up the wall was like that of a terrible beast from the ice-packs of the North. With majestic and graceful strides he disappeared from view down the passage, swallowed up by the inky darkness that threatened to engulf me, should the feeble light given off be extinguished. I blinked, and this light did go, for what felt like minutes until I opened my eyes. I had not yet moved my feet, nor could I – for they felt surely fastened to the ground where I stood, and time was slowed, my reflexes deadened. If I could lift my feet, walking would be impossible – I was in a stupor, and could not shake it off. There was a rustle of stiff material behind me. I could sense someone close to me, whispering in my ear with a mischievous, girlish voice, what the words were I didn't know – for they tumbled strangely from the lips like a child's mumbling. The person moved in front of my face and I saw it was little more than a shadow, a dark shape dancing around me like a nymph or spirit, dizzying my thoughts and confusing my sight.

I reached out to touch her as she spun past and she moved back, giggling. In the darkness I could not make out her movements but it seemed that she was floating, gliding with no effort at all. My hair was tweaked, and her tiny pale face stared up at me from behind my shoulder. I saw her eyes, black moons in an ivory sky, and for a moment they were sad. But then she smiled, went to the walls and blew out all the candles, until all but one were dead. Faintly, I saw her laugh as she reached up towards the light. There was darkness then, and

A coldness hit my cheeks and I gasped for breath. The floor's slippery oak boards slid from under me as I ran. My sudden motion hit me in the chest as a sharp pain but I kept running down the passage, until I felt nothing under my feet and my body ached. I wasn't conscious of time or distance; whether I was at the end or beginning. My head was rushing and all I could see was the black space in front of me. Too late I saw the door before me – a great wide door with its metallic and brassy handle just visible – I could not stop, and feared I would collide with it. But the door swung open, and as it did, my exhileration left me, my pulse slowed. I was sure my cheeks were burning, and I smoothed down escaped locks of hair which hung unruly around my face. Calm, I stepped through the door, not knowing why I was so impelled to enter.

My aunt turned her head, hesitating from drinking from the tea cup she held at her mouth. Her voice was polite, but without compassion. 'Jane Eyre. Come in. Do not think we were waiting for you.'

My eyes were fixed on Aunt Reed, her stout frame and her cold eyes, and somehow it was hard to turn away to look for a chair. There was one to my left which I sank into, finding it uncomfortable. My aunt watched me for a moment, then turned. 'Please continue, Mr Brocklehurst.'

I jumped at the name. Sitting opposite my aunt, by the fire, was Mr Brocklehurst. He was dressed all in black, making his body appear yet longer and thinner. He looked at me frankly, with grey eyes under bushy brows. Still looking at me, he spoke.

'I do not need to tell you, Mrs Reed, that the very devil is at work. She is an evil little girl. Our own Lord God turned her away, as she herself turned away the Christian generosity and selfless pity all have given her. She cares only to foul the pure air around her with wicked and shameful actions.' He sighed in distaste.

'Talk of her poisons my speech, madam. It saddens me that a girl in your care should have turned out like this.'

There was a sickening feeling in my stomach. I felt terror and indignation that he should say that. Aunt Reed had a sour expression and again glanced at me. The room was dark, drab and unfamiliar to me. I was cold, so far from the fire, and wanted to drag my chair forward – but I could not bring myself to take part in any way in this awful scene, so remained motionless, observing.

'She acts above her place here. A governess should not behave as Jane does: she has improper views for a lady. I have known her to paint for hours on end, she flirts with Mr Rochester: there's even talk of marriage. I cannot imagine how such grand ideas come from such a plain girl.'

Behind Mr Brocklehurst was Mrs Fairfax, sitting in her old stiff chair with her knitting. Worse, I saw standing by the chair in semi-darkness, Bessie, who avoided my eyes, and the portly figure of John Reed sat to my left near his mother. Thankfully, his attention was not directed to me as he gazed round the room. My head swam: I put my hands to my face. John's voice cut through the silence.

'Mamma, won't you send her away? She is a hateful, wild animal, always sneaking about and hiding: then more often than not flying into one of her mad rages. What is she to us? Why, only yesterday, she –'

Finally I cried out, screaming, 'Don't say any more!', and clenched my fists into my hair, but then relaxed them and sat back, and fell silent. For a moment I heard nothing but the hurried thud of my heart and the crackle of the fire. I lifted up my head, and saw them all look up at me, and I felt every stare upon me like a red-hot brand.

'You were right to warn me about this girl, Mrs Reed. She is indeed a fiery thing.' My fear and fury instantly returned to me at the sound of his voice. I got up from my chair, almost turning it over and stared wildly about, desperate to leave the room. With a cry I saw that the great door had gone. I spun round and went to the fire, trying to catch my breath. I was aware of my aunt speaking, but I did not hear her words as I had seen the mirror above the mantlepiece, and looked into it. I gasped: where was my face? All I could see in the mirror was the dull coloured walls behind me, where the door had been: I wished fervently it was not to be so: but not one part of me was reflected. I looked down at myself, and saw my grey dress, black shoes: I felt my face with my hand and it was certainly there, but looking back at the mirror, I could see nothing.

This terrified me: beyond caring now, I wrenched the tea cup from Mr Brocklehurst and flung it at the glass, shattering it; then stood there, dropping my hands to my sides. For minutes, no one spoke. I heard a mutter, and saw it was Mr Brocklehurst, now pale and uneasy. A great change had come over him. My aunt shot a terrified look and I realised my outburst had upset her. I felt great power surge through me: they were all shocked. John Reed scowled with dislike as I looked at him, but he had lost his bullying nature, now sullen and uneasy. Mrs Fairfax seemed unconcerned, her head still low as she knitted. Bessie though, at her shoulder, looked up, and our eyes met. For a moment I was angry, but then she smiled, and I was calm, not at all sorry for what I had done. I stood there, by the fire, watching, then I went to the door – whose appearance I had expected and did not shock me. I reached for the handle, swung open the door and stepped out into

The silvery night. I was enchanted by the sublime colours of the deep indigo sky, the luminous moon and the purple hills rising like waves along the horizon. Nothing stirred: I was alone in my own world, and never wanted to leave. I felt insulated, secure and free. I heard the sound of water rushing nearby, I was drawn to it, and ran: never stumbling or tripping, as if I knew every tree root, boulder and shrub. As I ran, the sound grew ever closer, until I was sure it was just over the rise of the hill and I could not distinguish the water from the blood rushing in my head. I effortlessly climbed the hill which didn't feel in the least slippery though I was sure there was dew all around.

I knew what I would see before I looked out across the land, but I still gasped at the sheer force of the waterfall, falling with a roar at least eighty feet to the river, which was so far below I could not see it from my lofty vantage point. For many minutes I stood enthralled by the waterfall, until I heard a noise. I turned, and listened for a moment, but the sound of the waterfall was deafening, drowning out any other noises. I turned back, but the spell was broken; I came away from the hilltop ledge, and went to sit by a tree, moving from the waterfall so that I could be free from the booming in my ears. I had not sat long before I heard something again, and now it was clearly defined as a shout. Frowning, I walked swiftly across fields, guided by more cries which were obviously a man's. I reached a path – and broke into a run when I saw him lying by his horse, which was gently nudging him to stand.

The man was slim, and tall. I drew near and saw that he was young, and his features were like those of an animal's, with an aquiline nose and ruffled black hair. He looked up at me then, and I have never seen eyes of such colour before, hazel, almost yellow, flecked with gold. Oddly, his looks and gallantry did not trouble or threaten me; rather pulled me closer so that I knelt by him, and asked if I could help. He looked up at me and smiled.

'That's very kind of you, but I'm perfectly fine. If you could just help me to stand –' I put my arms around his shoulders and helped him to his feet. He winced as he set weight on his left ankle – it seemed as though he had twisted it. We said nothing for a minute, and although I did not feel awkward there was a strange, intense atmosphere. Our eyes locked – but then I looked away and spoke:

'It's an eerie night to fall from your horse, sir.'

'Indeed – it is as though we entered another world when the moon entered the sky. Even my horse seems under a spell tonight.'

We were both smiling as we spoke, and I knew our conversation was little more than a game, as if we were acting out parts in a play. He turned slightly to face his horse, and said,

'Could you steady her, do you think?'

I was not afraid to hold the horse's head and gently stroke her neck, while the man put his bad foot into the stirrup and swung his right leg. I looked at him, and though he was flushed and slightly out of breath, he laughed.

'We make a good partnership, you and I. What's your name?'

'Jane.' He leaned forward in his saddle and watched me intently. The laughter left him and he became thoughtful.

'What grey eyes you have; like a new moon. I knew a girl called Jane once –.' I knew he was mocking me, but wasn't sure how. I just smiled and looked into those molten gold eyes. Suddenly he sat up.

'I must go, sister mine,' he said.

'Goodnight,' I said.

'I do not like to think of you outside and alone on this strange night. Promise me you will be careful.'

I smiled – what had I to fear from my own world? 'I promise.'

He looked at me one last time, then I watched him turn his horse and ride away along the path, his horse's breath misting in the cold air. I shivered and wrapped my arms around me for warmth. The pale moon slowly glided behind a cloud, its luminosity lost, and the land was plunged in darkness. There was a faint whistling in my ear, and a breeze began to lift my hair and skirts. The breeze became icy wind which pushed against me with a shrieking noise, until I stumbled back, gasping for breath, with my hair blown across my face. As the air rushed round me I felt a shudder, as if I had been lifted into the sky and flung about. I could see nothing now – all was black – and I was numbed by the screaming wind.

My stomach was heavy with nausea and my head reeled. Someone flashed by, too quickly to identify. Another face came before: this time I could see it was Helen Burns, pale and smiling. She held out her hands to me, and I was struck by her goodness, her angel-like quality that washed over me. I reached out – but she was fading as I fell. Someone else: Georgina Reed, adult and pretty – her eyes closed, head turning jerkily away from me, lips moving.

As the noise died and my senses slowed, I saw a woman standing above me in the darkness, watching over me. She was slim but not tall. She stood very straight and restfully with her hands clasped before her. Her hair was in a long thick plait. She did not smile, but was beautiful.

'Mother,' I said.

Suddenly I jerked back and felt myself pulled through the air at great speed, with the same burning, breathless sensation. The darkness slowly lifted around me, and there was the cool grey light of dawn. My fall ended – I dropped into my bed.

Outside there was a shrill noise like a peacock's cry, then all was quiet and still.

O cara luna, al cui tranquillo raggio danzan le lepri nelle selve...

[O cherished moon, beneath whose quiet beams the hares dance in the woods ...] Giacomo Leopardi

(Calvino 1988: 25)

A letter from Rebecca

The stories *Dodecahedron* and *Girl Today, Hare Tomorrow* were written by Rebecca during her final year at Harwell School. *Jane's Dream* followed five years later, as part of her coursework for the General Certificate of Education. Shortly afterwards, I wrote to Rebecca, asking permission to include a discussion of *Girl Today, Hare Tomorrow* in a lecture which I was revising for publication. I wondered whether she remembered the story and what she made of it now that she was five years older. This was her reply:

Dear Mr Armstrong,

I am sorry to write on such horrible paper etc anyway thank you very much for thinking to send me your talk. I agree with a lot of what you say, and find it really interesting. When you're a child [Rebecca was now sixteen] you don't realise just how much your stories reveal about yourself. I'm happy for you to use my story however you want and feel quite privileged to have so much attention put on it.

I hadn't forgotten the story at all – nor any others I wrote at Harwell. Reading it again, however, I was struck that it was so short and find it a bit irritating. I had, and still have, such an incredibly vivid picture of the hare jumping away in the moonlight purple and silver; and my words just seem to clumsily imprison the scene. I remember at Harwell hating using reality in stories and always tried to escape from what seemed to me boring events like '*I went to call for my friend ...*' I am more proud of so-called fantasy works than those such as *The Patient*, about being sick at school, and *Exaggerated Story*.

Because of this the early part of the story is uncomfortably familiar, at least to me. I think you'd probably argue that you need the 'factual' part to contrast with the later, magical developments – and perhaps the story would be worse if it was completely alien. But because the first half is basically real memory, I find it hard to accept it in the story. It is for this reason that I think I prefer *Dodecahedron*, although I haven't read it for a while. Obviously it is less interesting for you in terms of narrative and insights into my character (whether my character deserves to be delved into is another thing); but it seems to express my ideas better and is more of an escape. Recently I had difficulty with GCSE English coursework about a piece on Jane Eyre's dream. I saw it in my mind, rather like a film, and again, all that I wrote seemed to entrap the pictures I wanted to convey. I suppose that that is what writing is all about. I'm not sure if you've read my English work [I had not read any of Rebecca's work since she had left Harwell School], but I realised today how alike *Jane's Dream* is in terms of background to *Girl Today, Hare Tomorrow* – at least in my mind. I'm not sure if I conveyed it, but I was thinking of the same purple skies, silver moon and enchanted atmosphere.

Anyway. I tried to implicate the father as merely a shadow, a reliable but uneventful figure. The point of his final shake of the head is to show his complete unconnection with the hare and his daughter. The idea that his daughter has just grown ears and leapt over a hedge never occurs to him. Whether this reflects my own view of parentage at the time, I'm not sure; more likely that is how I wanted Rachel to feel. There is almost resentment of his narrow vision, total uncomprehension for fantasy, and failure to recognise his own daughter. I actually feel angry towards this stupid man as I'm writing now – how can he not see? She has left one world and left him behind, bemused but unsuspecting. I see that Mary [a graduate student who had written about Rebecca's story a year or two earlier and whose essay Rebecca had read] seems to think he knows about the metamorphosis. Although she is very perceptive throughout she doesn't seem to treat the change as I do. It IS more sinister as you suggested – I was fascinated by 'darkness' eg *Dodecahedron*, and wouldn't have wanted the metamorphosis to have been either acknowledged or a sparkly magical thing. Incidentally, there is no full stop between '. . . a march hare' and 'he thought' [as I had mistakenly suggested in my lecture], which would imply a twist such as that seen in Lydia's story. [Rebecca is referring to Lydia's story *I Found It in My Bowl of Cereal*, which was also discussed in the lecture I had written.] I think it makes my story slightly tackier, though Lydia's far better.

I don't think I would ever use the term 'magic' to describe what was going on. That seems to imply innocence and imagination. I wanted the change really to happen, rather than have Rachel turn into a rabbit in her mind and end the story on a limp 'all a dream' ending – falling back to the reality I tried to escape in my stories.

Oh I've gone on too much and have gone all reminiscent and intellectual. This is why I would have liked to have done English A Level – but
I'm not so keen on Chaucer, Shakespeare and endless essay writing. I
would like to try being a film producer to see if I could capture my ideas
better than words. What do you think? Anyway. Do you think that
children have the same ideas as adults, but just can't express them as
well? Or maybe their naivety (now I sound pompous like my dad,
shadowy Mr Slatter – I wonder how he'd like to be called shadowy) helps
them express them better? If I had written this story last year, would it
have been better or worse?

Oh Anyway (my last anyway of the evening) I've gone all silly as I do
by the end of my letters. I hope this shows you a bit more of my view of
the story. I'm very impressed by how perceptive your comments were.
I'm taking Grade 7 Piano in a couple of weeks [?!?] as a result of highly
expensive lessons and love Geman A Level. I'm being very vain now but
did you ever predict I would like language/anthropology?

Sorry I'm so self centred.
(rather an odd thing to write to your old headmaster – shows how silly
my letter is)
Thanks again,

Rebecca

Rebecca's letter, at once disarming and provocative, offers a storyteller's
critique of her own story. She looks on *Girl Today, Hare Tomorrow* with a
quizzical eye, placing it within the context of other stories which she wrote at
the age of eleven and documenting its continuing relevance to her more
recent work. I want in this chapter to follow her lead, exploring the narrative
thread to which she draws attention by examining in turn each of the three
stories on which her argument rests. At the age of 11 Rebecca was a child in
the full flow of literary consciousness. *Dodecahedron* and *Girl Today, Hare
Tomorrow* represent the narrative thought of the primary school in its most
advanced and adventurous form, the crown of a young child's literary
achievement. My aim is to describe that achievement and to consider its
aftermath as Rebecca moves through childhood into adolescence. The
account I have to give will eventually lead me back to the searching questions
which Rebecca asks at the end of her letter: 'Do you think that children have
the same ideas as adults, but just can't express them as well? Or maybe their
naivety ... helps them express them better? If I had written this story last
year, would it have been better or worse?'

Like Laura, Rebecca is haunted by the powers and dangers of the imagination but her work achieves a passionate intimacy which Laura never
attempts. Laura plays lightly with her readers' attitudes and expectations;
Rebecca seeks to entangle the reader in the plot. It is as if Laura's fanciful fairy
tale has evolved into an all too real and urgent drama. As Rebecca acknowledges in her letter, she was 'fascinated by "darkness" '. She was by no means a
gloomy eleven year old but in her writing there was never a doubt that
darkness prevailed. Here, for example, is a poem which she wrote some time

towards the end of the year. Originally she called it *Darkness* but later she changed its title to *Black*:

Black is the night and the bad things in it
Black is disappointment when you didn't win it
Black is a witch soaring high on her broom
Black is the evil in a world of doom
Black is the heart which is starting to break
Black is the fear which keeps you awake

Black is nothing, black is fear
Black is a hole where nothing appears
Black is death, cutting life away
Black is the hatred when SHE comes to stay
Black is a trap waiting to spring
Black is a bat flying on its wings.

Black is the water which trickles down the pane
Black is when you're walking down an empty lane
Black is a cat, its green eyes looking mean
Black is a strict lady, tall and lean
Black is the stallion which runs on the grass
Black is the silence when there's peace at last.

Darkness, however, was not necessarily a negative attribute from Rebecca's point of view. The night belonged to darkness but also to the moon and the moon offered an enchantment that might either terrify or thrill. Above all, darkness prefigured escape, as Rebecca explains in her letter, although escape of a kind that is always in question. The three tales that form the subject of this chapter may be seen as so many variations on darkness and the worlds that darkness exposes, successive attempts, the first two close together, the third at five years' distance, to explore a territory which, as we see from her letter, no less than from the stories themselves, Rebecca had chosen to make her own. The earliest of these stories, and five years later her favourite it seems, was *Dodecahedron*.

Dodecahedron

Dodecahedron was written towards the middle of the school year. Before she began the story Rebecca came to me to ask for the name of a certain kind of three-dimensional geometrical shape which she remembered making a few weeks earlier. We had been exploring the Platonic Solids and constructing models of them out of cardboard. The word she was looking for was dodecahedron. As soon as I suggested it, she recognized the name and went off to begin her tale, writing down the title in the familiar elegant script which had become her trade mark. Whether she was attracted by the strangeness of the name or the mathematical rigour of the form, it seems clear that the image of a Platonic Solid was the source out of which Rebecca's story grew. The story, as the title suggests, derives a new, literary, meaning from the geometrical shape. In his book *Six Memos for the Next Millennium*, a book that seems to touch on many of Rebecca's preoccupations, as we shall see, the Italian novelist Italo Calvino writes of the primacy of the visual image in the construction of all his stories:

> In devising a story ... the first thing that comes to my mind is an image that for some reason strikes me as charged with meaning, even if I cannot formulate this meaning in discursive or conceptual terms. As soon as the image has become sufficiently clear in my mind I set about developing it into a story; or better yet, it is the images themselves that develop their own implicit potentialities, the story they carry within them.
>
> (1988: 88)

The dodecahedron would appear to have been charged with meaning for Rebecca in just this way. Out of the austere beauty of the polyhedron which she had recently modelled in white card, she now constructs the story of an orphan child's fateful journey to a new and alien world, formally flawless but inhuman and enslaving, a world in the sharpest possible contrast with the village world of Minah in which the story opens.

The narrative goes out of its way to emphasize the sleepy, old world charm of the earthly village. Sebastian opens 'the old window on the landing', climbs onto 'the old ivy below', scrambles over 'the old rickety fence at the bottom of the garden' and lands on 'the cobbled lane that led out of the streets and down to the docks'. The word 'old' is repeated again and again, emphasizing the length and weight of established tradition. Beyond the docks, beneath the waves, lies another, unearthly world, unimaginable to the villagers: the savage metallic world of the dodecahedron. The 'metal noises' which Sebastian hears during the night remind him of 'the tin miners in an old tin mine hundreds of years ago' but the world into which he is drawn has nothing in common with the tortuous historical landscape of Minah. The story is poised between these two worlds as between alternative forms of consciousness; the docks beside which the village lies mark the boundary, the hinge on which the narrative turns.

'A scream broke the silence of the quiet village Minah, next to the docks.' For all the visual drama of the 'huge Dodecahedron' covered in metal or the picturesqueness of the 'quiet village Minah' with its weathercock and its cobbled lane, sound rather than sight is the sense that dominates Rebecca's narrative. The opening scream introduces a symphonic tale in which sound accompanies each successive moment of adventure. That scream, like the 'fearful shriek' that awakens Jane Eyre 'in the dead of night' in Thornfield Hall, never fades from the reader's mind, even as it is followed by a multitude of other sounds (Brontë 1985: 235). Each new sound – the wailing, the 'curious metal noises', the 'loud crack of thunder', the cursing villagers, the small boy's 'cry for help' – echoes that original, terrible note. It is the summons to a quest which is only completed in front of the Dodecahedron itself when the scream recurs and Sebastian finally grasps its meaning. This orchestration of sensation is characteristic of all three of Rebecca's stories. She seems to sense her stories whole as if the entire narrative might be captured in sight and sound and touch, without further literary means. Or, rather, her literary aim is to find verbal equivalents for the sensations that dominate her imagination. In her letter, she doubts her success while acknowledging the ambition. She fears that her words 'just seem to clumsily imprison the scene'. No wonder she refers to her desire to make films, 'to see if I could capture my ideas better than words'. The stories are already filmed in her mind.

The opening of *Dodecahedron* is unlike that of any of the stories described in earlier chapters, all of which open in the traditional 'once upon a time' or in the past of memory. Here the story opens in mid-adventure – 'that was the second scream he had heard that week' – with an immediacy that would have seemed alien to previous storytellers. It might be tempting to attribute this directness to Rebecca's age or level of maturity but I think this would be a mistake. It has more to do with the intricacy of narrative intention that directs each of these stories from start to finish. Just as Sebastian understands at last the significance of the opening scream, so, as readers, once we reach the end of Rebecca's story we understand for the first time the necessity of its opening sentence, the scream, the silence, the village, the docks. To follow the story is to embark on a journey that parallels Sebastian's quest, a journey already accomplished and organized by the narrator herself. The beginning achieves its full meaning only in the light of the end. Perhaps that is true of every well-told story. It is part of Rebecca's achievement that, in the self-conscious tightness of their construction, her stories make this truth singularly vivid.

Even before we discover that Sebastian is an orphan we know that he is isolated within his community, by virtue of the sounds, messages almost, that only he can hear. It is only 'himself' whom he asks where the screams come from: 'No one else heard those noises, Sebastian had found that out long before now.' Convinced, this time, that he has not been dreaming, he determines to set out on a secret and solitary adventure, uncounselled and unaccompanied: 'He simply had to see what was making those noises.' The narrative insists that the uniqueness of Sebastian's experience is not to be interpreted as unreal or dreamlike. Sebastian cannot be satisfied until he sees, until sound is matched with sight and he identifies its source, hence his journey. This is a first example of what Rebecca may mean when in her letter she denies the presence of magic in her stories. Magic, for Rebecca, implies 'innocence and imagination', a flight of fancy that might be exposed as no more than child's play, as the mother in Lydia's stories interprets her daughter's tales. The magical element in *Dodecahedron* is of a different order. There is nothing fanciful in Sebastian's journey, as Lydia's narrator implies there might be in her story *I Found It in My Bowl of Cereal*. His destination is terrifyingly real, a parallel world as palpable as the world he leaves behind when the whirlpool sucks him down. Five years later Rebecca calls her story an escape but the escape is not a relief from reality so much as an exchange of one reality for another.

We never discover who is looking after the orphaned Sebastian. All we know, all we need to know, is that the journey on which he now embarks has to be secret. No one but Sebastian hears the sounds he hears and no one else could accept the reality of his quest. The language in which Rebecca describes his escape is exact and considered as if he has always known just what he had to do. 'Packed a small breakfast', 'stole up the stairs', 'clambered down to the wet grass in the yard', 'scrambled up and over the old rickety fence'; the verbs are heavy with intent. But there is also something almost automatic about Sebastian's movements, as if he is acting under compulsion, possessed by the sounds that plague him. As he reaches 'the water's edge' the sense of compulsion overpowers him: 'Strangely, the metal sounds seemed to have got louder as the boy got nearer the docks. Now, as he got into a rowing boat, the noises seemed even lifelike in his head. They drew him in, closer and closer to the middle of the harbour.' Sebastian's quest is thus both chosen by him and determined for him. He affirms a destiny which is inescapable. It is at once his privilege and his fate.

The water's edge is the threshold between worlds. Once Sebastian steps into the boat he is at the mercy of the whirlpool and the underworld to which it is the passage. The 'constant wave', the clouds that 'darkened and joined together', the 'loud crack of thunder' and 'the torrent of rain' are the signs of a transformation which Sebastian is powerless to resist. We are at the critical moment in the story which Rebecca defines in the memorable image of 'the weathercock which spun in a blur on the very peak of the farmhouse's roof'. No wonder the angry villagers curse it for it is a magical object in the narrative, not so much the sign of the storm as the symbol for a metamorphosis which is taking place in front of them but which they cannot decipher. Like Mr Slatter, in *Girl Today, Hare Tomorrow*, as Rebecca's letter interprets him, the villagers of Minah are shadowy onlookers, unable to rescue Sebastian or even to recognize him, let alone to understand what is happening to him. It is the sound of thunder that wakes them from their slumbers, not the scream that woke Sebastian or the metal noises that now sound lifelike in his head. Their concern is more for the threat to their homes or the theft of a boat than for the 'small boy struggling in the icy water'. As they frown, argue, shake their fists, the child is lost. 'Then a whirlpool sucked the startled boy down, and all was quiet.' Sebastian, as we were told at the start of the story, had to see, the villagers are too set in their ways to see and now we learn that Sebastian's parents can't see: 'The villagers looked on, and as for Sebastian's parents they did nothing, for they were in heaven, long since dead.' With this soft, slow sentence the story takes leave of the world of Minah, returning the village to its slumber and enters the world of the Dodecahedron. The words 'as for' deceptively imply an afterthought but, as the narrator knows, the revelation is central to her story. News of the death of Sebastian's parents, artfully witheld until the moment of departure, shocks the reader by its brutal confirmation of Sebastian's isolation from the life and thought of his community. His experience is uncommunicable. There is no one with whom it can be shared. The parents to whom he might have told his tale are dead. The beyond must be entered alone.

The revelation that Sebastian's parents are dead brings the narrative to a momentary rest. The world that is Minah, quiet once more, vanishes from the story as Sebastian is sucked beneath the waves. A new world awaits him. Rebecca marks the passing from one world to the next by means of a single change of tense: 'Sebastian had been pulled down below the surface so suddenly he hadn't had time to take a breath and was now rapidly running out of air.' The absence of a paragraph break throws the full force of the shift in perspective onto the past perfect tense itself, making the narrative imitate the breathlessness of its hero. It is a device which Rebecca repeats, to even greater effect, in *Girl Today, Hare Tomorrow*, as we will see. The story has reached the moment of transformation. As Sebastian sinks, the water becomes 'cleaner and cleaner'. The detritus of earth, 'all the plants and mud', disappears and Sebastian finds himself floating, and breathing freely once more, in a 'black nothing'. There is an echo of Rebecca's poem *Black* – 'Black is nothing, black is fear/Black is a hole where nothing appears' – although the second of these two lines is about to be savagely contradicted. In her letter, Rebecca cites *Dodecahedron* as a prime example of her fascination with darkness, and the world into which Sebastian enters is dark indeed.

Rebecca's vision of an alternative reality is certainly no 'sparkly, magical thing', as in a story such as Lydia's *The Sparkling Star*, but, rather, a world that terrifies and binds. Floating in a black nothing Sebastian feels 'desperately hungry', a hunger which it is tempting to construe as the doorway to the imagination, but it seems that the world that this narrator imagines is incapable of feeding her hero's need. His breakfast pack has disappeared and as he searches for it he finds himself dressed as a slave, facing the huge metal frame of the Dodecahedron. So this is the 'new world' he is to be compelled to build, alongside a host of others, 'men, women, girls and boys, as old as 90, as young as 2', those whom the call of the beyond has entrapped. The language suggests the underworld of Greco-Roman mythology but this is no world of the dead. The perfection of its Platonic form is matched by the cruelty of the monsters that inhabit it. It is as if the imagination itself has turned hostile, imprisoning rather than liberating those who enter its dark world.

And yet we are never to know the full meaning of the world of the Dodecahedron. When Sebastian hears the girl scream and recognizes the sounds that have provoked his adventure, we are told that he 'understood everything' but later the narrator adds that he 'knew nothing'. That is to say, he understood that this was the world that had summoned him, that he had reached the goal of his quest, but the nature of that goal remained a mystery which he was not permitted to unravel: 'He knew nothing except to build the planet and that he would return to Earth when the dark moon came.' The dark moon is Rebecca's final image and it broods over her tale no less than the opening scream. Calvino writes of the moon as, above all, an image of lightness: 'As soon as the moon appears in poetry, it brings with it a sensation of lightness, suspension, a silent calm enchantment' (1988: 24). Rebecca's story undermines such ready confidence. The figure of a dark moon suggests weight, contradiction, the shadow of an eclipse, a troubled imagination. The dark moon heralds disenchantment, an eventual return to Earth, but the story carefully obscures the nature of that disenchantment. The last sentence, which the opening word turns into a kind of postscript, implies that the narrator already knows the truth: 'And in a hundred years time it did.' There is an extraordinary, almost frightening, finality about these words. But the reader is left to guess what that truth might be. The meaning of the sentence is at once categorical and inscrutable. The narrator acknowledges her own authority but denies the reader a sense of closure. The story ends in mystery. The final effect is one of deep disquiet.

Girl Today, Hare Tomorrow

Six months later Rebecca returned to her chosen theme. *Girl Today, Hare Tomorrow* was among the last of the stories that she wrote at Harwell School. Composed on a single day in late June, less than a month before she left for the summer holidays and a new career at King Alfred's School in Wantage, seven miles away, the story is a valedictory tale, a farewell to the school where she had learned to read and write and to spin her fantastic tales. It may not have been her favourite story but it seems to me to have been her finest, a tale in which the ideas explored in *Dodecahedron* achieve their most concentrated form. Economy of expression is a major source of its strength. It is a story of which it might well be said, as Tolstoy said of Fyedka's stories, that 'every word . . . calls forth a multitude of ideas, images and interpretations' (1982: 228). The command of detail is uncanny. Five years after she wrote it, Rebecca compared the story unfavourably with the visual image out of which it arose. 'I had, and still have,' she writes, 'such an incredibly vivid picture of the hare jumping away in the moonlight purple and silver, and my words just seem to clumsily imprison the scene.' Her doubt is understandable but surely misplaced, for the story dramatically enlarges the significance of its visual origin, transforming an evocative image into a narrative of extraordinary imaginative energy. The picture of the leaping hare remains in the reader's mind long after the story is ended but now it is charged with fresh meaning, derived from a distinctively literary imagination, inspired by the visual image.

Rebecca's story is written on one side of a large sheet of paper. The handwriting is incredibly neat. There are no corrections and no revisions of the text. The immaculate appearance of the manuscript, Rebecca's first and final draft, reinforces the impression conveyed by the tightness of the narrative argument that this was a story fully formed in Rebecca's mind before she sat down to write. At the top of the page she places her story's chosen title, apparently written down in advance of the story itself: *Girl Today, Hare Tomorrow*. The ingenious title does not name the visual source of the story, as *Dodecahedron* did. Instead it epitomizes the plot and its underlying significance. 'Here today, gone tomorrow', runs the familiar proverb, signifying, as the *Oxford English Dictionary* puts it, that which is 'short-lived, merely transient'. Rebecca's variation preserves the sound and rhythm of the original but wittily reverses the initial letters of the proverb's two halves in a manoeuvre that reinforces the revolutionary impact of her title. The linguistic conceit may be playful but its purpose is deeply serious. Tolstoy, in describing the origin of his pupils' story *He Feeds You with a Spoon and Pokes You in the Eye with the Handle*, writes of how among his unrealized dreams he had imagined 'a series not so much of stories as of pictures, written around proverbs' (1982: 223). Rebecca goes further. Her story is intensely visual but rather than illustrating the proverb she reinvents it. If, as Walter Benjamin argues in *The*

Storyteller, a proverb might be thought of as 'a ruin which stands on the site of an old story' (1968: 108), Rebecca, we might say, writes a new story that at once revives and challenges the proverb's original meaning. The merely transient acquires a darker implication, the passing from one world to another. In thus recasting her proverbial source, Rebecca mimics the tale she has to tell. It is the story of a metamorphosis. How better than to open it with the metamorphosis of a proverb. As readers we are immediately aware of the title's verbal play. Only the unfolding plot will clarify its sinister and subversive purpose.

'Saturday, June 13th. The time was 7.00 pm.' The story begins with a date, as a letter might. This date is genuine. Saturday, June 13th had just passed when Rebecca wrote her story. The choice of a historical date is no accident. A central concern of the story is the tension between reality and fantasy that so exercises Rebecca in her letter five years later. The world as we daily inhabit it is set against another way of being, the world into which Rebecca's heroine disappears. In *Dodecahedron*, Rebecca had already begun to explore this tension. *Girl Today, Hare Tomorrow* sharpens it. The narrative opens, not in a fabled village such as Minah, but in the all-too-familiar village of Harwell, here and now, at a precise historical moment. The opening directly challenges the convention of the folk tale's 'once upon a time'. Although Rebecca had avoided the traditional formula in *Dodecahedron*, her narrative had remained within the bounds of a purely imaginary time. Now she chooses to break these bounds by setting her new story in recorded time, a time that she will later describe as 'basically real memory'. Dating the story is a way of emphasizing its historicity, paradoxical though that might seem. We are not to be witnesses to a fairy story. This tale, we are warned, is for real whether or not we are able to recognize it as such. For the truth is that reality is not as commonplace as we ordinarily suppose in our uneventful lives, to borrow the word with which, in her letter, Rebecca chooses to characterize 'shadowy Mr Slatter'. The real embraces both ways of being, father's and daughter's, the mundane and the miraculous, shadow and substance, as time and the tale will show. As Rebecca explains, 'I wanted the change really to happen.' The folk tale is not abandoned then. Like the proverb, like reality itself, it is redefined.

Once date and time are established the story can unfold. 'Rachel Slatter was going to be in a play called Alice.' The name is intriguing. Wendy Slatter was Rebecca's best friend at school. By changing her first name to Rachel, Rebecca distances the reference while assimilating the name to her own. The fictional Rachel Slatter bears more resemblance to Rebecca than to Wendy and Mr Slatter, as he appears in the story, is modelled upon Rebecca's father rather than Wendy's. It was her own father who owned a Citroen Family Estate and had a mechanically minded friend named Pete, and the journey to Wantage begins on what is clearly her own front drive. These details are designed to enhance the story's verisimilitude but their significance should not be misconstrued as implying the identification of Rebecca with the heroine of her story. In her letter Rebecca raises the possibility only to dismiss it: 'Whether [the father's complete unconnection with the hare and his daughter] reflects my own view of parentage at the time I'm not sure; more likely that is how I wanted Rachel to feel.' The story is not to be read as one child's response to her own particular family situation. Its wisdom embraces a wider world of feeling.

Some three or four years earlier, both Rebecca and Wendy had taken part in a scene based on the Mad Hatter's Tea Party from *Alice's Adventures in Wonderland*, which had formed part of a school play in which each of the school's four classes had been involved. Rebecca had played the Mad Hatter, Wendy the White Rabbit. Lewis Carroll's masterpiece was certainly an influence on the story but less directly, I suspect, than Rebecca's memory of this play. The wonderland of Carroll's imagination is far removed from Rebecca's strange new world. Its function in the story is, as much as anything, to arouse suspicion, alerting a knowledgeable reader to the possibility of the fantastic. The play, on the other hand, lies at the story's heart. Playing and reality compose its theme. By the end, the world of the play will have turned into the heroine's real world, the world into which she disappears. Rachel Slatter becomes what she plays. Imagination takes her over while her father, like the villagers of Minah, looks idly on.

'She got in the car with her father.' It might seem that all is well as father and daughter set out together in the family car: 'their big Citroen Family Estate'. The capital letters suggest authority and security, the distinguishing marks of a solid social enterprise. But immediately the engine of the car adds a warning note: 'it shuddered.' The choice of the word 'shuddered' is an example of Rebecca's extraordinary narrative precision. The *Oxford English Dictionary* offers a variety of definitions of the verb 'shudder': 'have a convulsive tremor of the body caused by fear, abhorrence, cold, etc.'; 'feel repugnance or horror in doing'; 'vibrate; quiver'. Rebecca uses the word in all three senses. The vibration of the engine is a tremor of fear, a feeling of horror at the outcome of the journey ahead, an omen. In *Six Memos for the Next Millennium*, Italo Calvino suggests that 'the moment an object appears in a narrative, it is charged with a special force and becomes like the pole of a magnetic field, a knot in the network of invisible relationships ... We might even say that in a narrative any object is always magic' (1988: 33). Rebecca's Citroen Family Estate is an object of just this kind. Here at the start it is the magical means by which the plot is foretold. Later in the story, its breakdown may be read as a futile attempt to forestall the tale's predestined end. At the moment of breakdown Rachel Slatter's father himself personifies the car – ' "She's got the hiccups again" said Mr Slatter' – but his words are words alone, words without force, unentangled. The menace escapes him; the hiccups signify no more than a faulty engine; the metaphor is dead. 'It's not much,' he assures his daughter but by that time the reader may already have guessed that the car knows more than the father imagines.

The car is the first of many objects in the story to be charged with magic. Rachel Slatter, we learn, has left all her costume in the hall where presumably the play is to be put on, all, that is, except for the ears. 'My ears,' she calls them, as if they were already a part of her own body. Is it the presence of these ears which causes the car to shudder? They are the symbol of identity of the hare, the mark of the beast that Rachel is about to become. It may be significant, or it may be no more than a meaningful coincidence, that Harwell used to be known as Harewell. In either case, Rebecca would probably have seen around the village, at some time or other, the symbol of a hare's head, dominated by huge ears, decorating a commemorative pamphlet, pot, or church window. The ears reveal the silent presence of the hare from the moment the action begins. Does the heroine already sense this presence? As Rachel Slatter steps into the family car, the narrator's tone of voice momentarily resembles Rachel's own, as if she is sharing rather than witnessing her plight: 'She was a bit nervous.' At this point in the story the reader is inclined to put Rachel's nervousness down to thoughts about the forthcoming performance. But the narrator has a deeper cause in mind. Later, when the heroine's nervousness is mentioned a second time, halfway through the story, an attentive reader may begin to sense the truth at which the nervousness hints. By the end of the story we will be led to suspect that the stiffness of Rachel's reply to her father's question here at the start is in part at least the laboured response of a child whose metamorphosis has already begun. The narrator knows it and feels for her heroine even as she witholds the truth from her readers.

'"Right" said her dad' and the journey begins. The word 'right' is heavy with irony but it is an irony of which Mr Slatter is unaware. All is not right, as Rachel's stiffness has hinted. The consciousness of the father is already at odds with that of his daughter. For Mr Slatter the journey is just another errand, one more aspect of a familiar routine. If his daughter is a little nervous, that is only to be expected, a simple case of first-night nerves. Meanwhile for Rachel what is at stake is not a first-night's performance but consciousness itself. Father and daughter sit beside each other, lost in their own thoughts. The word 'right' signals nothing but trouble ahead. As the journey advances, the narrative quickens. A rapid succession of verbs sets the pace: 'let roll', 'swung round', 'drove', 'sped past', 'accelerated', 'went round', 'headed'. Familiar landmarks pass by in close order: the drive, the junction, the White Hart, the Grove Road, Rowstock, the roundabout, Wantage. The story's geography is as exact as its history. This is the very way in which Rebecca herself would have been driven to Wantage many a time. 'Basically real memory' again serves her well. Enumerating each landmark in turn becomes the indispensable means of establishing the authenticity of the tale, the spatial equivalent of the recorded date. And then, suddenly, within sight of the ostensible goal, the journey, the narrative, reality itself, all three are interrupted and overturned.

'They were nearly at Wantage when the car started hiccuping.' This apparently simple sentence bears close examination. Of all the sentences in the story, it is the only one that contains a subordinate clause. So it is that Rebecca halts the narrative flow, bringing her tale to rest on the image of hiccuping. Mr Slatter's comment, 'She's got the hiccups again' picks up the narrator's word but misconstrues it. For the character in the story, hiccuping implies merely a temporary setback. For the storyteller, it prefigures the metamorphosis to come, a seismic disturbance of space and time. The 'great spurt of steam' that 'came up from the car bonnet' continues the narrative imagery, though still Mr Slatter cannot read its meaning. 'It's not much,' is all he will say in answer to Rachel's cry. We have reached the parting of the ways.

They have stopped in a layby, as in a space between worlds. The narrative, like the journey, is momentarily suspended. What follows is a conversation between father and daughter in which the outcome of the story is determined. It is presented as a confrontation between future and past, between the daughter whose mind is absorbed in what is to come and the father who looks back complacently to the world that his daughter is about to leave behind. Rachel's opening cry, 'I can't be late', brings to mind the opening page of *Alice's Adventures in Wonderland* when suddenly the White Rabbit runs by, saying to itself 'Oh dear! Oh dear! I shall be too late' (Carrol 1927: 2). We remember being told at the start of the story that Rachel Slatter was going to be in a play called Alice and, at once, the narrator recalls the ears that Rachel had with her in the car: 'She fingered her felt ears nervously.' When Rachel got in the car, replying 'stiffly' to her father's question, she was already, as the narrator sympathetically put it, 'a bit nervous'. Now the nervousness deepens. 'Fingered', like 'shuddered', calls forth a multitude of interpretations. A reader is immediately struck by the power of the word in its particular context and once again a glance at the dictionary confirms and enlarges its resonance. To 'finger' means among other things to 'point at with the fingers', 'play on [a musical instrument] with the fingers', 'hold or turn about with the fingers', 'make restless movements with the fingers'. Each of these meanings finds an echo in Rebecca's melodic, alliterative sentence. The ears are of felt but they are also felt in the restless fingers, as a musical score might be felt, the significance of which Rachel Slatter could as yet barely anticipate.

Rachel's nervous cry makes no impact on her father, almost as if he had not heard it, as indeed, in its full significance, he had not. His mind is focused not on the visionary end that Rachel already senses, however dimly, but on the world left behind in Harwell, that uncomfortably familiar world of everyday. 'It's not much,' is all he can find to say, 'but I'll have to phone up Pete to tow us back.' The telephone is the magical object that binds Mr Slatter to the past. It links him back to Harwell, not forward to Wantage. Or is it just that Mr Slatter cannot imagine forewarning Wantage that his daughter is going to be late? Perhaps it makes no difference, for the telephone is itself a part of that past, no longer close at hand but in Ardington, a village which the car has already sped by on its journey, as Rebecca's local readership would surely have known. No wonder that she becomes desperate: ' "But Ardington's four miles back!" Rachel shouted. "And I've got a play to put on".' There is a hidden meaning to be found in those last few words, which the narrator is about to reveal but at this point in the story it is the shouting that commands the reader's attention. It is followed at once by silence and, within that silence, the fates of father and daughter, and of their story, are sealed.

'Her father thought for a moment. Five minutes later he had gone to find a telephone.' Every reader who attempts to read Rebecca's story aloud feels the need to mark in some way, whether by a change of voice, a slight pause, or a slower pace, the chasm that yawns between these two sentences. The distance between full stop and capital letter becomes the literary expression of a very particular moment, the moment of decision in which the drama of the plot is resolved. Once the boundary between one sentence and the next has been crossed there can be only one end to the story. Father and daughter are lost to each other. Whether or not they know it, their worlds have separated. As in her story *Dodecahedron*, Rebecca marks this separation by means of the past perfect tense: 'Five minutes later he had gone to find a telephone.' By the time he returns it will be too late. For all his efforts, there will be no going back. The story resumes, apparently seamlessly, yet the missing five minutes represent the space of a lifetime. The effect that Rebecca achieves is of a kind of narrative caesura. Until this moment, Mr Slatter and his daughter have travelled, however uneasily, together. Now they must journey on alone. The narrative is about to unwind. Reading the story, we sense that this is the climax, the turning point of the plot. We await the denouement uneasily.

The father's desertion of his daughter at her moment of greatest need signals the commencement of the metamorphosis for which, from the beginning of the story, the narrative has scrupulously prepared us. 'Rachel began to walk towards Wantage', we are told, and with these words we enter the story's dazzling finale. Wantage may be the heroine's destination but it is not given to her to reach it. In language of exceptional subtlety, Rebecca gently draws her heroine towards her fantastic destiny, action by action, thought by thought, sensation by sensation. 'She put on her felt ears.' We have known about these ears from the opening of the story, 'my ears' as Rachel called them then, ears which she later fingered nervously in her lap. Now at last she chooses to wear them. It is a momentous choice. The words 'put on' remind us of what she has just before shouted at her father: 'And I've got a play to put on.' But the words mean more now than we might expect. It is no longer an actor's role that Rachel is about to assume but a new identity. Putting on the ears is the first step in her transformation; she is to become what she has chosen to play. 'She sucked a travelling sweet hungrily.' Once again, as in *Dodecahedron*, the journey into another world is accompanied by hunger and as she sucks the travelling sweet Rachel ponders her fate. ' "I wonder if they'll miss me," Rachel thought. "After all, I am only the March Hare".' The words are apparently addressed to her fellow actors, emphasizing the insignificance of her part in the forthcoming play, but in the light of what follows they seem to have a deeper meaning. Is it her father, her family, her friends whom she has in mind? Is it her own significance that puzzles her, the girl who is about to be changed into the March Hare, no less but, after all, only a hare, no more. There is a note of sadness and resignation in her words which the story's conclusion will both confirm and complicate.

The seven short sentences that follow Rachel's musings take us into the very moment of metamorphosis itself. Here is the entire passage: 'Her nose began to itch. She twitched it. Her hands and feet tingled slightly, probably with cold. Rachel was still hungry. She picked some grass and chewed it thoughtfully. Her glassy eyes shone with the moon reflection. Her furry paws glistened with the dew of evening.' The magic of Rebecca's narrative, at this, the climax of her tale, is the literary equivalent of the magic of metamorphosis. It is not until the final sentence that we can be sure of the outcome, so unobtrusively calculated is Rebecca's language. In this respect it would not seem extravagent to compare Rebecca's achievement with that of the great storytellers within the Western tradition, rather as Tolstoy compares Fyedka's writing to the writing of Goethe. Here, for example, is how Calvino describes the poetic achievement of Ovid in his *Metamorphoses*:

> It is in following the continuity of the passage from one form to another that Ovid displays his incomparable gifts. He tells how a woman realizes that she is changing into a lotus tree: her feet are rooted to the earth, a soft bark creeps up little by little and enfolds her groin; she makes a movement to tear her hair and finds her hands full of leaves. Or he speaks of Arachne's fingers, expert at winding or unravelling wool, turning the spindle, plying the needle in embroidery, fingers that at a certain point we see lengthening into slender spiders' legs and beginning to weave a web.
>
> (1988: 2)

Rebecca's deceptively simple language has a comparable effect, for all her tender years. We are told how Rachel 'twitched' her nose, a word which suggests the involuntary or instinctive movements of a small animal, so much more evocative in this context than the more predictable 'scratched'. 'Her hands and feet tingled slightly,' the narrative continues, picking up the soft insistence, in sound and sense, of 'itch' and 'twitched'. 'Probably with cold,' the narrator seeks to reassure us but behind the word 'probably' lies that darker possibility which already by now her heroine has begun to sense. Hunger assails her again as she contemplates the future but it is no longer a manufactured travelling sweet but the grass across which she is walking that she picks and chews, 'thoughtfully'. 'Thoughtfully' strengthens the hint conveyed by the word 'probably', suggesting that by now the wandering child has understood what is happening to her. The next sentence confirms the truth. The 'glassy eyes' are the eyes of the animal she has become, eyes in which her new world is reflected, the world of 'the moonlight purple and silver' which Rebecca cites in her letter as the image out of which her story arose. It is as if the moon has entered through Rachel's eyes and taken her over, the very opposite of Alice's predicament in *Alice Through The Looking Glass*. And now, for the first time, the hare can make its candid appearance: 'Her furry paws glistened with the dew of evening.' Taken together, these final two sentences form a couplet which draws the metamorphosis to its haunting end. The paws are the final, unmistakeable mark of the beast. The passage from one form to another, one world to another, is complete and it would seem that there is no way back.

'Far away Mr Slatter returned.' The carefully ordered sentence evokes nostalgia, a sense of loss, of a world left behind, irretrievably. It is not as if the father, on his return, is that remote from his daughter, if only he knew. She is there, right in front of him, and yet she is no longer close at hand. The perspective from which the words 'far away' are written is that of the narrator who knows the truth that escapes the 'shadowy Mr Slatter'. His daughter has fled. It is from the world into which she has vanished that his own seems far away, no more perhaps, already, than a distant memory. All that Mr Slatter sees is 'a hare jumping away on the grassy bank'. He has not even noticed that his daughter has gone. We are told that he catches sight of the hare 'in the light of the moon', the same moon that shines in his daughter's new eyes, but for the father the moonlight is deceptive. He fails to read its hidden meaning, he only seems to see. Or rather, he cannot see beyond appearances. The hare he catches sight of is no more than the familiar creature of the downlands, as is clear from the narrator's switch, for the first and only time, from the pronoun 'she' to 'it': 'It leaped over the hedge and scampered on the cornfield.' The implications of that astonishing leap lie outside his comprehension.

The title of the story has a proverbial source, as we have seen, and now the story closes on another proverb: 'Mr Slatter shook his head and smiled. "As mad as a march hare," he thought.' The traditional words are preserved this time but their significance is dramatically reconstructed. For Mr Slatter the proverb is a conventional trope, a pretty turn of phrase suggested by the creature he has just caught sight of. Meanwhile, the truth, unknown to him, is that his daughter has become the proverb's subject. Rebecca establishes this bitter contrast through a simple, barely noticeable grammatical device. Within the proverb as pondered by Mr Slatter, the words 'march hare' are written in lower case. A few sentences earlier, the same words, as spoken by Rachel, were capitalized: 'after all, I am only the March Hare'. Such are the delicate means by which Rebecca makes an old proverb assume a new and startling life.

But who is it who is mad, the daughter who has leaped into the beyond, into the world of her own imagination, or the father who is too worldly to notice what is happening to his daughter? Characteristically, the story leaves it to the reader to decide. The ending is as mysterious as the ending of *Dodecahedron*. In the earlier story Rebecca acknowledges a return from the world beneath the waves but conceals its meaning. In this, her ultimate valedictory tale, she leaves her heroine alone within her new world, scampering across the cornfield into which she has leaped while her father looks on without suspicion, wrapped up in his own thought. 'He thought' are the story's last words, as if the narrator is prodding her readers to speculate and interpret in their turn. Terrified or thrilled, we are at the end left wondering. Underneath the last line of her manuscript, at the bottom of the page, Rebecca has written her name. As far as I know, it was the only time that she ever chose to write her name at the bottom of a story. It is as if she is signing off as she reaches the end of her life at primary school, which also marks in so many ways the end of childhood. Or is it, also, a final assertion of her own narrative authority, even her own identity, in the face of this passionate and fearful tale of escape and rebellion: the story of a child turned into a hare, enchanted by her own imagination?

* * *

Following Rebecca's hint, I have read her two late primary school stories as variations around a common theme, embodied in two images, the whirlpool and the leaping hare. In her letter, Rebecca describes her theme as that of escape, the flight from reality into fantasy. For Carlo Ginzburg, as we saw in the last chapter, it is the journey to the beyond; for Italo Calvino 'the sudden agile leap of the poet-philsopher who raises himself above the weight of the world, showing that with all his gravity he has the secret of lightness' (1988: 12). Rebecca's stories trace the creative tension between two levels of consciousness, two orders of being, the mundane and the miraculous. This theme is not peculiar to Rebecca. As we have seen, it is central to many children's stories: to Jessica's tale of playful magic that binds together the mother and child but excludes the father; to Lydia's exploration of children's privileged access to a visionary world; to Laura's carnivalesque romp around the Universe. But Rebecca is less at ease within the imaginary than her younger fellow storytellers. The thrill of the beyond is never free of an anxiety that can readily give way to terror. Imagination darkens as Rebecca conjures it. The undersea world of the Dodecahedron imprisons all who enter its savage domain; the enchantment of the moonlight into which the trans-formed heroine of *Girl Today, Hare Tomorrow* vanishes holds out no promise of return. Both stories are suffused with resentment at the social world's indifference to the solitary child, possessed by an imagination that may liberate but might also destroy. In Rebecca's stories, Calvino's lightness is always matched by weight.

Rebecca configures these perplexities in plots of rare authority, in language that is both extraordinarily inventive and extraordinarily precise. What, then, are we to make of the questions which Rebecca asks five years later: 'Do you think that children have the same ideas as adults but just can't express them as well? Or maybe their naivety helps them express them better?' As for Rebeccca's own ideas, we have already seen that they are shared by storytellers young and old, experienced and naïve, across diverse cultures. On the other hand, their particular expression in Rebecca's work is unique to her situation, on the threshold of adolescence. Her achievement is, in this respect at least, incomparable. 'If I had written this story last year,' she writes, 'would it have been better or worse?' There is no answer, for it would have been a different story. In effect, Rebecca acknowledges this herself by directing attention to the story that she *did* write five years later, 'thinking of the same purple skies, silver moon and enchanted atmosphere', *Jane's Dream*.

Jane's Dream

The tranquillity of Jane Eyre's first few months as governess to Mr Rochester's young ward Adele at Thornfield Hall was accompanied by a feeling of restlessness:

> Anybody may blame me who likes, [we read in Chapter 12 of Charlotte Brontë's novel,] when I add further, that, now and then, when I took a walk by myself in the grounds; when I went down to the gates and looked through them along the road; or when, while Adele played with her nurse, and Mrs Fairfax made jellies in the storeroom, I climbed the three staircases, raised the trapdoor of the attic, and having reached the leads, looked out afar over sequestered field and hill, and along dim skyline – that then I longed for a power of vision which might overpass that limit ... Who blames me? Many, no doubt; and I shall be called discontented. I could not help it; the restlessness was in my nature; it agitated me to pain sometimes. Then my sole relief was to walk along the

corridor of the third story, backwards and forwards, safe in the silence and solitude of the spot, and allow my mind's eye to dwell on whatever bright visions rose before it – and, certainly, they were many and glowing; to let my heart be heaved by the exultant movement, which, while it swelled it in trouble, expanded it with life; and, best of all, to open my inward ear to a tale that was never ended – a tale my imagination created, and narrated continuously; quickened with all of incident, life, fire, feeling, that I desired and had not in my actual existence.

(Brontë 1985: 141)

It is a critical moment in the novel, followed immediately by reference to the strange laugh which Jane would hear 'not unfrequently' as she paced up and down the corridor, and then by the account of her first meeting with Mr Rochester, with all its moonlit mystery, as of a fairy tale. Of all the major novels of the nineteenth and twentieth centuries, *Jane Eyre* is the masterpiece that corresponds most intimately to the young Rebecca's own narrative identity. Its concepts, images and values are those that Rebecca had begun to explore in her two late primary school stories and now revisits and extends. The consciousness of Charlotte Brontë's heroine, from the first to the last pages of the novel, is alive with vision, imagination, fancy, dream, enchantment. Moonlight and darkness are the novel's favoured elements, a world of shadowy thought and mysterious landscape. Solitariness and companionship, rebellion and acceptance, independence and reciprocity are the terms of the human condition which Charlotte Brontë scrutinizes. In *Jane's Dream*, Rebecca acknowledges and exploits this affinity. Her new story, written when she was sixteen years old, is a young reader's gloss or commentary on a canonical text. At one level it is a reflection around the novel, an entry into Jane Eyre's world, absorbing the novel's atmosphere, its characterization, imagery and language. But Rebecca is not content to reduplicate her source. Instead, she chooses to appropriate Charlotte Brontë's novel, after the manner described by Coleridge, as cited in Chapter 1, making use of *Jane Eyre* to illuminate further her own imaginary world, those purple skies she speaks of in her letter.

The story is cast in the form of a dream narrative, the kind of narrative summarily dismissed as 'limp' in Rebecca's letter. The challenge which she sets herself is to reanimate a tired and trite genre, turning it into a vehicle for further exploration of the fantasies that so deeply intrigue her. Her story recalls fragments of the many dreams scattered throughout *Jane Eyre* itself but, for all that, it remains a unique tale, combining figures and scenes from many different parts of the novel with entirely new elements of her own devising. The story opens in stillness, the stillness of a sleeping figure absorbed by a dream image, and closes with the stillness of dawn, broken by the cry of a peacock that might belong to either dream or waking life. Between these two still moments, in an indeterminate time and space, bounded neither by the ticking of a grandfather clock nor the length of a passage shrouded in 'inky darkness,' a drama is enacted of imaginative confusion, promise and denial, a journey through what Charlotte Brontë describes as 'imagination's boundless and trackless waste' (1985: 190). Of the three stories examined in this chapter *Jane's Dream* is the only one to be written in the first person. By assuming the voice of Jane Eyre, in creative mimicry of Charlotte Brontë's novel, Rebecca achieves a more personal engagement with the tensions that all three of her narratives explore. She turns herself into a participant observer, caught up in the action she describes, implicated and entangled within her own plot and subject, in imagination, to its disenchanted outcome.

'I became still; and watched the shadows thrown by candle light flickering against the panelled walls.' The opening sentence is at once a reminder and a confirmation of Rebecca's narrative skill. Once more, as in *Dodecahedron*, it is sensation that sets the story in motion and underlies its plot and once more the story opens in the middle of things, as is evident from Rebecca's choice of the word 'became.' Maybe we come across the narrator in the middle of a dream or maybe, more generally, in the middle of a troubled life, momentarily stilled in sleep, the life of a 'wanderer', as Charlotte Brontë's Jane describes herself (1985: 236). The opening scene is set in 'the long passage' of Thornfield Hall, which, in *Jane Eyre*, refers to the third storey, the site of Bertha Mason's imprisonment. Images of insecurity, anxiety, disorientation pervade the narrative. 'The disconsolate moan of the wind outside' is a direct quotation from the novel but its meaning is revised. In the novel, Jane derives from the wind's moan 'a strange excitement ... I wished the wind to howl more wildly, the gloom to deepen to darkness, and the confusion to rise to clamour' (1985: 87). For Rebecca's Jane the wind's confusion is a disquieting sign of inner turmoil, at one with the stupor she cannot shake off. The shadowy shapes that pass her as she stands in the passage, unable to move, represent her troubled imagination. The 'wolflike' Pilot, Mr Rochester's dog, 'terrible' yet 'majestic', even 'graceful', is still more fearful a creature than the 'North of England spirit, called a "Gytrash"' with which Jane compares Pilot as he glides past her for the first time in *Jane Eyre* (1985: 144). The whispering child seems to be an amalgam of the playful but wayward Adele, with her 'little freaks' (1985: 140) and the maniacal Bertha, whose 'goblin laughter' disturbs Jane's sleep on the night that Mr Rochester's bed is set on fire (1985: 179). Her eyes, 'dark moons in an ivory sky', echo the dark moon which concludes *Dodecahedron*, prefiguring the coming darkness as the last candle is laughingly extinguished.

The inky darkness that now engulfs Jane, as she stands rooted in the long passage, propels her into sudden motion, without direction or definition, an aimless escape far removed from the willing departure of Sebastian in pursuit of the sounds that awake him at the beginning of *Dodecahedron*. She does not seek the 'great wide door with its metallic and brassy handle just visible'. It simply appears before her, swinging open of its own accord as she approaches and appearing to beckon her in. 'Calm, I stepped through the door,' she tells us, 'not knowing why I was so impelled to enter'. This Janus-faced door presides over alternate scenarios, each of them a form of enchantment, though of opposite kinds, this first a terrifying picture of oppression.

The scene that follows is loosely modelled on the ten-year-old Jane Eyre's interview with Mr Brocklehurst in the breakfast room of Gateshead Hall in Chapter 4 of Charlotte Brontë's novel. On Mr Brocklehurst's departure at the end of this interview, Jane confronts her aunt in a passionate denunciation of her cruelty and deceit. 'Ere I had finished this reply,' she recalls, 'my soul began to expand, to exult, with the strangest sense of freedom, of triumph, I ever felt. It seemed as if an invisible bond had burst, and that I had struggled out into unhoped-for liberty' (1985: 69). Rebecca's Jane achieves an equivalent triumph within her dream but through deeds rather than words. The key to the scene is Aunt Reed's dismissive welcome on Jane's entry: 'Jane Eyre. Come in. Do not think we were waiting for you.' The room which she enters might as well be in Thornfield Hall as in Gateshead Hall. Mrs Fairfax, Mr Rochester's housekeeper, is sitting behind Mr Brocklehurst, 'in her old stiff chair, with her knitting', while standing beside her is Bessie, Aunt Reed's maid. Aunt Reed's son John is also present, apparently still a young child. What links all these figures is their common disregard for Jane. In one way or another, each of them despises, distrusts, or is disconcerted by Jane's fierce autonomy. She is a 'wild animal', an 'evil little girl', full of 'grand ideas' inconsistent with her social status, lacking in piety or gratitude. As Jane Eyre herself puts it at the opening of the novel, she is 'a discord . . . a heterogeneous thing . . . a useless thing . . . a noxious thing' (1985: 47). She will not accommodate to the demands of the society in which she finds herself. In presenting her heroine in this light, Rebecca sharpens the contrast drawn in *Dodecahedron* and *Girl Today, Hare Tomorrow* between the lonely protagonist and the adult, social world. In the earlier stories social conflict is the product of incomprehension or indifference. The adult world looks on in futility, seeing nothing, blind to the child's imagination. In *Jane's Dream*, on the other hand, incomprehension is rooted in social division and religious intolerance. Plain, poor, orphaned Jane has no right to paint, to flirt with Mr Rochester, to express her own ideas, to treat herself, or to be treated by others. as imaginatively or socially equal. Incomprehension is converted into ostracism.

Throughout the scene, Jane is excluded. The conversation proceeds as if she is not there. Mr Brocklehurst looks at her frankly but speaks of her always in the third person. Jane acknowledges her exclusion but feels powerless to contest it. 'I was cold,' she says, 'so far from the fire, and wanted to drag my chair forward – but I could not bring myself to take part in any way in this awful scene, so remained motionless, observing.' Even John's abusive cry – 'What is she to us?' – arouses her for no more than an instant. What finally moves her to act is not the voice of Mr Brocklehurst, declaring that 'she is indeed a fiery thing,' for all that it arouses her 'fear and fury', but the disappearance of the door and the sight of the mirror in which not one part of her is reflected. Door and mirror are the magical objects which declare her plight. She is trapped within a social order which does not recognize her. She has neither place nor even existence in this room. The world inhabited by Aunt Reed and Mr Brocklehurst is a world that annihilates her. Transgression is her only means of escape. She must smash the mirror which has revealed the truth, making use of the very tea cup that symbolizes the polite conventions of the hated world. Immediately, she restores her identity. A pause follows in which the various figures in the room lose their self-assurance while still failing to acknowledge Jane's presence. The suspense is eventually broken by Bessie, lowest ranked of all the assembled group. Previously she had avoided Jane's eyes; now, at last, their eyes meet and she smiles. That smile is both a sign of recognition and a sanction of Jane's transgressive act. The door returns, as Jane had known it would, the doorway to another world, an opposing enchantment. She swings it open and, with one step, she is free.

The world into which Jane steps, in mid-sentence, with all the ease and agility of Calvino's poet-philosopher, is, as Rebecca recognizes in her letter, the world of the leaping hare. That enchanted atmosphere, newly inspired by Charlotte Brontë's luxuriant prose, remains, nevertheless, uniquely personal. The fantastic romanticism of the mighty waterfall is unparalleled in the landscape of *Jane Eyre*. What the two authors share is the thrill, as of another world, that accompanies the rising of the moon. In the novel Rochester tells Jane, 'No wonder you have rather the look of another world ... When I came upon you in Hay Lane last night, I thought unaccountably of fairy tales, and had half a mind to demand whether you had bewitched my horse: I am not sure yet' (1985: 153). The nameless figure whom Rebecca's Jane discovers on the hillside echoes these sentiments: 'Indeed – it is as though we entered another world when the moon entered the sky. Even my horse seems under a spell tonight.' Rebecca's narrative identifies Jane wholeheartedly with the world of 'the luminous moon', 'my own world' as she calls it. She runs forward again but no longer blindly and insecurely as in the long passage: 'I heard the sound of water rushing nearby, I was drawn to it, and ran: never stumbling or tripping, as if I knew every tree root, boulder and shrub.' In the passage, as Jane described it, 'the slippery oak boards slid from under me as I ran.' Now she repeats the word slippery but only to emphasize the contrast: 'I effortlessly climbed the hill which didn't feel in the least slippery though I was sure there was dew all around.' Inner and outer worlds unite as she runs until, as she says, 'I could not distinguish the water from the blood rushing in my head.' Even before she reaches the crest of the hill she knows what she will see.

'The sheer force of the waterfall' is the equivalent, within the natural world, of the power of imagination within consciousness, an enchantment but also a trap. The imagination enthralls but, in enthralling consciousness, seems to demand a solitary and exclusive commitment. As soon as Jane is distracted by a faint human sound, the spell is broken. What follows is an idyllic but uneasy encounter. The meeting between Rochester and Jane Eyre on Hill Lane is here retold as a fantasy of companionship in imagination but it is a companionship that is no sooner offered than it is withdrawn. The man lying by his horse is not the dark-faced stranger 'of middle height and considerable breadth of chest' whom Jane Eyre catches sight of while 'the moon was waxing bright' (1985: 145). Rebecca's horseman is 'slim and tall', young and gallant, the kind of 'handsome youth' who would only have aroused Jane Eyre's fear: 'Had he been a handsome, heroic-looking young gentleman, I should not have dared to stand thus questioning him against his will, and offering my services unasked' (1985: 145). The Jane of *Jane's Dream* is altogther less anxious, almost as if Rebecca is intent on contradicting her source: 'Oddly, his looks and gallantry did not trouble or threaten me; rather pulled me closer so that I knelt by him, and asked if I could help.' The golden-eyed stranger and the girl strike up a conversation in which imaginative complicity is seen to be necessarily transient, almost frivolous. 'We were both smiling as we spoke', Jane recalls, 'and I knew our conversation was little more than a game, as if we were acting out parts in a play.' Suddenly the reality of Rachel's metamorphosis in *Girl Today, Hare Tomorrow* seems a long way away.

The young man, Rochester refigured, recognizes his fellowship with Jane but immediately discounts it. Her name reminds him of a past which somehow seems to unmask the present. 'I knew he was mocking me,' Jane admits, 'but wasn't sure how.' Acknowledging Jane as 'sister mine', her partner rides off alone. He will not risk imaginative brotherhood. Jane watches him leave, apparently without regret, responding readily to his demand that she promise to be careful: 'I smiled – what had I to fear from my own world?' But even as she watches, her world turns cold; she shivers. The loss of companionship shatters the dream of freedom: 'The pale moon slowly glided behind a cloud, its luminosity lost, and the land was plunged in darkness.' The ease with which she stepped out into the moonlight is matched by the violence of her fall. No longer in control of her destiny, she is the victim of 'the screaming wind', expelled by the force of her own imagination. Figures out of her past flit by her as she falls, like so many fragments of a world for a moment left behind: Helen Burns, whose patient suffering at Lowood Institution is the antithesis of Jane Eyre's determined resistance; Georgina Reed, the child 'universally indulged' in Gateshead Hall at Jane's expense (1985: 46); the mother whom she has never known, who would surely have cared for her, had she lived.

Reality returns; the weight of the world reclaims the poet-philosopher. 'My fall ended – I dropped into my bed.' The dream is over. In the 'cool grey light of dawn' all that remains to link the real world and the dream world, before the closing stillness, is 'a peacock's cry', the shrill shriek of a bird of dazzling plumage. It is Rebecca's final image and, in its terrifying beauty, the perfect sensation, visual and aural, with which to conclude her tale. It can also serve as the image that makes sense of Rebecca's entire narrative journey, over five years and more, as in story after story she ponders the beauty and peril of imaginative life.

7

THE PEDAGOGY OF THE
IMAGINATION

I have in mind some possible pedagogy of the imagination that would accustom us to control our own inner vision without suffocating it or letting it fall, on the other hand, into confused, ephemeral daydreams, but would enable the images to crystallize into a well defined, memorable, and self-sufficient form.

(Calvino 1988: 92)

The six preceding chapters have offered a series of interpretations of stories composed by children between the ages of 5 and 16, children from different cultures alike in their commitment to storytelling. In this concluding chapter, I want to answer three questions. What do these stories tell us about children's narrative thinking, about children as storytellers? What does children's narrative thinking tell us about intellectual growth, about the entry of children into culture? What are the implications of children's narrative achievement for education, for the shape of a curriculum, for teaching and learning, for the documentation and assessment of children's work, for education as a cultural project?

Children as storytellers

I want to examine the quality of children's narrative thinking by setting it in the context of one particular theory of narrative, that of the French philosopher Paul Ricoeur. The three volumes of Ricoeur's *Time & Narrative* (1984–1988) represent the most ambitious attempt in modern times to understand the nature of narrative and its relation to our experience of the world and of ourselves within that world. Following Aristotle, Ricoeur defines narrative in terms of mimesis, or make-believe, 'the creative imitation, by means of the plot, of lived temporal experience' (1984: 31). Ricoeur uses the word 'creative' advisedly. Mimesis, he argues, is not a replica of reality but, rather, a remaking or retelling of the world: 'I see in the plots we invent the privileged means by which we re-configure our confused, unformed, and at the limit mute temporal experience' (1984: xi).

Mimesis, as Ricoeur understands it, has a threefold structure. He speaks of three stages or moments, naming them *mimesis 1, mimesis 2* and *mimesis 3*. The central moment is the act of creation itself, that 'leap of imagination' which 'opens up the world of the plot and institutes the literariness of the work of literature' (1984: 53). Ricoeur calls this *mimesis 2*. But literary artifice is neither unprepared nor unaccountable. It arises out of experience, an experience already shaped by our understanding of the world of action, and it returns to experience as readers, including, I will add, the writer as reader, reconstruct the world of action in response to the experience of reading. These two stages, on either side of the mimesis of creation, frame the leap of imagination. Ricoeur calls them respectively *mimesis 1* and *mimesis 3*. The task of a theory of interpretation is to retrace the passage from each stage to the next, that is to say, 'to reconstruct the set of operations by which a work lifts itself above the opaque depths of living, acting and suffering, to be given by an author to readers who receive it and thereby change their acting' (1984: 53). This is the task which Ricoeur sets himself. I will follow his argument stage by stage, exploring the ways in which the children's stories presented in earlier chapters accommodate and appropriate the theory of mimesis which he proposes.

Mimesis 1

The origin of mimesis lies within experience. The world of the plot is constructed against the background of a prior understanding of the world of action. This 'practical understanding' implies, first of all, an understanding of the network of concepts associated with action. 'Every narrative presupposes a familiarity with terms such as agent, goal, means, circumstance, help, hostility, co-operation, conflict, success, failure, etc.' (1984: 55). At times, Vivian Paley's book *Wally's Stories* (1981) reads like a catalogue of this conceptual network. Wally and his classmates may not yet be familiar with words such as agent, goal, means or circumstance but the concepts already dominate their thinking as they debate among themselves the rights and wrongs of classroom behaviour, the uses of magic, or the origins of language. It is out of these classroom conversations, dense with the language of agency and purpose, enlivened by the children's play, that Wally draws his mythic tales. From time to time the semantics of action becomes, itself, a significant part of a story's theme, as for example in his own story about language where language is seen to depend upon the possibility of companionship, upon reciprocity; living, acting and suffering with others; a family environment; a public world.

As the recognition of a public world reminds us, practical understanding also implies a familiarity with the cultural symbols that articulate experience, the manners and customs by which we live. The drawings that accompany the written text of Jessica's story *The Poorly Mouse* are rich in symbols of this kind. Mother and daughter wait in line to see the vet; father, mother and daughter wave farewell as the mouse departs for home. In this, her final drawing, Jessica plays on the ambiguity and subtlety of a farewell gesture, as we saw in Chapter 3. The father keeps his arms by his side in a gesture of apology, almost a shrug. The mother raises her arm but her buttoned hand, apparently closed, implies a formal, muted goodbye. Only the daughter waves with feeling, her hand and fingers open and enlarged in a gesture of uninhibited friendship and good luck. Ricoeur points out that it is 'an inherent feature of action ... that it can never be ethically neutral' (1984: 59). Here, at the end of her story, Jessica seizes on the ethical complexity of action to create one of her most striking effects.

A third feature of practical understanding, and one that is decisive from the standpoint of narrative, concerns its relationship to time. 'The understanding of action', Ricoeur suggests, 'goes so far as to recognise in action temporal structures that call for narration' (1984: 59). Foremost among these is what Ricoeur calls 'the pre-narrative quality of experience'. 'Without leaving everyday experience, are we not inclined to see in a given sequence of the episodes of our lives "[as yet] untold stories," stories that demand to be told, stories that offer anchorage points for narrative' (1984: 74)? Ricoeur chooses examples from psychoanalysis and the law: 'The patient who talks to a psychoanalyst presents bits and pieces of lived stories, of dreams, of "primitive scenes", conflictual episodes. We may rightly say of such analytic sessions that their goal and effect is for the analysand to draw from these bits and pieces a narrative that will be both more supportable and more intelligible' (1984: 74). In a similar way, 'a judge undertakes to understand a course of action, a character, by unraveling the tangle of plots the subject is caught up in' (1984: 75). For teachers of young children, a more familiar example might be 'news time' or 'sharing time' (Cazden 2001: 10–29), when, in a school like Harwell Primary School, children gather round their teacher, often at the start of the school day, to swap experiences, talking about what they did at the weekend, or how a birthhday party or a football match went, or about something that happened in the playground or on the way to school. Sometimes these 'bits and pieces of lived stories' may provide the occasion for a more formal narrative. In Chapter 4, we saw how Lydia assembled, out of the fragments of memory which she had previously shared with the rest of her class, her first written story of a new school year, the autobiographical tale *I Remember,* a slender narrative of surprise and shock, yet configured with due care and, in effect, the seed out of which the most extravagant of her later tales would grow. For Ricoeur, the as yet untold story implicit in experience serves as 'a critical example for every emphasis on the artificial character of the art of narrating'. It teaches us that 'we tell stories because in the last analysis human lives need and merit being narrated' (1984: 75).

Mimesis 2

It seems clear from these examples that by the time they compose their earliest written stories children have already acquired the practical understanding which narrative presupposes. This, then, is the context in which

they enter 'the kingdom of the as if,' as Ricoeur describes the world of the
plot, opened up by the mimesis of creation. The world of the plot requires its
own form of understanding, 'poetic understanding', the art of composition.
Composition has a dual aspect. In shaping stories, we reshape experience. The
dynamism of the plot imposes order on the world of action. Ricoeur defines
plot as a 'synthesis of the heterogeneous'. Plot combines and integrates its
constituent elements in three ways. First 'it draws a meaningful story from a
diversity of events or incidents' (1984: 65). Because of this 'an event must be
more than just a singular occurrence. It gets its definition from its contribution to the development of the plot' (1984: 65). Second, plot gathers together
into a single story the heterogeneous factors that make up the conceptual
network of action: agents, goals, means, interactions, circumstances and all
those changes of fortune associated with the concept of *peripeteia*, such as
unexpected results, sudden reversals, surprising recognitions, violent uphea-
vals. In doing so, Ricoeur says, the plot draws concordance out of discordance, although concordance is never complete, discordance never wholly
overcome. Third, plot 'extracts a configuration from a succession' (1984: 66).
Two kinds of time are at work in every story. One is episodic time, in which
events succeed each other in an indefinite sequence, one after another, then
and then and then, linked by no more than 'the irreversible order of time
common to physical and human events' (1984: 67). The other is configured
time, the time of the 'fable and theme', by means of which past, present and
future are held together as one and time that passes gives way to time that
endures. Configuration 'draws from [the] manifold of events the unity of one
temporal whole', thanks to which 'the entire plot can be translated into one
"thought" which is nothing other than its "point" or "theme"' (1984: 66). It
'imposes the "sense of an ending" on the indefinite succession of incidents',
establishing 'the point from where the story can be seen as a whole' (1984:
67). We learn to read the ending in the beginning and the beginning in the
ending and in this way 'we also learn to read time itself backwards as the
recapitulation of the initial conditions of a course of action in its terminal
consequences' (1984: 68). In short, configuration is what makes a story
followable.

How do these large abstractions fit the stories told and retold in previous
chapters? I will consider each of Ricoeur's three syntheses in turn. How, first,
do the children's stories create a meaningful narrative out of a diversity of
events? Consider one of Wally's stories, the second of the nine stories discussed in Chapter 2, his 'lion pet' tale. Like most of Wally's dictated stories, it
is a family story, in mythic form, the tale of 'a man and a mother and two
sisters and a brother'. The story is made up of three sets of events. One by one,
the older members of the family disappear or run away; the younger
daughter, abandoned with her brother, learns to cook; along comes a lion and
asks if he can be the children's pet; the story ends. None of these incidents is a
singular occurence. The daughter's decision to stay home with her father,
only to be deserted by him, is the earliest sign of that autonomy which will
enable brother and sister to survive their parents' desertion while acknowledging their need for dependence. Learning how to cook means learning the
art of survival which is the proof of autonomy. The arrival of the lion who

asks to be a pet is a consequence of the daughter's wish, signifying that she recognizes that autonomy is not enough, that she and her 'little brother' need a guardian too. Autonomy and dependence, so the story tells us, are the complementary conditions of a happy family life, as the sister has implicitly recognized from the beginning: 'I was just wishing for a lion pet. You can carry us wherever you want.' Such are the means by which Wally devises, out of the simplest diversity of events, a structured tale of family life and its requirements, a story that renews the meaning of its conventional closure: 'So they lived happily ever after.'

Wally was five years old when he dictated this story. It was one of the earliest of all his stories. Rebecca wrote *Jane's Dream* when she was 16. Her ambitious dream narrative shows what happens to the definition of events as literary experience and life experience increase. *Jane's Dream* is a bravura display composed out of scattered fragments drawn either from Charlotte Brontë's novel or from Rebecca's own imaginative experience. The story opens with the stillness of a sleeping figure and closes in the stillness of dawn but between these two poles the narrative inscribes a fearsome journey through 'imagination's boundless and trackless waste', as Jane Eyre describes it in the novel. Each incident or scene, with its diverse array of figures, objects and settings, is bound to the others by the nature of the dreamer's quest for meaning: the long passage with its shadowy shapes; the room full of loud accusation and silent witness, where not even the mirror acknowledges Jane's presence; the enchanted landscape in which Jane encounters the gallant, golden-eyed stranger thrown from his horse; the final fall into waking life past an image of the dreamer's mother. The power of vision that Jane Eyre longs for is briefly glimpsed, only to be denied, and we are left with the peacock's cry, the story's final image which collects and concentrates the interlocking signifance of everything that has gone before, however uncanny.

How, next, do the children's stories integrate the conceptual network of action? Jessica's story *The Poorly Mouse* provides a good example. Each successive element in the network of action finds its fixed and appropriate place within Jessica's bold tale. The main agents of the narrative are the girl and her mother, although it is the wolf who initiates the action by hurting the mouse, and the father whose intervention draws the story to its close. The goal is the healing of the mouse, as the story's title indicates, but its achievement leads to fresh prospects and fresh unease. The means are the visit to the vet and, when that fails, the magic of pretence. Among the complex interactions which dominate the narrative, the most essential is that of mother and child, whose complicity is the secret of success, as shown in the drawing of the mother sitting beside her daughter in a gesture of solidarity as the two of them together pretend to be the vet. The circumstance that defines the means to the goal is the fact that the vet is 'busy', a circumstance dramatized in another of Jessica's visual representations of the story's plot. The unexpected result of mother and daughter's success is that they choose to keep the mouse, 'even now the mouse was better', as a consequence of which 'they had lots of fun'. A sudden reversal comes with the father's return from holiday. Jessica's drawing marks the moment of recognition and disquiet as father and mother confront each other alone across the page. The story ends with an upheaval which parallels the story's opening as the mouse is regretfully sent back home to live once again 'near where the wolves lived'. Taken as a whole, in all its inimitable assurace, *The Poorly Mouse* is a miniature narrative essay in concordance and discordance. The concordance of mother and child resolves the discordance caused by the wolf's action, abetted by the vet's preoccupation. But this concordance, which incorporates the healed mouse also, is, in turn, broken by the father's unwelcome response on his return from holiday. A fresh concordance is achieved on the final page as father, mother and child together bid the mouse farewell but it is now an uneasy concordance, as we can see in the ambiguity of the farewell gestures and the mouse's lonely departure towards its dangerous home.

The same interplay of concordance and discordance determines the course of action in Lydia's story, *The Magic Stone*. The story opens with the conspicuous discordance of mother and child, that generational conflict between the reasonable and the imaginable which the narrative sets out to resolve poetically, but as the tale is told new sources of discord are added: the nagging doubts of a sympathetic friend and, more urgently, the paradoxical signals of the magic stone itself, its constant changes of colour, its capriciousness, the way in which it teases the narrator, threatening to vanish or explode. As we saw in Chapter 4, the story's climax comes at the moment when the narrator, confronted by her mother's anger, begins to doubt herself, only to burst out defiantly: 'But I was not dreaming and I am not ill at all.' The unexpected eruption into the present tense represents the poetic triumph of concordance. From here on all that remains is to confirm the public status of the imagination by drawing all the agents together in recognition of the stone's magic power, including the blushing stone itself, the narrator's alter ego.

Lastly, how do the children's stories configure succession? Two of the stories are especially notable for their treatment of time: Rebecca's story *Girl Today, Hare Tomorrow* and Melissa's story *The Little Girl Who Got Lost*. The plot of *Girl Today, Hare Tomorrow* enacts, moment by moment, the process of configuration. Ricoeur argues that configuration 'transforms the succession of events into one meaningful whole' (1984: 67). In Rebecca's story this transformation of time is incorporated in the heroine's transformation. The story's title already hints as much. Rebecca has taken a familiar proverb signifying transience, time's passing, and recast it as time's reshaping. The word 'today' stands for the historical world, the world that is 'common to physical and human events'. 'Tomorrow' stands for the world of fiction, the reordering of time by the poetic imagination. The rewritten proverb in effect determines our capacity to follow the story. Rebecca's narrative opens in episodic time, to which she draws attention by her choice of a historical date and a chronologically precise time of day. The gathering speed of the car as it passes, one by one, the old, familiar landmarks evokes 'the so-called "natural" order of time', to use Ricoeur's phrase (1984: 67). But as we read, we begin to sense, behind the catalogue of events, the pressure of another temporal order, the hare's time, a time that secretly controls the narrative from the start. At first it is a matter of semantic hints: Rachel's nervousness as she climbs into her father's car, clutching her felt ears, 'my ears' as she calls them; the car's shudder. Then, mid-way to Wantage, mid-way through the story, the episodic sequence is brought to a sudden halt. The car hiccups, and time with it. As we saw in Chapter 6, this dramatic narrative caesura is signalled once again, as in Lydia's story, by a startling change of tense, accompanied by a final reference to the broken chronology: 'Her father thought for a moment. Five minutes later he had gone to find a telephone.' Between full stop and capital letter, the story enters the configured world, as Rachel steps out of the time of the here and now into a time from which the here and now is already 'far away'. Reading the rest of the story, it is as if we are granted a vision of the heroine's passage from form to form and time to time, a vision that at last resolves itself into the 'glassy eyes' and 'furry paws' of the leaping hare. And now we understand the story. The hare is the figure in which the tale completes itself. It has been lurking in the story from the start, waiting to be uncovered 'in the light of the moon'.

To see how a still younger child configures time within narrative we can turn back to the world that Melissa constructs in her story *The Little Girl Who Got Lost*. Melissa was half Rebecca's age and far less experienced a storyteller. Yet the tale she tells is even more directly a tale of time. In Chapter 3, I noted the variety of times invoked at the end of the story: time by the clock, time of day, time for bed, time to draw the story to a close. I now want to suggest that all of these times are integrated and configured under the concept of 'bedtime', the word reiterated time after time over the closing pages. From beginning to end, this is a story that insists on succession. All but one of the opening six pages mark a new episode in the order of events: 'one day ... but soon ... then one day ... then ... and when'. Then, in the last five pages, following the movement from third-person to first-person narrative, a shift of emphasis takes place. Each new page opens with a 'then' but as the thens accelerate, time slows down and succession is subordinated to a new and contrasted quality of time that finds its delicate and apt expression in the word 'bedtime'. On every page, the opening word 'then' is confronted, almost contradicted, by the closing word 'bedtime'. On the penultimate page, this confrontation is sharpened by the introduction of chronology – 'then it was ten minutes until my mum's and dad's bedtime' – and visualized in the drawing of a clock on the mantlepiece or shelf behind the seated parents watching TV. Bedtime, in Melissa' story, is the time that binds the day together, binds the family together, binds time together, imparting value to succession. Bedtime is also, we remember, the time for storytelling, the time when Melissa herself is most likely to have listened to stories for the first time. Significantly, the *New Shorter Oxford English Dictionary* cites a single idiom in its definition of bedtime – 'bedtime story'. It seems anything but fanciful to suppose that, in the word 'bedtime', Melissa's story finds its fulfilment and justification; fulfilment inasmuch as the story traces the passage from individual autonomy to collective fellowship; justification inasmuch as the story celebrates and validates this passage. 'Bedtime' is the last word in the story. Beneath it Melissa has drawn a bed and the scribbled heads of mum and dad asleep. The 'time for my mum's and dad's bedtime' is the time that, in completing the story, appears to complete time itself. Melissa does not necessarily know this, not in so many words. She doesn't need to. What she has done is to make the thought appear.

There is one further element that Ricoeur adds to his analysis of the plot. The various forms which plot assumes, its forms of configuration, are embedded within a historical tradition. Tradition is simultaneously derivative and innovative: 'Let us understand by this term not the inert transmission of some already dead deposit of material but the living transmission of an innovation always capable of being reactivated by a return to the most creative moments of poetic activity' (1984: 68). Originality is inseparable from convention:

> There is always a place for innovation inasmuch as what is produced, in the poiesis [i.e. the making] of the poem, is always, in the last analysis, a singular work, this work ... A work of art – a poem, play, novel – is an original production, a new existence in the linguistic kingdom. Yet the reverse is no less true. Innovation remains a form of behaviour governed by rules. The labor of imagination is not born from nothing. It is bound in one way or another to the tradition's paradigms.
>
> (1984: 69)

The interplay of innovation and derivation is characteristic of every narrative genre, even a genre as conventional as the folk tale. As Italo Calvino acknowledges in the introduction to his definitive collection of Italian folk tales, 'poetic creativity' plays its part 'in the very existence of a storytelling tradition ... The folk tale must be recreated each time' (1980: xxii).

Poetic creativity is at work in every example of children's engagement with narrative tradition considered in earlier chapters. We have found it in Wally's reinvention of myth, in Jessica's and Melissa's linguistic and visual play with the picture book, in Lydia's exploration of the narrative of magic, in Rebecca's adventures in metamorphosis and dream narrative, just as Tolstoy found it in Fyedka's fictional autobiography. But no example is more compelling than Laura's simultaneous assimilation and appropriation of the trickster tradition in her story, *Upsetter Finds the Four Leaf Clover Circuit*. As far as I know, she had never written a trickster tale before although the tradition would have been familiar to her from tales she had read or listened to. In any case, it was David Cox's workshop which made her aware of the significance of that tradition. Her own story is a variation on the trickster tale, almost a commentary in its self-consciousness, a kind of meta-narrative. By splitting the trickster's personality in two, cunning intelligence on the one hand, witless opportunism on the other, and assigning each aspect to a different character, Upsetter himself and the narrator who tells his story, Laura imparts fresh energy to the conventional genre, renewing the trickster's role as 'a character living on the cusp of reflective consciousness' (Hyde 1998: 56). The trickster, as Lewis Hyde presents him, lives up to Ricoeur's high ambition for narrative. He, or she, is the figure who understands the power of the imagination, with all its craft, to transform life, to reconstruct culture. Laura's story, the outcome of a workshop devoted to the art and craft of making and to the role of storytelling in making, bears witness to that power and to the innovative force of tradition in which it is grounded. It is a story which leads us directly to the far side of mimesis, its capacity to refigure experience.

Mimesis 3

The world configured by the plot is not self-sufficient. Narrative only achieves its full meaning, Ricoeur tells us, 'when it is restored to the time of action and of suffering' (1984: 70). This final moment of mimesis is dependent on the act of reading: 'It is in the hearer or the reader that the traversal of mimesis reaches its fulfilment' (1984: 71). It is the reader's privilege to make sense of the story by following its course, playing with its possibilities, comprehending, representing and completing its thought. But in making sense of the story the reader also comprehends its reference, 'that is, the experience it brings to language and, in the last analysis, the world and the temporality it unfolds in the face of this experience' (1984: 79). Literature is more than artifice. To suppose otherwise is to 'enclose literature within a world of its own and break off the subversive point it turns against the moral and social orders' (1984: 79). Every story, as Ricoeur sees it, 'unfolds, as it were, a world in front of itself ... a world that I might inhabit and into which I might project my ownmost powers' (1984: 81). In the act of reading we learn both to live 'in the mode of the imaginary' and to see how the imagined world responds to, represents and refigures our daily experience, the world of action. It is in the act of reading that we fulfil the narrative's intention.

Each of the studies undertaken in previous chapters has been a study in reading and yet I have had little directly to say about children themselves as readers. In many ways, however, the young writers whose stories I have set out to interpret might all be said to be their own readers. Reading stories, listening to stories, telling each other stories, dramatizing stories, talking about stories: these are the contexts in which each of these writers' stories has taken shape. Jessica's and Melissa's picture books reconstruct the experience of poring over the books that line the bookshelves of home or school. Rebecca revisits and exploits the fictional worlds of *Alice in Wonderland* and *Jane Eyre*. Often the children seem to invent or imagine their readers, as Laura does when she plays with her readers' anticipated responses to the tale her narrator has to tell. But it is in the movement from one story to the next, in the works of Wally or Lydia or Rebecca, that we can detect most clearly each writer's readerly response to their own narratives. So it is that we may trace in nine-year-old Lydia's successive stories the thread of a year-long speculation around the central concerns of her life, as experience grows with each new story, leading her from tale to tale. With this spiralling movement, winding back on itself again and again, linking storytelling to lived experience and lived experience to storytelling, Ricoeur's mimetic traversal is complete and the way is open to answer my second question: what does children's narrative thinking tell us about intellectual growth, about the entry of children into culture?

Entering the culture of narrative

The young writers whose stories have been the subject of this book are already at home within the culture of narrative. As we have seen, their stories fulfil each of the criteria of mimesis, as Ricoeur defines it. They presuppose a broad and developing understanding of action; they demonstrate children's capacity to configure experience by way of the plot; they illustrate the variety of ways in which, as readers of their own writing and the writing of others, children learn to interpret and reinterpret life in terms of narrative. These children are the young masters of make-believe. The plots which they invent are exemplary instances of what Ricoeur calls 'poetic understanding' and Tolstoy spoke of as 'conscious creativity'. In every story, we can recognize the leap of imagination, that 'sudden agile leap of the poet-philosopher' as Calvino describes it. Inventiveness places each of these writers at the heart of tradition in Ricoeur's sense of that term. They are simultaneously recipients and innovators, inheritors of a tradition which they recast in accents derived from their own experience, including the experience of immaturity. They assimilate tradition by appropriating it for their own particular purposes. This is the source of the innovative power that confounded Tolstoy as he read *The Life of a Soldier's Wife* and elicited the paradoxical title of his famous essay.

Children's achievement as storytellers has radical consequences for an understanding of intellectual growth. Education is commonly pictured as the initiation of children into culture, an 'initiation into the space of reasons' as John McDowell (1994: 123) puts it in a recent study of the place of minds within the world. But initiation is a misleading word, overlaid, as it is, with implications of passivity in the face of knowledge and the suspicion of a rite of passage into the realm of thought. The assumption seems to be that children stand outside the way of the world, awaiting culture. The role of education is to prepare them for culture so that, in due course, they can participate creatively and critically in its traditions. As the philosopher Michael Oakeshott once put it, with memorable extravagance, education, at least at the level of schooling, means 'learning to speak before one has anything significant to say' (1962: 306).

The evidence of the stories examined in earlier chapters contradicts these assumptions. Children like Wally, Jessica and Melissa are wholeheartedly engaged in the creative and critical practice of narrative from the moment they compose their earliest stories. They are cultural participants as well as cultural spectators. However immature, their stories are significant, both for themselves and for their readers, including their teachers. It is just because they have something significant to say that they are learning to say it so well. In a review of Jerome Bruner's cultural psychology, first published in *The New York Review of Books* (10 April 1997), Clifford Geertz enlarges the argument for significance as follows:

> Seeing even the infant and the preschooler as active agents bent on mastery of a particular form of life, or developing a workable way of being in the world, demands a rethinking of the entire educational process. It is not so much a matter of providing something the child lacks, as enabling something the child already has: the desire to make sense of self and others, the drive to understand what the devil is going on.
>
> (Bakhurst and Shanker 2001: 22)

The case set out in our studies of the tales children tell is that narrative lies at the centre of children's response to this desire.

Before turning to the educational implications of children's narrative thinking, I want to look briefly at the history of their narrative practice, as implied by the storytellers whose work we have been following. For Tolstoy, as we saw in Chapter 1, the history of intellectual growth is a ceaseless struggle to sustain creativity in the face of experience.I want to suggest that Ricoeur's theory of narrative shows us how to picture this struggle in its narrative dimension. According to Ricoeur, the stories that we tell are the way in which we make sense of the world of action, the world in which we live. By configuring life in terms of narrative we reconfigure experience, remaking our world. That is to say, we come to experience the world, and ourselves within it, in new ways. These new ways give rise in turn to fresh experience which leads to further narrative and so the cycle of mimesis renews itself. Ricoeur speaks of 'the hermeneutical circle of narrative and temporality' (1984: 72). 'That the analysis is circular is indisputable,' he tell us, 'but that the circle is a vicious one can be refuted. In this regard I would rather speak of an endless spiral that would carry the meditation past the same point a number of times, but at different altitudes' (1984: 72). The history of narrative growth in childhood might be described as the earliest phase of Ricoeur's endless spiral.

As suggested in my summary of *mimesis 3*, the 21 stories which Lydia wrote during her ninth year offer an instructive example. The six stories selected from this body of narrative and examined in Chapter 4 chart Lydia's own spiral of meditation as she passes from tale to tale over the course of a school year. Her opening fiction, *The Fire Alarm*, a tale of her own choosing, establishes a narrative environment and a narrative identity which will recur again and again in later stories. Place and person are at once familiar and imaginary, enabling her to exploit that quality of attentiveness to the world of everyday which gives access to the unexpected wonder. In *The Puppies*, a story written under the influence of one of Tolstoy's stories for children, she returns to the theme of the extraordinary world uncovered behind or within the ordinary. A dog jumps up at the narrator as she walks down the street: 'somehow it tried to make me follow her'. The dog leads her to the revelation of three puppies enclosed within a box down a dark alley way. 'An ordinary box', Lydia is careful to insist. But now she introduces a new figure, that of the sceptical mother whose presence alerts us to adult suspicion of the tales that children tell and the looming conflict between imagination and common sense. It may have been Tolstoy's cautionary tale, written from a decidedly adult point of view, that suggested to Lydia the struggle between parent and child. At any rate, her story turns the tables on Tolstoy's tale. It is the adults who are now to be cautioned by the child's 'good deed'.

With *The Magic Stone*, written shortly after the Christmas break, Lydia dramatically extends the range and power of her chosen theme. The generational conflict between mother and child is transformed into a passionate defence of childhood vision in face of the anxious disbelief of a chastened adult world. At the same time a residual anxiety on the child's own part is identified, in the capriciousness of the magic stone and in the narrator's insistent need for reassurance, a need which is only satisfied when the mother is able to confirm with the evidence of her own eyes the reality of her daughter's vision. The difficulty which Lydia experienced in ending her story is a sign of the complexity of her thought at this mid-point of the year. Resolving the difficulty engendered great confidence. Her next story, *The Sparkling Star,* is an expression of her developing assurance. The figure of the mother disappears, as if there is no longer a need to question the reality of childhood vision or its acknowledged status. In the new story, the narrator's authority is never in doubt. For this very reason, perhaps, the possessiveness that marked the earlier narrative, the child's desire to pocket the stone, let alone the stone's final consignment to a museum, now becomes the subject of a narrative critique. Vision is not to be entrapped or confined but glimpsed and released. Its value is inseparable from its transience, its 'winged life'.

Yet for all its beauty and authority, *The Sparkling Star* in no way concludes Lydia's speculative meditation. She no sooner resolves the conflict between the imaginative world and the world of everyday than she reopens it. *I Found It in My Bowl of Cereal* reads like an ironic reversal of *The Sparkling Star*. This time, there is no trace of the fleeting communion of worlds. Vision turns hostile, as if to take possession of the child who had at one time herself sought possession. It is only by spitting out the magic bubble gum she had swallowed that the narrator frees herself from magic's spell and can return home. The figure of the mother reappears and her return gives rise to a carefully ambiguous ending. Lydia now plays with the opposition between imagination and common sense, challenging her readers, herself included, to experience the story in alternate ways.

The same ambiguity, pushed to an extreme, marks her final tale, *The Talking Tree*. For the first time in this particular sequence of stories, Lydia alters the narrative setting and her own narrative identity. The story is told in the third person and cast in the form of a fairy tale. This shift of perspective allows Lydia to distance herself from her cherished theme and to meditate on its significance from a less engaged point of view. An elegiac note enters her writing, the resonance of a bedtime story, well suited to her purpose. The tale she has to tell is the tale she has been telling all year, circling around it from different points of view in the light of a developing experience, the story of a fundamental tension between two realms of being, magic and reality, the visionary world and the world of everyday. Once again she forces the reader, at the end of the story, to determine the outcome. Whom are we to believe, the child or the woodcutter? Who is it who has saved him, the working man or the talking tree? Does the story represent Lydia's farewell to the fairy tale or a warning to those who refuse to take it seriously? Characteristically, Lydia is content to pose the question without offering an answer. The meditative cycle is not to be closed. There will be more to be said, as experience is enlarged, new tales to tell. The Ricoeurian spiral has only just begun.

The pedagogy of imagination

In the Fogg Art Museum at Harvard University, there is a room devoted to the remarkable clay sketches of saints and angels made by Bernini and his workshop in preparation for the sculptor's various projects in Saint Peter's and elsewhere in seventeenth-century Rome. On the wall, just inside the entrance to the exhibition, a note informs the visitor that 'these clay sketches were tools in a collaborative enterprise. Their pressed forms and raked, prodded and gouged surfaces embody the inextricability of thought and making.' I have more than once been reminded of these words while reading and rereading Lydia's stories, remote though the world of Bernini and his collaborators may seem from that of Lydia and her classmates. As we have seen, her successive explorations of narrative over the course of a single school year both embody her thought and provoke it. Thought and making are indeed inextricable in her practice. The art and craft of composition is the critical and creative matrix in which her understanding evolves from work to work, the privileged form of her meditation on literature and on life, as it is with all her young fellow writers.

The inextricability of thought and making, that is to say the integrity of poetic understanding, has radical implications for education, as Tolstoy foresaw. Creativity moves to the centre of the curriculum. It is neither the end for which education prepares us nor a decorative accompaniment to the acquisition of knowledge and skill but fundamental to the process of learning at every age. This is the meaning of Tolstoy's refusal to distinguish between learning to read and write and learning to compose a literary work. The former implies the latter. Learning to compose a literary work is what learning to read and write amounts to. Creativity is the highway to skill. The stories of Fyedka and Wally, Jessica and Melissa, Lydia, Laura and Rebecca, have shown us some of the ways in which young children test their developing skills as they experiment with the dangers and difficulties of the written word. Jessica exploits the distinctive connotations of words such as 'busy' or 'pretended' in a young child's world. Melissa makes sense of an apparent inconsistency in the use of person in written narrative by shifting from the third-person 'they' to the first-person 'we' at the moment when the successful completion of her heroine's second walk, no longer alone but with 'the whole family', allows her to identify herself at last with the little girl who got lost. Lydia uses a sudden, brief and irregular movement from past tense to present tense to dramatize the climax of her story of the magic stone. Laura plays havoc with parentheses, capital letters, slang terms and sentence structures in her self-conscious determination to trick and tease. Rebecca matches the magic of metamorphosis with the magic of her own language in which the distance between a full stop and capital letter can capture the boundary between worlds. Such are the means by which skill is wedded to purpose at each separate moment of development. The literary context, where thinking and making coincide, provides both the motive for literacy and the method for its achievement. Outside this context learning becomes, as Vygotsky puts it in the essay quoted in Chapter 1

something self-contained, relegating living written language to the background. Instead of being founded on the needs of children as they naturally develop and on their own activity, writing is given to them from without, from the teacher's hands. The situation recalls the

development of a technical skill such as piano-playing: the pupil develops finger dexterity and learns to strike the keys while reading music, but
he is in no way involved in the essence of music itself.

(1968: 105)

Once the productive imagination is placed at the heart of curriculum
practice, children's works, the products of their imagination, become the
predominant focus of educational interest and attention and the classroom is
transformed into a workshop whose members, like the members of Bernini's
workshop as envisaged in the Fogg Art Museum, are partners in 'a collaborative enterprise'. Children's works and children as the 'makers of works'
are the subject of Patricia Carini's remarkable collection of essays *Starting
Strong: A Different Look at Children, Schools, and Standards* (2001). Carini
describes children as 'poets of our lives' and sees in the relationship between
makers and works 'a dialectic that discovers in works and the making of works
the self's medium and animating energy' (2001: 19). Jerome Bruner, in *The
Culture of Education* (1996), takes a broadly similar view, emphasising the
collective nature of works and reconceiving the classroom as 'a collaborative
community ... engaged in producing a joint product, an oeuvre' (1996: 76).
Both of them see the school itself as a work, 'a work that is ever in the making'
(Carini 2001: 93). Children's works – their stories and poems, their art and
music, their dance and drama, their experiments, investigations and spec-
ulations in the arts and sciences – represent the 'externalization', to use
Bruner's term, of their imaginative engagement, the public face of creativity.

The works examined in this book represent just one particular sub-set of
children's works: their written stories, the products of their narrative thinking
and making. My focus has been on the stories of individual children rather
than on the collective culture of the classroom. Yet it is a collective enterprise
that nourishes these children's achievements. Storytelling is, of its nature, a
companionable art. Tellers seek listeners, writers have their readers. As Walter
Benjamin puts it, 'a man listening to a story is in the company of the storyteller; even a man reading one shares this companionship' (1968: 100). The
companionship in question here is anything but passive. There is always an
interplay between teller, listener and tale. It is the listener no less than the
teller, the reader no less than the writer, whose task it is to bring the tale to
life, by following its plot, enjoying its pleasures, confronting its perils, playing
with its constraints and opportunities, reconfiguring its meaning, placing it
alongside experience including the experience of other tales. Reading or listening is itself an act of composition, a remaking in the company of the
storyteller and his tale.

Companionship was a notable feature of each of our young writers' narrative environments. Wally's classroom was awash with stories: the stories
that enlivened the children's classroom play, the fairy tales they listened to in
the darkened room at rest time, the picture books they pored over together,
and, above all, their own stories, dictated to their teacher and subsequently
read aloud, discussed, criticized, elaborated, revised, and acted out, there and
then, on the rug around which they sat, reinventing mythology in tale after
tale. Jessica's and Melissa's stories were written and drawn at the table they

shared, looking over each other's work, chatting to each other from time to time, swapping ideas, exploring their diverse visions by common visual and literary means in a shared idiosyncrasy of form. Laura's trickster tale was the product of a visiting artist's workshop in which narrative, craft and drama were combined in the exploration of an ancient literary tradition. Companionship was the unspoken premise of Laura's and her schoolmates' achievements as classrooms were redesigned so that young and old, brothers and sisters, children and teachers might work as one, alongside each other, in an enactment of the topsy turvy world of the trickster, listening to David Cox as he spun his tales, or exchanging stories of their own as they constructed their rattles, masks and cardboard figures under the artist's authoritative but indulgent gaze.

Inevitably companionship finds its way into the childrens' stories. Sometimes it provides the major theme, as in Wally's lion pet story or Melissa's family drama. Sometimes it breeds trouble, as in Lydia's stories with their opposition of mother's and child's perceptions. Sometimes the interplay between writer and reader itself becomes an element in the narrative intention, most notably in Laura's tale with its introduction of the reader as a character within the fiction. Even Rebecca's stories, for all their authorial control, seem deliberately designed, in their inquisitive endings, to leave to the reader the task of puzzling out the significance of the tale that has been told, as is equally true of Lydia's tale of the talking tree. It is as if these young writers are determined to implicate their readers in the tales they have to tell.

Within the company of storytellers assembled in the classroom, it is the teacher's privilege to organize and animate the work in progress, 'orchestrating the proceedings' as Bruner (1996: 22) puts it. The act of reading, by which I mean the business of interpretation, stands at the forefront of this responsibility. Teaching, in the context of works and the making of works, is, above all else, an interpretive art. I want to emphasize four moments in the process of interpretation, four aspects of scrutiny in the study of children's narrative works, each of which I have sought to illustrate in one form or another in previous chapters. The teacher's first task, as I understand it, is to inhabit the work and the world which it represents and projects, in the spirit of Goethe's remark, cited by Walter Benjamin in his *Little History of Photography:* 'There is a delicate empiricism which so intimately involves itself with the object that it becomes true theory' (1999a: 520). Living in the work means acknowledging its authority, however elementary the work may initially appear. A story by Wally or Jessica or Melissa has no less power to challenge our understanding, to put our knowledge to the test, than a story by Rebecca. This intimacy of engagement with the world of the work leads on to the teacher's second task which is a drawing out of the work's narrative intention, both as consciously recognized by the author and as implicit within the text. Here is where the teacher explores the ramifications of the story's language, the interplay of form and content, the thematic development and the story's underlying significance, the light it throws on life, including the author's own sense of life.

These first two moments correspond to Ricoeur's 'act of reading' and together they govern the teacher's imaginative response to the work as a configuring of experience. The third moment comes when the teacher, sometimes independently and sometimes in collaboration with other members of the class, fellow readers and writers, redescribes or represents to the author her or his understanding of the work. This is the moment for questioning the author or authors, for sharing perceptions, exchanging interpretations, speculating together about the story's plot or its language, its characters and their circumstances, its twists and turns, its significance as a story. It is the time at which children and teachers, in conversation with each other, come to a broader understanding of narrative, both the stories which they write and the stories and books which they read. Representation, discussion and speculation lead on, in their turn, to the final moment of interpretation which looks to the future as implicit in the work of the present, both the individual work of particular children and the collective work of the class as a learning community, its narrative corpus. The focus of attention may be on the development of verbal or grammatical skills in the light of the existing, always momentary, equilibrium of skill and purpose in the children's work. It may be on the introduction of new genres or new techniques, perhaps already implied in the tales that the children have told. It may be on the literature which responds to the work in hand: novels to be read, folk tales to be told, picture books to be examined. It may be on the further exploration of the subject matter of the children's stories, the human predicaments which they have been confronting in narrative form. It may be on the extension of the narrative work of the class into other areas of the curriculum than language and literature: into drama, dance, music, art, history. In looking forward, as at every moment of interpretation, the distinctive role of teachers within the culture of the classroom is to bring all their accumulated knowledge to bear on the task of helping the class to move ahead. Teachers are both representatives and critics of the wider culture. No knowledge is too rarefied to be of value in interpreting young children's narrative thought, just as no intuition, on the part of a young writer, is too elementary to challenge the teacher, as reader, to think again.

In classrooms devoted to works and the making of works, interpretation becomes synonymous with assessment and evaluation. To identify with the work, draw out its intention, meditate on its significant form and anticipate the direction of future work is to render the work its due value, whether within the process of learning or as learning's product. Value is made visible through the documentation of individual and collective thinking and making within the classroom workshop. In a fascinating study by two teams of researchers from Harvard University's Project Zero and from the Municipal Infant–Toddler Centres and Pre-schools of Reggio Emilia, entitled *Making Learning Visible*, Carla Rinaldi describes documentation as 'visible listening, as the construction of traces (through notes, slides, videos, and so on) that not only testify to the children's learning paths and processes, but also make them possible because they are visible' (Project Zero and Reggio Children 2001: 83). The documentation of children's narrative thought takes many forms. It includes children's individual portfolios of stories, selected, illustrated and presented by children in collaboration with their teachers and classmates; anthologies, in manuscript or published form, of the class's stories; wall displays; exhibitions of narrative work in a variety of media; public readings and performances; tape and video recordings; photographs and films; computer programmes. The selection, presentation and publication of work is itself a form of interpretation but documenting the work of an individual child or a class of children also calls for a variety of annotations, linked to the display of finished products: teachers' and childrens's writing journals; interpretive notes and comments; recollections, reflections, proposals and projects; reading lists and critical commentary. As Carla Rinaldi reminds us, the purpose of documentation is not only to make children's achievement visible to themselves and others but to promote further learning through reflection on the nature of that achievement. Works build on works and on the meditation that accompanies their making. Documentation seeks to place the meditation on public view, bringing to life, in and around the classroom, Ricoeur's speculative spiral.

To document the work of the classroom, its 'oeuvre' as Bruner calls it, is to tell the story of learning and at the same time to put on display the classroom's contribution to the larger culture. For children's works, as we have seen, are not so much the means of preparing for culture as cultural statements in their own right, adding to the sum of knowledge, however tentatively and provisionally. This is what makes the documentation and assessment of works so remote from the prevailing educational ideology of standardized assessment. Standardized assessment depends upon quantification and upon the selection of a set of tests and tasks which are presumed to act as simulacra of learning. Whatever their merits, such tests and tasks tell us nothing about the quality of children's thought as demonstrated in their works. They offer no challenge to our own authority; they never put us on the spot. In effect, they treat children's works as if they were empty of significance. Documentation, by contrast, is the narrative of a culturally significant achievement, traced through the succession of works and their interpretation over the course of a term, a year, a school lifetime. The two forms of assessment may be complementary but they are not to be confused.

In his essay *The Storyteller*, Walter Benjamin describes storytelling as the exchange of experience. The story of learning, as I have sought to present it in this book, is itself a story of experience exchanged, between writer and reader, pupil and teacher, child and adult, in the company of each other. Among his educational essays Tolstoy includes a story which brings to vibrant life the nature of this companionship. It is a tale about storytelling, about meditation and interpretation, about the mutuality of learning and teaching, about art, about children's lives and children's thought, and, of course, about Tolstoy himself, in all his contradictions. Once again, Fyedka is the hero; once again Tolstoy's own literary future is at stake. The story comes in the middle of a long essay, originally published in serial form under the title *The Yasnaya Polyana School in the Months of November and December* (Tolstoy 1982: 87–184). Tolstoy has been describing, with numerous digressions, the school's daily routine. The last lesson of what appears to be a very long school day is devoted to what Tolstoy calls 'physics experiments'.

This lesson, [he tells us,] as regards the character it has assumed in our school, is the one best suited to the evening, the most fantastic lesson, entirely appropriate to the mood which is evoked by reading fairy tales. Here the fairy tale world passes into reality – they personify everything: the juniper berry which is repelled by sealing wax, the magnetic needle which repels, the filings scurrying across a piece of paper underneath which a magnet is drawn, all these represent living creatures to them. Even the cleverest boys, who understand the explanation of these phenomena, get carried away and start to mutter at the needle, the berry and the filings 'Hey you! Where are you going? Stop! Hey! On you go!' and so on.

(1982: 102)

What follows, as he begins to describe the end of the school day, is Tolstoy's own story of the pedagogy of the imagination.

WALKING THROUGH THE WOOD

Usually the lessons end at eight or nine, unless carpentry keeps the older boys back longer, and the whole gang runs shouting together as far as the servants' quarters and from there on begins to make off towards various quarters of the village in groups that shout across to one another. Sometimes they take it into their heads to coast downhill to the village on a big sledge which is parked by the gate – they tangle with a snowdrift, go slap into the middle and disappear from view with a shriek into the powdered snow, leaving here and there on the road – black patches – boys that have tumbled out. Outside school (in spite of all its freedom), in the open air, new relations are established between teacher and pupil with more freedom, more simplicity and more trust, the kind of relations that appear to us to be the ideal towards which a school should strive.

Recently we were reading Gogol's *Vii* in the first class; the last scenes had a strong effect and excited their imagination; some of them mimicked the witch and kept on remembering the last night.

It was not cold outside – a moonless, cloudy, winter night. At the crossroads we stopped; the older ones who had been at school for three years, came to a halt around me, asking me to go further with them; the little ones looked on for a bit – and started sliding downhill. The juniors had started work with a new teacher, and there was not the same trust between me and them as between me and the seniors.

'Well then, let's go to the plantation,' (a copse about two hundred paces from the dwelling houses) said one of them.

Fyedka begged me to hardest of all, a boy of about ten years old, a tender, receptive, poetical and dashing nature. It seems that for him danger is the most important condition of enjoyment. In summer it always used to be frightening to watch him swimming out with two other boys into the very middle of the pond, which is about a hundred yards across, and occasionally disappearing altogether in the warm reflections of the summer sunshine, swimming across the deep stretch, turning over on his back, spurting out streams of water and calling out in a thin voice to his friends on the bank to see what a fine fellow he was. Now he knew that there were wolves in the wood; that is why he wanted to go into the plantation. The others supported him, and we four went over to the wood together. Another one – I shall call him Syomka – a lad about twelve years old, healthy both physically and morally, walked on in front and kept shouting and making warbling calls to somebody. Walking beside me was Pronka, a sickly, meek and unusually gifted boy, a son of a poor family, sickly, it seems, mainly from lack of food. Fyedka was walking between me and Syomka and kept on making remarks in a specially soft voice, now telling how he had guarded horses here in summer, now saying that there was nothing to be afraid of, and now asking 'What if one did jump out?' and demanding categorically that I should say something in reply to that.

We did not go into the middle of the wood – that would have been too frightening, but even near the wood it had grown darker: the path could scarcely be seen, the lights of the village had vanished from sight. Syomka stopped and began to listen.

'Stop lads! What's that?' he said suddenly.

We fell silent, but there was nothing to be heard; even so it added to our fear.

'Well, what are we going to do when he jumps out and chases us?' asked Fyedka.

We talked about Caucasian robbers. They remembered a story about the Caucasus which I told them long ago, and I began to tell them again about abreks and cossacks and Hadji Murat. Syomka was walking in front, striding out in his big boots and swaying his healthy back in rhythm. Pronka was about to try to walk beside me, but Fyedka pushed him off the path, and Pronka, who always gives in to everybody, no doubt on account of his poverty, came running up to one side only in the most interesting parts, even though he sank up to his knees in the snow.

Anyone who knows a little about peasant children will have noticed that they are not used to and cannot bear any sort of caressing, soft words, kissing, stroking with your hand and so on. Once I happened to see a lady in a peasant school, who wanted to make much of a boy, say 'Then I'll give you a kiss, darling!' and kiss him, and I could see the boy who was kissed was shamed, insulted, and unable to understand why *that* had been done to him; even a five-year-old boy is above these caresses – he is already 'a lad'. I was therefore particularly struck when Fyedka, who was walking beside me, suddenly, at the most frightening point of the story, touched me lightly with his sleeve; he then gripped two of my fingers in his whole hand and did not let them drop. As soon as I fell silent Fyedka began demanding that I tell more, and in such an imploring and excited voice that I could not do anything but carry out his wish.

'Here you, get out from under our feet,' he said angrily to Pronka, who had come running forward; he was absorbed to the point of cruelty, he felt so creepy and happy holding on to my finger, and nobody should dare to disturb his pleasure. 'Now some more, some more! It's *fine*.'

We walked through the wood and started to approach the village from the other end.

'Let's go further,' they all said as the lights came in sight. 'Let's go through again.'

We walked in silence, stumbling here and there on the unfirm, badly worn pathway; it was as if a white darkness were swaying before our eyes; the clouds were low, as if something were pouring them down upon us; there was no end to that *whiteness* in which we alone were crunching over the snow; the wind roared in the bare tops of the aspens; but for us it was quiet on the other side of the wood. I finished my story by telling how the abrek, having been surrounded, burst out singing and then threw himself upon his dagger. Everyone was silent.

'But why did he burst out singing when he was surrounded?' asked Syomka.

'You've been told – he was getting ready to die, of course,' replied Fyedka irritably.

'I think he started singing a prayer,' added Pronka.

Everyone agreed. Fyedka suddenly stopped.

'And what did you say about your aunt being murdered?' he asked – he had not had enough of terrors.

'Tell us! tell us!'

I told them once more the terrible story of the murder of Countess Tolstoy, and they stood around me in silence, looking into my face.

'That was a brave chap,' said Syomka.

'It must have been frightening for him walking around at night with her lying murdered,' said Fyedka, 'I would have run away!' And he once again grasped my two fingers in his hand.

We stopped in a copse behind the barns, on the very edge of the village. Syomka picked up some brushwood from the snow and hit the frosty bole of a lime-tree with it. Hoar frost showered down from the branches onto his cap, and the noise resounded, solitary, through the woods.

'Lev Nikolayevich,' said Fyedka (I thought he was going to speak about the countess again) 'why do we learn singing? I often think, really, why sing?'

How he had made the leap from the horror of murder to that question Heaven knows, but everything: the sound of his voice, the seriousness with which he sought an answer, the silence of the other two made us feel that there was a very vital and legitimate connection between that question and the preceding conversation. Whether the connection was that he was replying to my explanation that crime may be due to lack of education (I had been telling them that) or that he was testing himself by identifying himself with the murderer and remembering his favourite occupation (he has a wonderful voice and an immense talent for music) or whether the connection was that he felt that now was the time for sincere talk and all the questions which were calling for an answer arose in his mind – at any rate none of us was surprised at his question.

'And why drawing, why write well?' said I, not knowing in the least how to explain to him what art is for.

'Why drawing?' he replied meditatively. He was in fact asking 'Why art?' I did not dare to explain, I did not know how.

'Why drawing?' said Syomka. 'You put everything down in a drawing – you can make anything from that.'

'No, that's technical drawing,' said Fyedka, 'but why draw figures?'

Syomka's healthy nature saw no difficulty. 'Why a stick, why a lime-tree?' he said, still rapping the lime.

'Well then, what *is* a lime-tree for?' said I.

'To make rafters with,' replied Syomka.

'And what else, what is it for in summer, before it's chopped down?'

'Why nothing.'

'No, really,' Fyedka continued obstinately to ask, 'why does a lime-tree grow?'

And we started to talk about the fact that utility is not everything, but there is beauty, and art is beauty, and we understood one another, and Fyedka quite understood why a lime-tree grows and why we sing. Pronka agreed with us, but he understood better moral beauty – goodness. Syomka understood with his great intelligence, but he would not admit beauty without utility. He doubted, as often happens with people of great intelligence who feel that art is a force but who do not feel in their hearts any need of that force; like them he wanted to approach art with his intellect and was trying to light that fire within himself.

'Tomorrow we're going to sing "Ije", I can remember my line.'

He has a good ear but lacks taste and refinement in singing. But Fyedka understood perfectly that a lime-tree in leaf is beautiful, and it is good to look at in summer, and nothing more is needed. Pronka understood that it's a pity to cut it down, because it too is a living thing.

'You know it's just as if it was blood when we drink the sap out of a birch tree.'

Syomka, although he did not say so, evidently thought that it was not much good when it was rotten. I find it strange to repeat what we said then, but I remember that we talked over – as it seems to me – everything that can be said about utility and about plastic and moral beauty.

We walked to the village. Fyedka still did not let go of my hand, out of gratitude now, I thought. We were all so close that night, as we had not been for a long time. Pronka walked beside us along the broad village road.

'Look, there's still a light at the Mazanovs!' he said. 'As I was walking to school today Gavryukha was riding away from the pot-house,' he added, 'as dr-r-r-unk as drunk, his horse was all foaming and he was flogging it . . . I always feel sorry. Really! what does he want to beat it for?'

'And the other day,' said Syomka, 'he gave his horse its head out of Tula and it took him off into a snowdrift, and him asleep drunk.'

'And Gavryukha does whip him across the eyes so . . . and I felt so sorry for it,' said Pronka once more. 'Why was he beating it? There were tears, and he goes on whipping it.'

Syomka suddenly stopped. 'Our folks are asleep by now,' he said, peering into the windows of his crooked black cottage. 'Won't you walk some more?'

'No.'

'Goodby-y-ye Lev Nikolayevich,' he suddenly shouted and, as if he were tearing himself away from us with an effort, trotted up to the house, lifted the latch and vanished.

'So you'll see us back, first one and then the other,' said Fyedka.

We walked on. There was a light in Pronka's place; we looked in at the window: his mother, a tall, beautiful but worn woman with black brows and eyes, was sitting at the table and peeling potatoes; in the middle of the room a cradle was hanging; the mathematician of the 2nd class, Pronka's elder brother, was standing by the table, eating a salted potato. The cottage was black, tiny and dirty.

'You've been gone long enough!' shouted his mother to Pronka. 'Where've you been?'

Pronka gave a meek, pained smile, looking at the window. His mother guessed that he was not alone and at once changed to an ugly, false expression. Only Fyedka was left.

'We've got the tailors sitting up in our place, that's why there's a light,' he said in the softened voice he had that evening. 'Goodbye Lev Nikolayevich,' he added quietly and tenderly and began to bang the ring on the locked door. 'Open up!' his thin little voice sounded through the wintry silence of the village.

It was a long time before they opened to him. I looked in at the window: the cottage was a big one; logs could be seen on the stove and benches; his father was playing cards with the tailors; a few copper coins were lying on the table. A woman, the step-mother, was sitting by the light and staring hungrily at the money. The tailor, a young peasant who is a hardened rogue, was holding his cards, which were bent right over, on the table, and gazing in triumph at his partner. Fyedka's father, his collar undone, all frowns from the intellectual tension and vexation, was shuffling his cards and in his indecision waving his workman's hand over them.

'Open up!'

The woman got up and went to unlock the door.

'Goodbye,' Fyedka repeated once more. 'Let's always go walking like that.'

Translation by Alan Pinch
(Tolstoy 1982: 102–8)

REFERENCES

Armstrong, M. (1980) *Closely Observed Children*. London: Writers and Readers Cooperative Society.

Bakhurst, D. and Shanker, S. G. (eds) (2001) *Jerome Bruner: Language, Culture, Self*. London: Sage Publications.

Benjamin, W. (1968) *Illuminations*. New York: Schocken Books.

Benjamin, W. (1999a) *Selected Writings* Vol. 2. Cambridge, MA: Harvard University Press.

Benjamin, W. (1999b) *The Arcades Project*. Cambridge, MA: Harvard University Press.

Berlin, I. (1978) *Russian Thinkers*. Harmondsworth: Penguin.

Blake, W. (1966) *Complete Writings*. Oxford: Oxford University Press.

Brontë, C. (1985) *Jane Eyre*. London: Penguin Classics.

Bruner, J. (1996) *The Culture of Education*. Cambridge, MA: Harvard University Press.

Calvino, I. (1980) *Italian Folk Tales*. Orlando, FL: Harcourt Brace & Co.

Calvino, I. (1988) *Six Memos for the Next Millennium*. Cambridge, MA: Harvard University Press.

Carini, P. (2001) *Starting Strong: A Different Look at Children, Schools and Standards*. New York: Teachers' College Press.

Carrol, L. (1927) *Alice's Adventures in Wonderland*. London: Macmillan.

Carter, A. (1992) *The Second Virago Book of Fairy Tales*. London: Virago Press.

Cazden, C. B. (2001) *Classroom Discourse*. Portsmouth, NH: Heinemann.

Christian, R. F. (1978) *Tolstoy's Letters*. London: The Athlone Press.

Coleridge, S. T. (1969) *The Collected Works of Samuel Taylor Coleridge*. London: Routledge & Kegan Paul.

Eikhenbaum, B. (1982) *Tolstoy in the Sixties*. Ann Arbor, MI: Ardis.

Ginzburg, C. (1990) *Ecstasies: Deciphering the Witches' Sabbath*. London: Hutchinson.

Goethe, J. W. von (1970) *Theory of Colours*. Cambridge, MA: The MIT Press.

Hyde, L. (1998) *Trickster Makes This World*. New York: North Point Press.

Jacobs, J. (1968) *English Fairy Tales*. London: The Bodley Head.

Kearney, R. (2002) *On Stories*. London: Routledge.

Keynes, G. (1976) *William Blake's Laocoon: A Last Testament*. London: The Trianon Press.

Lomas Garza, C. (1991) *A Piece of My Heart: The Art of Carmen Lomas Garza*. New York: The New Press.

Maude, A. (1929) *The Life of Tolstoy*. Oxford: Oxford University Press.

McDowell, J. (1994) *Mind and World*. Cambridge, MA: Harvard University Press.

Oakeshott, M. (1962) *Rationalism in Politics and Other Essays*. London: Methuen.

Paley, V. G. (1981) *Wally's Stories*. Cambridge, MA: Harvard University Press.

Paley, V. G. (1990) *The Boy Who Would Be a Helicopter*. Cambridge, MA: Harvard University Press.

Project Zero and Reggio Children (2001) *Making Learning Visible: Children as Individual and Group Learners*. Reggio Emilia: Reggio Children.

Propp, V. (1968) *Morphology of the Folk Tale*. Austin, TX: University of Texas Press.

Ricoeur, P. (1984) *Time and Narrative* Vol. 1. Chicago: University of Chicago Press.

Sontag, S. (1983) *A Barthes Reader*. New York: Hill & Wang.

Tolstoy, L. (1965) *Stories for Children*. Moscow: Progress Publishers.

Tolstoy, L. (1982) *Tolstoy on Education*. London: The Athlone Press.

Vygotsky, L. S. (1968) *Mind in Society*. Cambridge, MA: Harvard University Press.

Wittgenstein, L. (1953) *Philosophical Investigations*. Oxford: Basil Blackwell.

INDEX

MAKING SENSE OF CHILDREN'S DRAWINGS

Angela Anning and Kathy Ring

'If you know and love young children, find a way to read this book. Here you will discover the hidden talents of young children for complexity, design, and tenacity for learning ... This book is a wonderful addition to the too-small library of quality books on young children's learning through art.'

Shirley Brice Heath, Professor Emerita, Stanford University and
Professor at Large, Brown Universitys USA

'This book is unique in giving an in-depth account of the way young children approach drawing at home and at school. It shows the cognitive value of drawing in children's intellectual and emotional development and sets out the truly extraordinary range of drawing types that are used and understood by three to six year olds ... It is an invaluable experience.'

Professor Ken Baynes, Department of Design and Technology,
Loughborough University

This book explores how young children learn to draw and draw to learn, both at home and at school. It provides support for practitioners in developing a pedagogy of drawing in Art and Design and across the curriculum, and provides advice for parents about how to make sense of their children's drawings.

Making Sense of Children's Drawings is enlivened with the real drawings of seven young children collected over three years. These drawings stimulated dialogues with the children, parents and practitioners whose voices are reported in the book. The book makes a powerful argument for us to rethink radically the role of drawing in young children's construction of meaning, communication and sense of identity. It provides insights into the influence of media and consumerism, as reflected in popular visual imagery, and on gender identity formation in young children. It also offers strong messages about the overemphasis on the three Rs in early childhood education.

Key reading for students, practitioners and parents who want to encourage young children's drawing development without 'interfering' with their creativity, and who need a novel approach to tuning into young children's passions and preoccupations.

Contents

152pp   0 335 21265 4 (Paperback)   0 335 21266 2 (Hardback)

THE EXCELLENCE OF PLAY
Second Edition

Janet Moyles (ed.)

The second edition of this bestselling book encapsulates all the many changes that have taken place in early childhood in the last ten years. While retaining its original message of the vital importance of play as a tool for learning and teaching for children and practitioners, it consolidates this further with current evidence from research and practice and links the most effective practice with the implementation of recent policies.

New contributions for the second edition include:

- Children as social and active agents in their own play;
- Practitioners' roles in play and adults' enabling of play;
- Play and links with Foundation Stage and FS Profile/legislation and policy;
- KS1 links (and beyond);
- Birth to three matters;
- Outdoor and physical play, including rough and tumble;
- Gender differences;
- Play and observation/assessment;
- Special Educational Needs and play;
- Parents' perspectives on play;
- Child development links and play.

The importance of curriculum and assessment is retained and extended. *The Excellence of Play* supports all those who work in early childhood education and care in developing and implementing the highest quality play experiences for children from birth to middle childhood. All the contributors are experts in their fields and all are passionate about the excellence of play. The book will stimulate and inform the ongoing debate about play through its powerful – and ongoing argument – that 'a curriculum which sanctions and utilizes play is more likely to provide well-balanced citizens of the future as well as happier and more learned children in the present'.

Contributors
Lesley Abbott, Ann Langston, Sian Adams, Angela Anning, Pat Broadhead, Tina Bruce, Tricia David, Sacha Powell, Bernadette Duffy, Hilary Fabian, Aline-Wendy Dunlop, Rose Griffiths, Nigel Hall, Stephanie Harding, Jane Hislama, Alan Howe, Dan Davies, Neil Kitson, Theodora Papatheodorou, Linda Pound, Peter Smith, David Whitebread, Helen Jameson

Contents
Introduction – Play and curriculum – Birth to three matters and play – Supporting creativity/identity – Play and SENPlay, language and gender – Impact of play on storytelling – Play, literacy and the teacher – Role play – Outdoor play – Physical and rough and tumble play – Play and science/technology – Playing music – Art in the early years – Mathematics and play – Play in transitions – Play and different cultures – Reflecting on play, the universe and everything – Afterword

c.288pp   0 335 21757 5 (Paperback)   0 335 21758 3 (Hardback)

EXPERIENCING REGGIO EMILIA
Implications for Pre-school Provision

Lesley Abbott and Cathy Nutbrown (eds)

Early education, internationally, is the focus of much challenge and debate. Various approaches to teaching young children are being developed and advocated, but the focus is often on curriculum content with the processes of learning as a secondary issue. The most important consideration in early education is the way in which young children learn. Their transferable skills of communication, collaboration and investigation can underpin all aspects of learning, These elements form the main focus of work in a group of pre-schools in an area of northern Italy that has earned an international reputation for innovative practice and pedagogy.

The experience of Reggio Emilia, in providing challenges to accepted approaches to early childhood education in many countries, is widely acknowledged. Since 1963, when the Italian municipality of Reggio Emilia began setting up its network of educational services for 0 to 6 year olds, the 'Reggio approach' has gained worldwide recognition. Numerous visitors have been impressed by the acknowledgement given to the potential of children, the organization and quality of the environments created, the promotion of collegiality and the climate of co-participation of families in the educational project.

This book reflects the impressions and experiences of the Reggio Emilia approach gained by a range of early childhood educators following a study visit to the region. It focuses on key issues such as staffing, training, working with parents, play, learning, the culture of early childhood and special educational needs, from a variety of perspectives, and will provide a welcome challenge to thinking for both practioners and policy makers.

Contents

176pp   0 335 20703 0 (Paperback)   0 335 20704 9 (Hardback)